Worth-Focused Design, Book 2
Approaches, Contexts, and Case Studies

Synthesis Lectures on Human-Centered Informatics

Editor
John M. Carroll, *Penn State University*

Human-Centered Informatics (HCI) is the intersection of the cultural, the social, the cognitive, and the aesthetic with computing and information technology. It encompasses a huge range of issues, theories, technologies, designs, tools, environments, and human experiences in knowledge work, recreation and leisure activity, teaching and learning, and the potpourri of everyday life. The series publishes state-of-the-art syntheses, case studies, and tutorials in key areas. It shares the focus of leading international conferences in HCI.

Worth-Focused Design, Book 2: Approaches, Contexts, and Case Studies
Gilbert Cockton

Worth-Focused Design, Book 1: Balance, Integration, and Generosity
Gilbert Cockton

Usabiity Testing: A Practitioner's Guide to Evaluating the User Experience
Morten Hertzum

Geographical Design: Spatial Cognition and Geographical Information Science, Second Edition
Stephen C. Hirtle

Human-Computer Interactions in Museums
Eva Hornecker and Luigina Ciolfi

Encounters with HCI Pioneers: A Personal History and Photo Journal
Ben Shneiderman

Social Media and Civic Engagement: History, Theory, and Practice
Scott P. Robertson

The Art of Interaction: What HCI Can Learn from Interactive Art
Ernest Edmonds

Representation, Inclusion, and Innovation: Multidisciplinary Explorations

Worth-Focused Design, Book 2: Approaches, Contexts, and Case Studies
Gilbert Cockton

ISBN: 978-3-031-01102-3 print
ISBN: 978-3-031-02230-2 ebook
ISBN: 978-3-031-00210-6 hardcover

DOI 10.1007/978-3-031-02230-2

A Publication in the Springer series
SYNTHESIS LECTURES ON HUMAN-CENTERED INFORMATICS
Lecture #47
Series Editor: John M. Carroll, Penn State University

Series ISSN 1946-7680 Print   1946-7699 Electronic

Worth-Focused Design, Book 2

Approaches, Contexts, and Case Studies

Gilbert Cockton
University of Sunderland

SYNTHESIS LECTURES ON HUMAN-CENTERED INFORMATICS #47

ABSTRACT

This book introduces the concept of worth for design teams, relates it to experiences and outcomes, and describes how to focus on worth when researching and expressing design opportunities for generous worth. Truly interdisciplinary teams also need an appropriate common language, which was developed in the companion book *Worth-Focused Design, Book 1: Balance, Integration, and Generosity* (Cockton, 2020a). Its new lexicon for design progressions enables a framework for design and evaluation that works well with a worth focus.

Design now has different meanings based upon the approach of different disciplinary practices. For some, it is the creation of value. For others, it is the conception and creation of artefacts. For still others, it is fitting things to people (beneficiaries). While each of these design foci has merits, there are risks in not having an appropriate balance across professions that claim the centre of design for their discipline and marginalise others. Generosity is key to the best creative design—delivering unexpected worth beyond documented needs, wants, or pain points. Truly interdisciplinary design must also balance and integrate approaches across several communities of practice, which is made easier by common ground. Worth provides a productive focus for this common ground and is symbiotic with balanced, integrated, and generous (BIG) practices. Practices associated with balance and integration for worth-focused generosity are illustrated in several case studies that have used approaches in this book, complementing them with additional practices.

KEYWORDS

worth-focused design, value-centred design, value-sensitive design, design synthesis, critical creative design, interaction design, innovation

Contents

Preface

Computers are now everywhere, supporting websites, in mobile devices, on desktops, and in public information systems, ticket sales kiosks, home appliances, in car-systems, and much more. Our digital age can feel radically different to previous ones, but continuities reach back decades, centuries and even millenia. For example, the many professions involved in design and development of digital artefacts all predate computers in some way. Visual designers have been with us for millenia, engineers for several centuries, and modern professional (business) managers for around one century. Human factors (ergonomics) barely predate the invention of the stored program computer approximately seven decades ago. Professions bring value systems that shape both their attitudes toward design and also their expectations for design practice. These value-driven expectations begin with education and are refined and reinforced by the professional bodies that steadily superseded craft organisations during the Industrial Revolution.

Design is inherently *axiological* (Biedenbach and Jacobsson, 2016): value trumps fact. Disciplines that construct themselves as objectively value-neutral cause friction in multi-disciplinary settings, as they lack the critical reflective practices that expose and acknowledge unavoidable value orientations. A companion book, *Worth-Focused Design, Book 1: Balance, Integration, and Generosity* (Cockton, 2020a), developed a basis for the co-existence of the different disciplinary value systems that have joined the software design mix since the 1950s.

Initially, computers were the domain of engineers, focused mostly on hardware, at first, and then increasingly on software. Once computers became important commercial and administrative tools, business schools developed Management Information Systems as a specialty. Once consumer markets developed for hardware, software, and computer services, established management disciplines such as marketing and innovation extended their interest to digital products and services. With digital convergence for all existing audio-visual media, design and media educators and professionals extended their interests and expertise into multimedia and interaction design (IxD). At least three value systems now overlap in software design practice. At the risk of oversimplification:

- engineering seeks demonstrable solutions (preferably optimal) to clearly specified problems;

- management stresses outcomes, with digital artefacts judged by their value achieved through ownership and use by organisations and individuals; and

- creative design stresses delight and appreciation, with consumers being surprised by, admiring, and enjoying outstanding imagination and realisation.

While optimal solutions, achieved value, and audience delight can and do overlap, it is possible (and very common) for one or two to be achieved without the other. An engineering solution can have no obvious value for any human activity and will not excite possible consumers. Similarly, designers can be outstandingly original and creative but overlook specific user needs and technical realities. Also, management strategists can champion new product or service propositions for which there can be no viable technical and/or creative realisation in any foreseeable future.

Brown's (2009) framing of design thinking as something that "brings together what is desirable from a human point of view with what is technologically feasible and economically viable" is not systematically achieved in practice. Unfortunately, current approaches to developing digital products and services tend to be firmly rooted in one value system, as manifested in their preferred work products:

- problem analyses, requirements specification, and analysed designs of solutions (engineering);

- business cases and value propositions (business management); and

- radically novel artefacts that have not been previously envisaged (creative design).

Each discipline would like to own the single "centre," but this makes it hard to balance respect for values of capability, rationality, and desirability. However, a hybrid methodology that aims to blend the best of disjoint value systems will introduce new problems of integration across different professional work streams. This book exploits a new framework for progressing designs from its companion book. With it, it covers the details of balancing and integrating design work around a Wo-Fo. This book presents practical approaches and support for reflection with support from several detailed case studies.

TAKING LEAVE OF OUR CENTRES

For much of my research career, and in my teaching and practice, I was uncritical of the risks associated with championing one set of disciplinary practices as "the centre" for design work. A centre was a good idea. We just had to find the right one. I came to argue that we should stop centring on users and usage, and centre instead on value. This radically new value-centred design (VCD) would focus on experiences and outcomes from use of digital products and services.

Value too turned out to not be good enough as a centre. Worth was much better, as it expresses a balance between positive and negative values (Cockton, 2006). As I was moving from users and usage to value and worth, John Heskett was moving his graduate seminar on Design and the Creation of Value with him from Chicago to Hong Kong (Dilnot, 2017). However, Heskett and I had different aims.

Heskett sought to improve design's ability to communicate how it creates and adds value by drawing on economic theory, although for Dilnot (2017, p. 11), Heskett "never conflates 'economic value' with value or values per se." Interestingly, his focus on economic value was often turned to other perspectives on value and values (Heskett, 2017, Appendix B). Heskett's audience were governments and C-level management.

My audience was design teams in both research and development. I sought to improve design teams' understanding of worth and their explicit ability to make use of it when designing interactive systems. Heskett was carrying out research *into* design, and I was carrying out research *for* design (Frayling, 1993).

My attempts to shift the focus of design, first to value and then worth, were supported by a UK NESTA fellowship from 2005–2008. I was mentored by two distinguished design researchers and educators, who awoke a dormant interest in creative design practice. However, even toward the end of this fellowship, when I spent three months at Microsoft Research Cambridge, I failed to support concurrent creative practices (Cockton et al., 2009a). Centring on worth was effective for integrating across completed design work on a digital Family Archive, but not for directing, balancing, and scheduling additional work. A better balance was needed for design work.

I began to explore balance through the concepts of design choices within Abstract Design Situations (Cockton, 2009a, 2010), which involved four different *design arenas* (Cockton 2013a, 2013b). This developed into the framework presented in the companion book. The concurrent work on design arenas in this framework lets creative design-led activities go generously beyond known needs, wants, desires, and dreams of identified beneficiaries to a more open and broad design purpose. Design could thus be BIG—Balanced, Integrated, and Generous—by balancing design activities across a project and also integrating these activities in ways that left room for creative opportunities alongside well-grounded insights about beneficiaries.

Changing design's centre from users via value to worth was less effective than supporting multiple foci, being worth-focused (Wo-Fo) some, but not all, of the time (and actually, not much of it, relatively). Multiple changing integrated foci increase the manageable complexity of factors under consideration during design. Rather than:

- placing all our trust in a single centre (such as users, usage, value, values or worth), BIG expects, and supports, multiple dynamic foci; or

- focusing predominantly on positive or negative outcomes, a Wo-Fo considers the balance of both, based on the understanding that positives can outweigh, or compensate for, negatives.

This book brings these two positions together. The first was developed in the companion book. The second is developed in this book using the context from the first.

The resulting complexity may feel very challenging, with so many factors under consideration. A key aim of this book is to communicate how such complexity can be managed and thus avoid the (often unacceptable) compromises that methodologies with centres and fixed processes (such as HCD) impose on design teams. BIG design combines existing perspectives from human-centred design (HCD), value-centred design (VCD), and worth-centred design (WCD). The last two are variants of HCD, but BIG design subsumes them all. User-centred design (UCD) and user experience (UX) practices co-exist alongside (or either side of) Wo-Fo and design-led practices.

The case studies illustrate how the complexity of a Wo-Fo in combination with three others can be managed in design projects. One case study combines the full BIG framework with a Wo-Fo (George, 2016). This Ph.D. is online and can be consulted for details of a complete design research project, as can another Ph.D. thesis (Camara, 2012) and a Master's dissertation (Vu, 2013).

WHO SHOULD READ THIS BOOK?

This book is for everyone who is aware in any way of limitations of current approaches to IxD at their current career stage. Students or professionals working within constraining engineering or innovation (design thinking) methodologies can learn how to open up their work to more creative practices while maintaining a focus on worthwhile experiences and outcomes. Similarly, designers working in loosely structured practices such as agile development or unconstrained exploratory design can learn how to add useful and productive structure to their work, especially a clear sense of design purpose coupled with the ability to ground this in understanding of beneficiaries and evaluations of usage. Managers and directors can learn practices and perspectives that take them beyond the limitations of current design thinking, design-led, agile, and lean practices and improve their tracking, scheduling, and subtle direction of concurrent design work.

LETTING GO WITHOUT LOSING YOUR GRIP

One advantage of focusing on worth in design is that it applies to the progression of design work as much as the outcomes of design. If we are generous with our beneficiaries as designers, then we must also be generous with our own design teams. We need to understand what is worthwhile about a range of disciplinary and professional practices. We then need to take the best of each and reduce their drawbacks. Benefits can make drawbacks worthwhile, but when drawbacks are reduced or even removed, design practices become even more worthwhile.

Thinking in terms of worth means that we must assess both the positives and negatives of specific disciplinary and professional practices and respond appropriately. As designers, we primarily serve others, and not our disciplines or professions. We must critically reflect on the values into which we have been socialised by education or professional practice. We should be comfortable with having our values challenged and be able to assess their impact on our design practices. We need a strong grip on how we get design work to work, and that means letting go of values that cannot be demonstrably realised by effective action.

Gilbert Cockton
April 2020

Acknowledgements

This book has its roots over 25 years ago in the work of my first two Computing Ph.D. students at Glasgow University. Steven Clarke (1997) responded to second-wave HCI (Rogers et al., 1994) by exploring the nature of links (connections, in this book) between contextual research into beneficiaries and the design of software artefacts. He moved away from assumptions of synchronised clean interfaces between phases of software development cycles to incremental asynchronous connections. Darryn Lavery developed methodological resources for the systematic study of evaluation work that was to develop into a resource-based approach to design work. Clarke's Ph.D. work is the first case study in this book.

Ph.D. students and colleagues in computing at Sunderland University built on Lavery's research from 1997–2009. Alan Woolrych and Mark Hindmarch developed an understanding of informative and expressive resources in evaluation work. Sharon McDonald and Kelly Monahan demonstrated the flexibility of HCD methods by repurposing contextual research approaches for evaluation. Alongside this continuing work on evaluation, specialised approaches and resources for contextual research were developed for accessibility (Eamon Doherty, Paul Gnanayutham, Brendan Cassidy), culture (Fuad AL Qirem), and e-learning (Susan Jones).

From 1999–2005, I directed regional support projects for the digital sector in the northeast of England. Industrial board members on three projects improved my understanding of business strategy. I became more aware of the limitations of HCD approaches to contextual research and usability evaluation in the broader context of developing and marketing digital products and services. I thus chose to focus VCD for my UK NESTA fellowship. I had the very good fortune to be mentored by Gillian Crampton-Smith. Gillian and her husband, Phil Tabor, developed my understanding of perspectives from creative design education and research. During this fellowship, I was seconded to Microsoft Research Cambridge (second case study on this book) and was an international advisor to the Finnish TEKES VALU project (third case study). At Microsoft, Abigail Sellen, David Kirk, and Richard Banks were particularly helpful with the development of worth sketching and mapping, which Sari Kujala and Piia Nurkka developed Wo-Fo resources further on the VALU project. I developed a range of Wo-Fo resources during my NESTA fellowship.

The rejection of fixed design and evaluation methods, and their reconceptualization as approaches and resources, developed during two European COST networks, MAUSE and TwinTide, with applications in consultancy as part of the regional CODEWORKS digital support project. Resource functions underpinned work by my Ph.D. students in Northumbria University's School of Design from 2010 onwards. Malcolm Jones discovered multiple resource functions (rather than types) in his Ph.D. on storytelling resources (Jones, 2020). Jenni George's Ph.D. applied a wide range of new design theory to a Wo-Fo case study (George, 2016). The Why-Frames in Chapter 4 were invented at Northumbria University's former Centre for Design Research by Louise Taylor and Joyce Yee.

The research framework that was refined within the TwinTide project and by Ph.D. students has been the basis for teaching undergraduate and postgraduate students in Italy, Slovenia, Iceland and the Netherlands. It has also been the basis for workshops and courses at conferences in Finland, Germany, Estonia, U.S., Sweden, Canada, and the UK. I have gained much from the hundreds of participants on these courses, and share some experiences as a final case study in this book. My framework has also been extended in response to several Ph.D.s that I have examined, and collaborations arising within the TwinTide COST network, in particular with Kasper Hornbæk, Erik Frøkjær, Marcin Sikorski, Igor Garnik, Marta Lárusdóttir, and Åsa Cajander.

This book is thus the result of dozens of collaborations and several funded projects. I have also benefitted from independent use of the approaches that I have developed, as covered in Chapter 6. I have been very fortunate to have received advice, ideas, knowledge, and guidance from a wide range of colleagues in academia and business, as well as the trust and enthusiasm of colleagues who have independently applied my approaches. Most recently, as Co-Editor-in-Chief of ACM *Interactions* magazine, I have had the opportunity to interact with colleagues at all stages of their careers, which has refreshed and extended the framework presented here.

Gilbert Cockton
April 2020

CHAPTER 1

Wo-Fo Success Needs Appropriate Design Progressions

This book's companion, *Worth Focused Design 1: Balance, Integration and Generosity* (Cockton, 2020a), co-evolves a new lexicon and framework for design *progressions* rather than *processes*. Such RILED processes are Rational, Idealised, and Linear, originating in Engineering Design, but superseded for over three decades now by concurrent engineering (Umemoto et al., 2004). As argued in Book 1 (Cockton, 2020a), agile development and Design Thinking methodologies remain closer to RILED than to concurrent engineering. Neither are appropriate contexts for a Wo-Fo, but design progressions based on concurrent engineering are.

Concurrent engineering developed from studies of innovation in Japanese manufacturing (Takeuchi and Nonaka, 1986), as did knowledge management, since the loss of a rigid linear staged development process will make it harder to manage the knowledge inputs and outputs from design work. Having a Wo-Fo is an innovative practice as it focuses on experiences and outcomes, and not artefacts or the detailed practices of their beneficiaries. Innovative practices have to be creative. Creative work cannot be planned up front, not only at process level, but also at the level of iterations in agile development. In creative work, you do not know exactly what you are going to do, and thus you cannot fully plan it in advance. RILED processes are thus associated with obstructing innovation (Christensen and Kaufman, 2008). Any process that is drawn with a simple chain of boxes and arrows is a linear process, irrespective of any iterative loops, backtracking, and notes about arrows that have been left out to simplify a diagram. Calling it agile or Design Thinking makes no difference to the fact that such a process is more RILED than wholly concurrent.

The companion book argues for three key realities of creative work: co-evolution, backtalk, and generosity. Rather than follow an orderly rational sequence, design work co-evolves. Originally, this was seen as co evolution of problem and solution spaces, as in Wicked Problems (Rittel and Webber, 1973). However, what evolves cannot be a problem and a solution, since a defining characteristic of a wicked problem is that its final framing is impossible until a solution has been accepted. This is not problem solving. It is not even problem setting. As long as we keep words such as "problem" and "solution" in our design lexicon we will always be prone to linear thinking, since problems must precede solutions.

Book 1 (Cockton, 2020a) instead argued that what co-evolves is an artefact and its *memoranda*. At the start of a design progression and subsequently, no final artefact is under development. Instead, various *antefacts* are developed as sketches and a broad range of prototype forms. Work on *a_tefacts* happens in one *design arena* (a_tefact generalises antefact and artefact). The other design arenas are memoranda, things to be borne in mind when working on a_tefacts. What co-evolves are all the arenas in a design progression.

The companion book derived for design arenas from Heskett's (2005) analysis of the origins of design outcomes. As well as choices about "means" (a_tefacts) there also choices of "ends" (purpose), "who benefits," and evaluations. This gives us four design arenas: a_tefact, purpose, anyficiaries, and evaluations. As with a_tefacts, anyficiaries generalises beneficiaries and maleficiaries, since all benefits require some sacrifices in turn. However, a_tefacts do not distribute benefits and sacrifices equally. Some benefit more than others, and others suffer more than some.

Design arenas provide the bases for balance and integration that are obstructed by a fixed process in RILED. Work on a design arena is no longer restricted to a single stage. Instead, design arenas are worked on concurrently, so attention must be paid to their balance. This can be supported by tracking representations for design progressions. Moving away from RILED moves away from fixed interfaces between process stages, which is a simple mechanism for (hopefully) integrating work from different design arenas. In concurrent design work, connections can be made in any way at any time. There are no fixed forms of connection. Instead, connections are formed by backtalk from one design arena to another.

Co-evolution and backtalk are symbiotic. Backtalk is a shorthand for Schön's (1992) "reflective conversation with the materials of a design situation." This both co-evolves and connects design arenas. It also enables the third key reality of creative practice: generosity, In the absence of a fixed set of upfront requirements, and also the lack of a rational value system that sees delivering to specification as the highest form of achievement, design teams are free to deliver the most worth possible. The purpose design arena is the focus for this worth. Generosity results when design teams can frame purpose from several perspectives. The purpose of design is not only to create something, nor just to have a successful validation, nor just to meet users' needs and wants while removing their pain points. The purpose of design is all of these *and more*. "More" here is generosity, going beyond what is specified or (implicitly) requested to a vision for product strategy that delights.

This book present concrete approaches, practices, and examples of Wo-Fo approaches within BIG design contexts. Chapter 2 introduces the concept of worth, advocates best practices, and reviews approaches to researching and communicating design purpose as worth. Chapter 3 examines balance for the other three design arenas. Chapter 4 presents a broad and versatile range of approaches and resources for integrating across all four design arenas. Chapters 5 and 6 present several case studies. Chapter 7 reviews the past, present, and future of BIG Wo-Fo design.

Having replaced process with progression, we have one other RILED word to remove from the design lexicon: *method*. This is replaced in the design lexicon by approaches, resources, and functions.

1.1   APPROACHES, RESOURCES, AND FUNCTIONS

This book takes a broad informed view of design work. It extends its companion book's rejection of fixed re-usable processes in its high-level framework by rejecting fixed re-usable design and evaluation methods. These may be managerially attractive, but desiring control (Dorst, 2017) and actually having it are different. Managers value control, but critical creative work control cannot be achieved through heavy handed planning of process or activities. Takeuchi and Nonaka (1986) thus stress *subtle* management control. There is no subtlety in fixed procedures slotted into fixed top down box and arrow processes. A significant design project is a unique design project. All bets are off at the outset.

A method is a complete sequence of steps for achieving a result. It is a process in miniature, but as Gedenryd (1998) has shown, method has a much longer history, beginning with ancient Greek philosophy and foregrounded in Descartes' fourth Rule for The Direction of the Mind:

> *…by a method I mean certain and simple rules, such that, if a man observe them accurately, he shall never assume what is false is true, and will never spend his mental efforts to no purpose, but will always gradually increase his knowledge and so arrive at a true understanding of all that does not surpass his powers.*

Descartes regarded mathematics as the ideal model of reasoning, as did Alexander (1971) when looking back on the failure of the 1960s design methods movement, and Parnas and Clements (1986) when arguing for faking a rational design process.

We must side with Alexander, Jones, and other pioneers of design methods who all owned up to failure. Methods, like processes, devalue "people, product, and content" (Fallman, 2003). We reject fixed re-usable methods in favour of *approaches*. Approaches are incomplete procedures supported by incomplete sets of resources (Woolrych et al., 2011). Resources too are typically incomplete and are used alongside as well as within approaches. They are critical to effective work in arenas (Cockton, 2020a, Section 4.1.1). Approaches and their resources must be adapted and completed in design work. Just as wicked problems can only be defined once a solution has been adopted, so too do "wicked" methods only look complete in a rear-view mirror: looking forward, they are stepping stones when an approach is chosen, often with large gaps or tiny footholds. Designers must work to get methods to work. In reality, methods are achievements, not premonitions. However, this openness and incompleteness makes them open to "people, product and content" to an extent and in a manner beyond fixed upfront processes and methods. Designers need "to invent ad hoc approaches, or draw inspiration from unorthodox sources or take inexplicable creative leaps" (Gaver and Bowers, 2012), but later explanations of such leaps do help!

This alternative realistic framework of approaches and resources is completed by *functions*. Work with approaches and resources is typically communicated in some way (expression, performance). Approaches and resources have potential functions that are realised by both intent and surprise during design work. Five functions were used as examples in Book 1 (Cockton, 2020a, Section 4.1.1), and nine others were used previously without comment, but as nouns (e.g., integration, association, invigoration). Functions are typically indicated adjectivally, i.e., directive, expressive, ideative, informative, inquisitive, integrative. While many functions are cognitive, others are affective (invigorative, protective), social (affiliative, deliberative, performative), or axiological (ameliorative). The 14 current functions are:

1. *Adumbrative*: scopes all design work from enduring paradigms to improvised design moves;

2. *Affiliative*: strengthens bonds and common ground within design teams;

3. *Ameliorative*: targets specific worth at all extents of design work, supporting disciplinary and professional values with specific practices;

4. *Deliberative*: triggers and supports discussion with design teams;

5. *Directive*: guides design and evaluation activities;

6. *Expressive*: externalises design work;

7. *Ideative*: triggers creative moves within design work;

8. *Informative*: provides data, knowledge, and insights to support design work;

9. *Inquisitive*: triggers questions about current and future design work;

10. *Integrative*: forms connections across design arenas;

11. *Invigorative*: provides confidence and energy for ongoing design work;

12. *Performative*: presents design work to audiences beyond a core design team;

13. *Protective*: redirects current and ongoing design work to maintain its worth; and

14. *Reflective*: supports design team members' individual reflections on design work.

These 14 functions are not exhaustive, but are finer grained than functions used elsewhere, e.g., investigative, explanatory, explorative, and persuasive (Vistisen, 2015); Lawson and Dorst's (2009) five general groups of design activities: formulating, representing, moving, evaluating, and managing. "Representing" corresponds to expressive above and "managing" to directive, but the other three have no obvious counterparts. They are above resource level: "formulating" corresponds to framing of arenas or connections; "moving" to design transitions at any level from moves to episodes; and "evaluating" to a design arena. A problem with such heterogeneous frameworks is that gaps are hard to spot, since a clear low-level omission could be argued to be covered by an existing higher-level group. In contrast, resource functions have the same level of abstraction. They are not restricted to resources, and also apply to approaches and episodes as overall cumulative function (George, 2016), but nevertheless remain homogeneous at their level of application. This has made omissions easy to spot, with ideative, reflective, deliberative and affiliative functions added since Cockton (2013c).

Some may take issue with the names of some functions, particularly adumbrative, ameliorative and invigorative. I would argue that these are appropriate as regards precision (e.g., an umbra, or shadow, is less sharp than a boundary line) and they also have reflective and inquisitive functions that reasonably prompt thoughtful responses from designers and researchers. Four alternative name sets for different audiences and uses were provided in Cockton (2013c). A further action-oriented name set for the current 14 is: scoping, affiliating, valuing, deliberating, directing, expressing, ideating, asking, informing, integrating, invigorating, performing, protecting, and reflecting.

Functions replace the types in Woolrych et al. (2011) where, for example, a report produced toward the end of a user testing activity was an *expressive* resource. However, a test report may be: *informative* about possible design changes; *performative* as a social resource; *invigorative* for its target audience; and *protective* against project risks. Rather than having a single type, a resource can have multiple functions. This was the basis for developing *resource function theory*. The difference is that *expressive resource* no longer refers to a fixed type resource, but to a resource and one of its potential functions. This is much less wordy than "resource with a potential expressive function." An expressive informative resource is like a long red scarf, which is not a type of scarf but one with two non-exclusive highlighted attributes. The scarf can also be woollen and woven, just as an expressive informative resource can also be performative, invigorative, and protective.

Textbook methods tend to have two primary functions: to direct and express. They are often supported by resources with informative functions. For example, Heuristic Evaluation is primarily an informative resource (its heuristics), but extends to an approach when combined with a directive procedure for applying the heuristics (Woolrych et al., 2011). A problem report format (Cockton et al., 2004) adds an expressive resource for further support. Fallman (2003) contrasted "first-generation" design methods that aim to systematize and formalize (i.e., have a directive function), with "second-generation" ones that support learning, collaboration, and creative practice (i.e., have informative, affiliative, performative, and ideative functions).

A resource may have one primary function, often informative, but further functions can be realised. Indeed, careful resource use can achieve ten or more functions. This is how design work manages complexity by addressing multiple important concerns in a single move. Just as resources are mobilized for success in political arenas (Renn, 1992), so design resources are mobilized by activating their potential functions. Resources can give design organisations a strong competitive advantage (Stevens and Moultrie, 2011), and this includes resources for design purpose (Winkler and

Spiekerman, 2019). Some economic theories address resource advantages (e.g., from specific design co-products) better than others (Weber, 2017). Takeuchi and Nonaka (1986) exposed the importance of human capital, skills, and knowledge. In practical terms, resources and the approaches that develop and apply them form a palette (Friedland, 2019) that can be structured into a playbook for specific project and programme settings (Gajander, 2019).

As with process plans, there are no guarantees from textbook resources. Design teams must work to get resources to work. Teams only know what their methods were, never what they will be. Every method realisation is unique. Approaches are templates.

Human-centred design (HCD) methods focus on primary research to inform design work using empirical human science practices that are primarily directive, with ameliorative functions focused on process more than outcomes, with the assumption that a badly used method can have no good outcomes. This overlooks the many possibilities for "repair" in design work, which follow from the use of spoken language, where repair is a common feature of dialogue. Again, such adaptive uses of language can realise resource functions: "inquiry is an aggregate process with several component functions" (Gedenryd, 1998). Gedenryd notes how the interactive structure of design work brings important advantages over working *intramentally*, i.e., wholly within a single designer's head

Primary research will figure in most substantial IxD work. However, it is not the only research mode, especially for the a_tefact design arena, where much research is secondary, which is focused on standards, trends, innovations, and technology. Similarly, other arenas draw on secondary research, as well as personal resources, and also on critical and creative practices. Whatever the mode of research, expression and sharing of outcomes is important. Such outcomes can be framed as results, findings, insights, proposals, requirements, opportunities, and more, but whatever we call them, they need to be captured, shared, discussed, and used.

Book 1 (Cockton, 2020a) developed a template for good BIG progressions, having set processes aside. Similarly, this book presents not methods, but approach and resource templates that realise their potential functions through thoughtful creative work. There are no guarantees. Instead, there are challenges that effective design teams routinely overcome through judgement, wisdom, and courage.

CHAPTER 2

Framing Design Purpose as Worth

Book 1 (Cockton, 2020a) considered design work that progressively departs from a normative process as design problems get less tame. Differences between ideals and realities are primarily ones of structure. RILED phases each focus on a single design arena. Problem phases must logically precede "solution" phases. Systematic interfaces between adjacent phases are imagined, with phase outputs acting as inputs to generation, derivation, translation, or other design activities that are conceived as quasi-mechanical operations. None of these RILED assumptions hold in creative design practice.

A focus on worth or any other consideration will only be effective if it is "at home" with a range of design practices. This is why Book 1 (Cockton, 2020a) addressed these first. Its Chapter 2 considered creative design practice. Its Chapter 3 used fiction to critique uncritical positions of engineering design management and its HCD offshoot. Its Chapter 4 developed BIG design paradigms that can give due weight to creative, engineering, and management considerations. Its Chapter 5's tracking and reflection practices make space for critical creative work while keeping room for the rational values of engineering design management. Much of this tracking initially has an *adumbrative* function, i.e., to roughly outline the scope of current design work at decreasing levels of abstraction. To adumbrate is to overshadow (*umbra* is Latin for shadow). As with any shadow, the edges provide the main detail. It is only with such an open "zoomable" programme and project infrastructure that we can consider how a Wo-Fo approach to design purpose can be "at home" within appropriately broad design practices.

This book focuses on advancing and integrating design arenas without losing sight of their locales of use, i.e., the broader assemblages of projects, organisations, and communities of practice. This chapter focuses on purpose as a relatively underexplored design arena. Chapter 3 surveys approaches to a_tefacts (antefacts then artefacts), anyficiaries (beneficiaries and maleficiaries), and evaluations. After that, Chapter 4 focuses on integration across design arenas. Chapters 5 and 6 present case studies that use the approaches introduced in Chapters 2–4.

Making decisions is not the only way to advance design arenas. Indeed, when observing design work it can be difficult to see whether, when and how design decisions are being made. Chapter 4 has examples of how design decisions occur implicitly through integration, especially during Davies and Talbot's (1987) *imago* when an idea is experienced as THE right idea. Unlike much research on abstract disembodied decontextualized "creativity," having "original" ideas is of little interest to design research. Creative designers ideate prolifically. They are unlikely to be admitted to Design Schools if they cannot already demonstrate and discuss the geneses and development of their ideas up to and beyond an imago experience.

Design School studio education practice has emergent creative progressions with "crits" (critiques) at their heart. Critique in design education and professional practice is wide ranging. It is not wholly an evaluation activity. Often, there may be no evaluation of an a_tefact in a crit. While evaluative feedback from peers and tutors can provide valuable direction, much direction actually arises from questions rather than statements. Design work is advanced in many ways. This includes advances through: questions (inquisition); discussion (deliberation); suggested research or experiments (direction); new ideas (ideation); possible connections (integration); designer's knowledge (information); and social (association) and emotional functions (protection, invigoration).

Initial design work is both open and focused. For Darke (1979), designers "fill boxes with concepts." Knowledge ranges from Dorst's (2015) open generic themes to focused craft knowledge about making final artefacts. All forms of knowledge can be in play at the same time (Guindon 1990).

2.1   WORTH AND THE AXIOLOGY DESIGN

Simon (1969) views design as "changing existing circumstances into preferred ones," which requires resources with ameliorative functions. Amelioration improves something (*melior* is Latin for better), as required for preferred outcomes. Worth is the balance of (ameliorated) positive experiences and outcomes over (alleviated) negative ones. Worth is a universal framing for design purpose.

Axiology is the philosophy of value. The term "represents an attempt to bring together, and critically examine, a wide variety of already existing and overlapping questions related to the essence of goodness, right conduct, value, and obligation" (Hiles, 2008). Given Simon's "preferred" circumstances, design research, and practice both require an axiological basis.

As the balance of achievable benefits over possible costs and risks, worth is a matter of judgement. There has been no improvement on Bentham's (1789) proposed calculation over 200 years ago:

> *Sum up the values of all the pleasures on one side and of all the pains on the other. If the balance is on the side of pleasure, that is the over-all good tendency of the act with respect to the interests of that person; if on the side of pain, its over-all bad tendency.*

Bentham's calculus has various names (felicific, utility, hedonic, or hedonistic), complemented by terms for units of pleasure (*hedons*) and pain (*dolors*), which came later, not from Bentham. Bentham and followers' failure to deliver on a quantified calculus has led to his thinking being replaced by a simpler focus on positive value or undifferentiated utility, which has drawbacks.

There are a few empirical approaches to specific utility. In marketing, *conjoint analysis* elicits consumer data on relative preferences for features, functions, or benefits (Green and Srinivasan,

1978). However, the "rigorous" mathematical basis of this analysis can be undermined by unwarranted distorting assumptions. Rigour has little value without ecological validity. Some recent Human-Centred Informatics (HCI) research has applied economic approaches on utility to the worth of a sorting feature in an investment task (Nov and Su, 2018). The cost of using the sort feature was varied between 0% and 10% of the investment gains, letting price elasticity be investigated. Younger, less experienced investors made more use of the sort feature, but all usage declined as costs increased. Use of the sort feature was associated with higher investment gains. Although this study has a very narrow scope, the use of economics concepts generalises to considerations of worth. Price elasticity explains why users can accept costs in return for benefits, since any purchase or use involves foregoing costs for benefits. However, costs and risks can become too much for the benefits received. Usage is not worthwhile there.

The challenge is to extend consideration of price denominators beyond experimental uses of "money," which admits mathematical rigour, to a broader range of costs and risks that do not reduce to numbers. Breadth is very important for the purpose arena. Nov and Su's study avoids a single valence by considering benefits (investment gain) and costs (percentage of gain foregone to use sort). They avoided one of three drawbacks associated with axiological HCI.

2.1.1 AVOIDING THE SINGLE VALENCE DRAWBACK

A first drawback appears when only positives or negatives are explicitly in focus, but not both. Bentham's approach to utility considered both, as did Doblin (1978), with good/bad analysis identified as a tool for innovation. Much Value-Sensitive Design (VSD; Friedman et al., 2006) focuses on avoiding negatives. In contrast, value-centred design (VCD; Cockton, 2004b, 2005) mostly focused on achievement of positives. We should consider both positives and negatives, as well as neutrals. The occupational psychologist Herzberg (1966) developed a two-factor theory for workplace motivation. The first factor (group) of motivators leads to satisfaction. The second, hygiene factors, leads to dissatisfaction. However, absence of motivators leads not to dissatisfaction, but to a lack of satisfaction, which is not the same as dissatisfaction. Similarly, removal of adverse hygiene factors leads not to satisfaction, but to undissatisfaction. The important point here is that there is a neutral middle ground with no positive or negative valencing. Thinking only in terms of positives and negatives is not enough. We must consider three valences when designing for worth.

Herzberg's workplace motivators were achievement, recognition, the work itself, responsibility, advancement, and growth. His hygiene factors were company policy, supervision, relationship with boss, work conditions, salary, relationship with peers, and security. Tuch and Hornbæk (2015) have identified Herzberg's factors in relation to user experience (UX). They studied smartphone ownership and usage, identifying technical quality and price as hygiene factors, and utility and convenience as motivators. Utility, being able to do useful things with a smartphone, was qualitative in contrast to Nov and Su (2018). Convenience was often expressed in terms of efficiency.

The need to focus on polyvalent worth, not monovalent value or values, is understood in design, economics, marketing, and also ethics, where the controversial principle of *double effect* is relevant in many contexts (Woodward, 2001). Design teams need not resolve the general ethics of double effect, where an intentional positive goal can compensate for a (known) negative consequence. Instead, they can focus on balances of worth and decide whether users and other stakeholders can forego specific costs in return for specific benefits. A worthwhile balance, however, does not mean that attempts to reduce adverse consequences should stop. Nor should the latter be exaggerated (as dystopian), but nor should there be excessive celebration of benefits (Gaver and Bowers, 2012).

2.1.2   AVOIDING THE ABSTRACT VALUES ONLY DRAWBACK

Anti-utilitarian thinking often narrows *utility's* meaning down to narrow instrumentalism. This introduces a second drawback, where mundane instrumental values are seen as being less worthy than noble "human values." The former become hedonic and transient, unlike the latter ethical and spiritual guides for people's highest achievements. Kheirandish (2018) thus restricts her design resources to human values in contrast to Boztepe's (2007) instrumental "product" values. Human values are one of a family of terms for a realist universalist position on values, others being "substantive values," "deeper values," and "inner values." Walker (2017) refers to all three, but without examples when each term is used. To her credit, Kheirandish (2018) tested her belief in fundamental values and could not be empirically validate many as resources for design work.

Street (2012) reviews the arguments for substantive values that follow from the argument that "valuing beings" must have reasons in their humanity for what they value. To avoid an infinite regress of reasons, it is attractive to propose a fixed set of terminal values for all people at all times in all places, which are "deep" enough and personally "inner" anytime anywhere. The reality of means-ends chains is that an infinite regress can only be avoided by deciding where to stop. At the extreme, this is a single value, such as Aristotle's *eudaimonia*, translated simply as happiness or welfare, or drawing on the Greek (*eu* means well, *daimonia* is "spiritness"), as human flourishing or prosperity (Anscombe, 1958). This is far too abstract a place to stop. Design teams need to be more concrete.

High status values are much more abstract than the worth achieved through ownership and use, regardless of how superficial some may find that. Achievement of more concrete user value (e.g., Boztepe, 2007) is easier to design for and evaluate than satisfaction of more abstract human values. Noble values may make a design team feel worthy in political or spiritual terms, but such values must direct work in support of improvability. If values are not evaluable, then e-valu-ation work is severely constrained. Similarly, within the a_tefact arena, it must be possible to appraise the likely impact of specific capabilities as designed on achievement of desired values for stakeholders.

When framing worth through positive values (benefits) and negative ones (costs, risks), abstract values can provide scope, whereas concrete values direct attention to specific usage experiences and outcomes and their evaluation. Abstract values are best used to group more concrete ones, so work on design purpose be both top down and bottom up. Such an approach has been developed by van de Poel (2013), who "translates" values into design requirements via more concrete mediating *norms*. Similarly, Winkler and Spiekerman (2019) associate overarching values with one or more of five dimensions, and refine each value into specific aspects.

This second drawback is compounded by confusion between value and values. VSD is strictly *values*-centred design, in that it focused design on human values of ethical import, and not on the broader and more concrete value of a digital product. Worth-centred design (WCD) avoided this confusion by combining VCD and VSD. Concrete value (VCD; Cockton, 2004b) is combined with abstract (ethical) values (VSD). Achieving positives (VCD) is combined with avoiding negatives (VSD). VCD and VSD overlap in the sense that VSD also addresses positives, even though its ethical focus connotes avoidance of negatives. However, there is little overlap on the range of abstraction, with VCD focused on specific valuable concrete outcomes in the world, and VSD focused on abstract ethical values that span many possible usage outcomes. A Wo-Fo spans all these differences.

2.1.3   AVOIDING THE INDIVIDUALS' VALUES ONLY DRAWBACK

A third drawback arises from the loss of Bentham's consideration of both individual and collective worth elements (e.g., association, friendship, benevolence, power, malevolence, enmity), some of which can be either positive or negative (e.g., reputation, memory). Much research for design focuses on what is worthwhile for individuals, whereas Cockton (2006) covered both individual and collective worth, as did Rokeach (1973) in his landmark study, where he defined a value as

> *an enduring belief that a specific mode of conduct or end-state of existence is personally or socially preferable to an opposite or converse mode of conduct or end-state of existence*

Rokeach also highlighted the textually obvious connection between values and individuals' evaluation: values are "relatively general and durable internal criteria for evaluation." In design, such criteria need to be externalised whenever possible.

Social innovation work inevitably develops collective value, but consumer-oriented products can be overly individual in focus, missing opportunities arising from a balanced value proposition that includes collective worth. While a narrow focus leaves fewer values to be reconciled during design, these values still need to be reconciled in the world. It is best to anticipate this and design for this. Difficulties of incommensurability are bound to arise (Heskett, 2017) and judgement and wisdom are the best resources to apply here. There are no objective procedures that can help. Even so, Davies and Talbot (1987) identified individual/collective as a common theme in designers' work, so risk of over individualisation is reduced by such personal design resources.

Heskett (2017) spent decades studying the relationship between design and economics. He assessed major economic theories for their ability to include design competence as a source of competitive advantage. Collective value extends to the organisations that develop and market digital products. Important values here are technical feasibility, financial viability, and compatibility with the product range. Strategic Design can combine these into whole new business cases (Stevens and Moultrie, 2011). Such values and business cases are not restricted to commercial for profit organisations. Worth in Strategic Design primarily results from design work practices that in turn improve the worth of digital products developed by or for an organisation. However, design research practices do bring additional considerations, such as aesthetic knowledge and scientific value and communication with audiences through books, exhibitions and other expressive and performative resources (Gaver and Bowers, 2012).

This book mostly focuses on the worth of digital products and associated design work practices. Chapter 7 considers worth in relation to design progressions.

2.2   WORKING ON DESIGN PURPOSE

It is worth making BIG design Wo-Fo, but only if worth is broadly scoped to avoid the three drawbacks above by being:

1. *trivalent* by considering a balance of positives, negatives, and neutrals. Value propositions wholly focused on positives risk ignoring potential negatives. The anyficiaries arena concept keeps both maleficiaries and beneficiaries in scope;

2. *multi-layered* by ranging from the most abstract noble values to concrete and instrumental value, avoiding confusion between value and values, and not favouring "deeper" values over instrumental or experiential value; and

3. *multi-len*s by considering collective as well as individual value(s).

Dilnot (2017) notes the complexity of realistic value propositions

> *Design is therefore ... the creation and or the addition not just of "value," but of complex multiple "values" that embody, express and enable capabilities.*

The "emphasis is very emphatically on the plural" (Heskett, 2017), which requires a broadly scoped concept of worth that can involve any mix of positive, neutral and negative, abstract and concrete, noble and mundane, and individual and collective. Such a concept can preserve the scope of Bentham's ranges of pleasures and pain without committing to forms of calculation that underlie much classical economic (choice) theory. Worth extends the simple value propositions of much business practice to become multi-layered (value consistent with values) and multi-valenced (positives, neutrals, negatives). The concept of worth as a design resource is potentially both informative and directive in function, sensitising design teams to, and directing them to contemplate, many value considerations.

Design teams who are informed and directed by the concept of worth can immediately recall potential positives and negatives that may be relevant for a new project. Working on design purpose can thus begin with the design team, understood broadly as all those who will be involved in a project and ideally will contribute to its inception. Not all team members are creatively educated designers, but include a wide range of stakeholders and specialists. Approaches are needed that can include a diverse team in design work. Managers' desire for early control can delay the involvement of a broad team, leading Winkler and Spiekerman (2019) to defend their values resource as a tool for management when developing an initial value proposition before involving system designers who "can probably arrive at such a list with a little reflection." The evidence is that designers can definitely articulate values. Heskett (2017) illustrates this with seven words from one paragraph by Gordon Russell, a furniture designer who was the first head of what is now the UK Design Council: healthy, good, quality, sham, standard, seemly, satisfying. Section 2.4 adds scores of publicly shared experiential values from architecture and interaction design.

Over the last decade, a wide range of *canvas* resources have been developed that are very well suited to multidisciplinary project inception. The Value Proposition Canvas (Osterwalder et al., 2014) lets a multi-expert design team collect ideas about *pains* and *gains* in the context of *Jobs to be Done* (Kalbach, 2019). "Jobs" represent work and similar goals, while pains and gains represent the negatives and positives associated with pursuit of these goals. This canvas avoids a risky sole focus on positives common in too much business work on value propositions.

The starting point of work on any design arena is subjective (inter-subjective for teamwork). Rational design polemics often devalue the subjective, but all well-grounded studies of creative design work treasure it (e.g., Darke, 1979). In (well) under an hour of brainstorming or similar activities such as brainwriting (Warfield et al., 1975), a design team can fill out an initial Value Proposition Canvas.

Ultimately, subjectivity cannot be avoided. It is better to value it as hardwon expertise when faced with a complex set of positives, neutrals, and negatives. A team must make judgements on the acceptability of a resulting balance of worth on the basis of benefits that have been achieved (motivators) or unachieved (neutral) and of costs and risks that have been removed (neutral) or reduced (hygiene factors). The absence of an intended benefit is not a negative for stakeholders from Herzberg's (1966) perspective. As regards unachieved benefit, relevant stakeholders will be unsatisfied rather than dissatisfied. Similarly, costs and risks that are reduced or even removed will leave relevant stakeholders undissatisfied rather than satisfied.

Judgements of achieved worth must weigh achieved positives against persisting negatives. There is no calculus for this yet, and one cannot be expected soon given lack of progress since Bentham's initial attempts over two centuries ago. However, subjectivity can be balanced by evaluation work. Similarly, the relevance of intended positives and negatives to stakeholders can be addressed by stakeholder research within the anyficiaries arena.

2.3   RESEARCH ACTIVITIES FOR DESIGN PURPOSES

Reviews of modes of research for design purpose as worth begin with secondary research resources, then critical reflective resources, then primary research approaches, and lastly expressive resources.

Primary research is not sufficient for design purpose, especially when only focused on users. Potential users do not have the proactive innovative vision of product management and design teams. User research must be augmented with a project sponsor's product goals. Current technology usage and experience may be of limited relevance. For major innovations, design purpose needs to go beyond empirically grounded needs, wants and similar. Similarly, user studies may not provide majority support for purpose in projects motivated by political or environmental values, e.g., promoting intersectionality (Erete et al., 2018) or sustainability.

2.3.1   SECONDARY RESEARCH RESOURCES

In May 2019, a Google search for "Lists of Needs and Wants" reported 229 million hits. Over a month later, this had dropped to 179 million, but a search for "Lists of Human Values" reported 1.17 billion hits. No design team should ever be short of inspiration when reflecting on possible purposes for a design! Worth spans a range of psychological constructs such as values, needs, wants, drives, dreams, nightmares, pleasures, pains, lacks, and motivations. These are all in scope for intended worth as positive benefits to deliver and negative costs and risks to avoid. Despite this veritable tsunami of information, researchers in HCI have drawn up their own proprietary lists. VSD has drawn on an evolving set of "human values with ethical import," such as these 13: Human Welfare, Ownership and Property, Privacy, Freedom from Bias, Universal Usability, Trust, Autonomy, Informed Consent, Accountability, Courtesy, Identity, Calmness, and Environmental Sustainability This list is not assumed to be comprehensive. As the authors note, "the list of other possible moral and non-moral values could get very long very quickly" and could include "peacefulness, respect, compassion, love, warmth, creativity, humor, originality, vision, friendship, cooperation, collaboration, purposefulness, devotion, loyalty, diplomacy, kindness, musicality, or harmony" (Friedman et al., 2006). This more than doubles (from 13 to 32) the values that could be considered.

There is no need, however, for a single list, even less so for a short one. For example, Shneiderman (2003) reported that his "quest for clearer statements of human needs led me to a simple formula for life: Living, loving, learning, leaving a legacy" (Covey et al., 1994). Rationalist values are clear here: statements must be "clear" and formulae need to be "simple." In contrast, creative design practices thrive on ambiguity and complexity. Both originate in the world. There is less and less chance of escaping them. As the challenges addressed by design become more open, complex, dynamic, and networked (Dorst, 2015), preferences for simplicity veer toward escapism.

There is no clear upper limit to the number of values that can be considered during the course of a design project. If there is one, it is not less than 10 or 20, which tend to be the upper bounds for what some researchers imagine design teams can manage. Winker and Spiekerman (2019) assembled a list of 31 overarching values relevant to sustainable design. Each was associated with a range of 2–32 specific aspects, resulting in a list of over 200 possible considerations. This value collection is intended for "innovation teams and engineers … [to] consider during requirement engineering," groups who are too often inappropriately assumed to need simple clarity.

Lists of values of any length can be used alongside each other. There is no need to merge and integrate them into one resource for use on all design projects. A selection of lists can be placed on a double-sided sheet of paper for use in projects and courses. I have done so without problems with almost 200 course attendees over the last 5 years. Adopting specific values from lists has ameliorative and adumbrative functions: the former *expresses* design purpose (as an initial DAN); the latter *scopes* it. Juxtaposition of lists has a potential deliberative function that prompts design team discussion on the directive value of each list.

The lists on the following pages show Rokeach's (1973) list of Instrumental and Terminal Values, Kahle's simplification of these for consumer product design (Homer and Kahle, 1988), and Schwartz's (1992) Basic Values. The lists are from the Center for Nonviolent Communication (CNVC, 2005). These four lists have been chosen to undermine each other as standalone informative resources. Their differences promote inquisitive and reflective responses. For example, Kahle's reduction of Rokeach's list from 36 to 9 values, and the loss of Rokeach's *instrumental-terminal* distinction prompts design teams to reflect on what is lost and gained in a quest for clarity and simplification. The CNVC list (75) is more than double Rokeach's combined value lists (36). The groupings of values in Rokeach, Schwartz, and CNVC are an additional informative resource.

The four lists can be further augmented with ones that have been explicitly developed to support design work, e.g., Kheirandish, (2018) and Kujala and Väänänen-Vainio-Mattila, (2009). However, the benefits of juxtaposition should not be lost. Dorst's (2015) open, complex, dynamic, and networked design challenges must be matched by requisite variety (Ashby, 1958) of design resources, which must also be *open* and *complex* through choice, *dynamic* through adding and changing resources during a project, and *networked* through reflection and deliberation that expose synergies and tensions between different lists of values.

In summary, existing lists of values, need, and wants or other axiological resources can be used to achieve some or more of the following functions (and possibly others):

- *Informative*: by alerting team members to values that they have not yet considered;

- *Inquisitive*: by prompting questions in relation to gaps, overlaps, different vocabulary and groupings, and other contrasts between published lists and personal constructs;

- *Ideative*: generative by spotting gaps in lists and filling them;

- *Reflective*: by reconsidering, prioritising, triaging, or otherwise considering the relative importance (if any) of different values to a design project, a quasi-predictive use;

- *Deliberative*: by the design team discussing any results of the preceding four functions;

- *Affiliative*: by the preceding two functions providing a design team with initial common ground. Aliasing (alternative names for values) can respect vocabulary differences;

- *Directive*: by framing with values, an exploratory role that can "go some way to uncovering aesthetic and socio-political values" (Gaver and Bowers, 2012); and

- *Adumbrative*, *Ameliorative*, *Expressive*, and *Directive*: by noting (prioritised) values in a purpose DAN for further investigation. This cluster is typical of successful design work, where multiple functions are realised simultaneously.

Rokeach Instrumental

Cheerfulness	Courage	Broad-mindedness
Ambition	Politeness	Logic
Love	Honesty	Obedience
Cleanliness	Imagination	Helpfulness
Self-control	Independence	Responsibility
Capability	Intellect	Forgiveness

Rokeach Terminal

True friendship	Freedom	National security
Mature love	Pleasure	Sense of accomplishment
Self-respect	Social recognition	A world of beauty
Happiness	Wisdom	A world at peace
Inner harmony	Salvation	A comfortable life
Equality	Family security	An exciting life

Kahle

Fun and Enjoyment	Sense of accomplishment	Sense of belonging
Excitement	Self-Fulfilment	Being well respected
Security	Warm relationships	
Self respect	with others	

Schwartz's Basic Values

Openness to change	Achievement	Tradition
Self-direction	Power	Self-transcendence
Stimulation	Conservation	Benevolence
Self-enhancement	Security	Universalism
Hedonism	Conformity	

CNVC Needs Inventory (2005) (http://www.cnvc.org/Training/needs-inventory)

Connection	**Physical Well-Being**	**Meaning**
acceptance	air	awareness
affection	food	celebration of life
appreciation	movement/exercise	challenge
belonging	rest/sleep	clarity
cooperation	sexual expression	competence
communication	safety	consciousness
closeness	shelter	contribution
community	touch	creativity
companionship	water	discovery
compassion	**Honesty**	efficacy
consideration	authenticity	effectiveness
consistency	integrity	growth
empathy	presence	hope
inclusion	**Play**	learning
intimacy	joy	mourning
love	humor	participation
mutuality	**Peace**	purpose
nurturing	beauty	self-expression
respect/self-respect	communion	stimulation
safety	ease	to matter
security	equality	understanding
stability	harmony	**Autonomy**
support	inspiration	choice
to know and be known	order	freedom
to see and be seen		independence
to understand and		space
be understood		spontaneity
trust		
warmth		

There are many ways to use lists of values in a design project, which extend beyond theory's roles as explanatory, predictive, or generative (Löwgren, 2013). The wide range of potential functions makes it unwise to offer any method for using lists of values and other secondary research in design work. Lists may be used in breakout groups in project inception workshops, but can also be used individually or collectively during reflective activities (e.g., Sprint Retrospectives in Scrum software development). Values may also be encountered indirectly through a team's "previous eclectic research" (Gaver, 2011). For the Equator 1 design workbooks, this spanned "possible views on the home ranging from previous work in HCI, sociology, and the arts to psychoanalytic accounts of the home, descriptions of the home as a hiding place for contraband, and popular news articles about unusual domestic activities." Such eclectic reading is not wholly within the purpose arena, but instead forms a concourse. It challenges close adherence to Lévi-Strauss' position on the universe of instruments in bricolage being closed (Fallman, 2003). There is no need to stick with whatever is at hand, bringing into question the appropriateness of bricolage as a model for design work, which forges both new means and new ends, especially in IxD where concerns have expanded beyond functionality and usability to the emotional, aesthetic, cultural, and critical (Gaver and, Bowers 2012).

Overall, the functions of secondary research for design purpose are primarily some mix of informative, inquisitive, ideative, and expressive. They support, following Darke (1979), *filling the design purpose box with concepts*. Having concepts to hand helps.

2.3.2 CRITICAL AND REFLECTIVE RESOURCES

Design teams are never without some resources. Each individual member joins a project with relevant knowledge and experience. Secondary resources in design work can, will, and should be augmented with autobiographical ones. A key aspect of Strategic Design is leveraging the existing intuitions and judgement of creative designers (Stevens and Moultrie, 2011). This extends to design research portfolios, where annotated highlights "reflected our own views, focusing on what they would want to promote in the future," "political theorizing in a sense," but "grounded in people's specific experiences and identities" (Gaver and Bowers, 2012).

Davies and Talbot (1987) stressed the importance of RDI designers' careers to understanding how and why they form and accept the ideas that become the "right" ones, and how they draw on a range of themes such as public/private *en route* (Cockton, 2020a, Section 2.1.4). Subjective personal perspectives should never be excluded in principle, especially in co-design contexts where participants can be new to design work. Only right ideas come with risks, but designers spend much time testing and challenging before committing to them (Darke, 1979; Davies and Talbot, 1987). However, initial transcendence of client dreams may not be grounded in user research, but in the vision, empathy, and receptiveness of the design team. Generous design goes beyond evidenced needs.

Creative designers augment published secondary lists of values, etc., with their own experience. Le Dantec et al. (2009) discussed their own research experiences with a values focus in design and then collated a list that did not match that of Friedman et al. (2006). Unsurprisingly, "many of the values that were expressed locally in each of our case studies can be connected to one or more of the values of ethical import," but not in a value-norm hierarchy as in van de Poel (2013). However, additional values were important in their case studies, e.g., pride, durability, justice, being knowledgeable, being normal, independence, identity control, and staying connected. These arose in specific project *locales*, i.e., technology for the homeless, acceptable RFID use in ubicomp, and domestic technology. The values in Le Dantec et al. (2009) added to the secondary literature.

Lists from secondary research clearly have limitations. The well-grounded critical reflection of Le Dantec et al. (2009) reminds us of the need for teams to be aware of their past practices and to draw on these judiciously as resources. Le Dantec et al. also argue for appropriate empirical research, which we will turn to next after considering a "discount" approach to concepts for design purpose.

I developed a resource (Cockton, 2009b) that acknowledges a need for simplicity when time or other resources such as budget are short and there is not time for involved inception workshops or extensive research on beneficiaries. Such resource gaps introduce major risks, which can be mitigated to some extent with appropriate activities.

The starting point for a quick approach is a locale where an envisaged digital product will be used. Webs of worth spin out from co-located anyficiaries who experience the locale differently. Such *worth webs* locate anyficiaries in overlapping contexts of individual and collective (de)motivators. A very simple approach to individual motivation is taken by adopting Alderfer's (1972) motivational categories of Existence, Relatedness, and Growth (ERG). Collective motivation is addressed as IKK social structures: *institutions*, *kin* (family), and *kind* (community). Relatedness links individual to collective worth, as do Locales (L), multiple places in a single space.

The resulting L-ERG-IKK (Locales for Existence, Relatedness, and Growth, and Institutions, Kin, and Kind) framework (Cockton, 2009b, for those allergic to theory!) relates places and social structures to individual needs and wants. A third dimension of Mind–Body–Spirit was subsequently added as a further inquisitive resource for thinking about possible purpose. While many will take issue with a Mind–Body dualism, and others with adding Spirit too, these common sensemaking categories extend the range of individual and collective (de)motivators considered for design purpose beyond more focused concepts such as Bourdieu's field as used by Dorst (2015).

Figure 2.1 shows this extended L-ERG-IKK+ model as a Rubik's Cube. L-ERG-IKK+ is primarily an inquisitive resource with an ameliorative focus. It is adumbrative as it effectively begins, critiques, or extends the scope of design purpose. It is barely informative, doing little more than foreground worth web locales that relate minds, bodies, spirits, and associated existence and growth needs to relatedness needs in the context of families (kin), communities (kind), and institutions. It is important to relate individuals to the intersecting biological and societal contexts that make then unique.

Figure 2.1: Locales for Existence, Relatedness, and Growth, and Institutions, Kin, and Kind (L-ERG-IKK).

A commonsense view of institutions is taken of them as formal organisations, rather than adopting New Institutionalism and its blurring of boundaries (Meyer and Rowan, 1977). This is not to deny that marriage is an institution in one sense, nor that institutions as cultural practices underpin communities: both kin and kind have institutionalized aspects to them (North, 1991) as formal rules (constitutions, laws, property rights) and informal restraints (sanctions, taboos, customs, traditions, codes of conduct). While as social structures, kin, kind, and institutions all have things in common, there are also important differences between them.

Conceptual blurring in L-ERG-IKK+'s does not impact its main inquisitive function, since its superficial (and somewhat fraught) "information" rapidly transitions into questions structured around the axes and their intersections. Each of the 27 cells is essentially a question to a team, e.g., is "spiritual growth" in "families" a focus for your design? What about maintaining "bodily existence" needs in some "community"' context? Creative moves here are not bisociative (Koestler, 1964) but *trisociative*.

Lists of values, etc., provide more structure and content than L-ERG-IKK+, and are thus better used first in team settings, to avoid a looking at blank sheets of paper for too long. Used once an initial purpose DAN is populated, L-ERG-IKK+ is a compact quick way to scan for gaps, especially ones that can be filled by team knowledge. L-ERG-IKK+ can be used during project inception and at reflective points at the end of design episodes.

2.3.3   PRIMARY RESEARCH RESOURCES AND APPROACHES

Secondary research and reflective resources are relatively low cost, but with risks that can be addressed by primary research. Formative evaluation of prototype use is one way to do this and can become summative in Lean UX experiments with Minimal Viable Products (MVPs; Gothelf with Seiden, 2013). The latter evaluations are used to test assumptions about purpose and whether an

MVP can deliver it. Where assumptions prove to be mistaken, primary "just-in-time" research can improve understandings of anyficiaries. In ISO 9241-210 (ISO, 2019), all research underpinning user requirements must be completed before design begins. However, this can only hold for the first release of a digital product or service, as from that point there is always a fielded system in use. Lean UX's just in time approach to primary research (Gothelf with Seiden, 2013) is more realistic.

Primary research approaches for design purpose overlap with those for anyficiaries. The main difference is their outputs. For design purpose, only benefits, costs, and risks are of interest, expressed at relatively high levels of abstraction. Other important aspects of beneficiaries or maleficiaries are left for the anyficiaries arena. These can be very concrete and make or break a design, but even so they are not strategic as a focus for design purpose.

Table 2.1: Potential values by locus of manifestation for family archive design purpose (values prefixed new or newly offered innovation opportunities since no existing systems could be identified that would plausibly deliver on these values)

PEOPLE: A Happy Family	PLACE: A Nice Home	OBJECTS: Treasures
Manifest identities	**Newly** less cluttered	Treasures sold/passed on
Increased family empathy	Nurturing: somewhere you want to be	Protected heirlooms
New shared times as a family	Living family heritage: a past you want to revisit	Well displayed
Manifest status for external social standing	Enviable: somewhere others want to be	Materialisation with enhancements
Stronger family past		
Stewardship obligations discharged		
Stronger roots in past		
Achievement of closure		
New pride in improved organisation, enhanced		
Caring for each other		

A wide range of empirical research approaches can be used to fill design arenas with evidence as well as concepts. For the Family Archive programme at Microsoft Research Cambridge (Cockton et al., 2009a), a draft report of ethnographic research (published later as Kirk and Sellen, 2010) was used to identify values relevant to a family's archiving of physical and digital possessions. A list of values was assembled, used, and revised in workshops. This was then collaboratively triangulated against a large corpus of field photographs of possessions in people's homes taken by the field researcher. No revisions were required to Table 2.1, and many photos evidenced each manifested value. As with culture, values can only manifest themselves through people (words, deeds), places, and things. Toward the end of my role in the Family Archive research, a list of candidate values was organised into a table using these three categories. Table 2.1 shows ten values that would manifest themselves in people, and four each for values that would manifest themselves in changes to a home or to the precious objects within it. Many of these values remained in scope for family communication research at Microsoft Research Cambridge for several years.

Table 2.1's header is a basis for a Design Arena Frame (DAF) (Cockton, 2020a, Section 5.3): *A Happy Family in a Nice Home with Treasured Objects.* The values in the three lists are sufficient as basic DAN (Cockton, 2020a, Section 5.4) for design purpose, organised into three subarenas: people, place, and objects. They can all be marked as interfaces from purpose to evaluation as measures and thresholds can be developed for each. Questionnaires have also been used for research on purpose. In the VALU project (Cockton et al., 2009b), online sentence completion questionnaires were used to interrogate the gambling experiences of two demographically distinct groups. Answers to each question (in Finnish) were grouped by similar meaning for each group. Table 2.1 shows histograms of responses for each group. Two collaborative workshops later grouped responses into values for design purpose that abstracted over users' responses (Chapter 5). For commercial reasons, these were not published (a few can be seen in Chapter 5), but as above, they are a basis for a DAF and DAN for purpose.

Primary research methods need to fit project cultures. Ethnography was used with a research group that was primarily qualitative in the research underpinning (Table 2.1). Sentence completion was used for an online gambling organisation that strongly preferred quantitative research, hence the histograms in Figure 2.1 and subsequent analyses and uses of quantitative data.

Laddering interviews have also been used in values-focused user research. Zaman and Abeele (2010) used laddering to explore young children's game preferences. In a laddering interview, respondents are asked *why?* questions, with the answer to one question forming the focus for a subsequent one. This moves the respondent from a focus on attributes (here game features and qualities) to usage experiences and onto values (with specific prompting if required). In Zaman and Abeele's study, questions did not proceed beyond the consequences of playing different games for children. These are a basis for researcher generalisations to values if this is appropriate (as in collaborative generalisations from sentence completion in the VALU project). Laddering here was not used as part of a research through design project, but as with sentence completion, it can provide axiological data below the level of values that can inform the formation of design purpose.

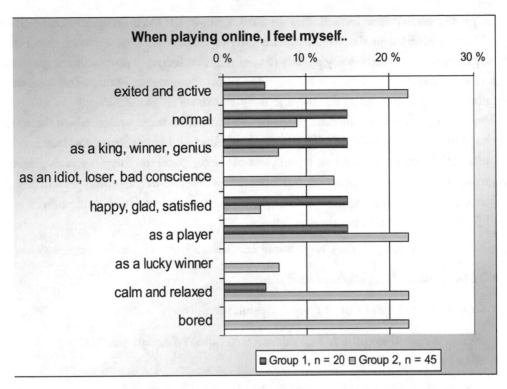

Figure 2.2: Sentence completions on gamblers' feelings (Cockton et al., 2009b).

Similarly, Le Dantec et al. (2009) used interviews in their design research. Their retrospective analyses revealed gaps and overlaps between Friedman et al.'s (2006) values and the espoused values in their interviews. Even so, there were overlaps with VSD's human values of ethical import.

Secondary and primary research can be combined. It is not an either/or situation. Secondary and personal resources can seed initial thinking for an arena and support subsequent reflection points. Also, what is primary research for one project becomes secondary for future ones, as with Table 2.1.

2.3.4   EXPRESSIVE RESOURCES

The resources for design purpose above are mostly ameliorative, adumbrative, informative, and inquisitive, with possible reflective and deliberative functions, and some suggestions for directive procedures. The lists of values, when printed on a double-sided sheet of paper, are also given an expressive function as inputs to work within the purpose arena. Alternatives forms to plain printed text include cards such as the HuValue tool (Kheirandish et al., 2019) and Envisioning Cards (www.envisioningcards.com/; Friedman and Hendry, 2012).

The outputs of design purpose activities can also be expressed visually, perhaps sharing the mental imagery behind design ideas (Davies and Talbot, 1987). Visual resources are also well suited to co-design and early evaluation activities. In 2015, I taught BIG Wo-Fo approaches to Industrial Design Master's students at the Technical University of Eindhoven. One approach that I outlined was to express intended worth using adverts to communicate intended purpose. One group created a brand (*We Luisteren*—We Listen) that integrated across three arenas. Four posters were designed to communicate a mix of artefact features and usage outcomes (Figure 2.3).

These four posters were the main outcome of a one-week design project where these students also chose to use: an early form of PADS (Proportional Abstract Design Situations) based on Keller's (2005) research process visualisation; stakeholder research; paper prototyping; high fidelity wire frames; worth mapping (see Chapter 4); and formative evaluations of the prototypes and posters.

The value groups guiding the *We Luisteren* concept were openness, helping others, community and feeling heard, grouping values as follows.

- *Openness*: Sincerity/Trust/Cooperation/Truth/Seeing consequences of actions/*Control*

- *Helping others*: Altruism/Service/Caring

- Community: Sense of Belonging/Cooperation

- *Feeling heard*: Recognition/Reflection/React/Equality/Acceptance/Making a Difference/Power/*Control*

The student groups were given Kahle's and the CNVC lists of values on the third day of teaching, as well as Herzberg's motivators and hygiene factors. Only six of the above 15 values are in one of those lists (all from the largest, CNVC), demonstrating the value of personal knowledge and group deliberation in scoping purpose. There is repetition (*Control*) and poor wording ("react" is not a value, but responsiveness would be), but there was no evidence of adverse impact.

The posters hint at features of a proposed app, as well as the value that can be delivered. A common advertising structure is in use here, with *messages* about valuable outcomes *supported by points about* app features (except the bottom right poster). These posters span express a two-arena concourse (purpose, antefact), unlike the posters prepared by student groups using the HuValue tool (Kheirandish, 2018).

Visual representations of values can have a valuable expressive function. Visual expression was used for the Family Archive (Cockton et al., 2009a), where photos from field work (Kirk and Sellen, 2010) were collaboratively grouped by the values in Table 2.1. The photos were organised into a Powerpoint stack with title slides at the start of each group. Each title was a value from Table 2.1. Collage versions of this stack were proposed as "worth boards," replacing the visual and branding elements of "mood boards" in creative design with strategic purpose elements.

Figure 2.3: Four Wo-Fo student posters (Manon Barendse, Nicky Liebregts, Danielle Smits, and Rachel van Berlo).

Textual and visual representations are thus expressive resources for inputs to, and outputs from, design purpose activities. While design and evaluation methods have tended to only have been communicated textually, visual representations are being used more. For example, approaches associated with the Value Proposition Canvas (Osterwalder et al., 2014) have rich visual representations, with the last author (Trish Papadakos) designing their presentation.

2.4   EXPERIENCES, OUTCOMES, AND THE BALANCE OF WORTH

The previous section focused on worthwhile outcomes, which complement worthwhile usage experiences. HCD has mostly focused on quality in use and fit to context (Cockton, 2004a, 2004b), which has been, and remains, very valuable. The overall worth of an interactive digital product is its balance of worthwhile experiences and outcomes (Cockton, 2008c). User experience varies in its contribution to what makes an interactive product worthwhile. For some applications, for example games or media players, user experience can be a major determinant of worth. For others, such as productivity software for office work or applications for creative professionals, outcomes outweigh experience. There should be an appropriate balance of worthwhile transient UX and lasting outcomes: positive outcomes can outweigh, or compensate for, some negative UX; similarly, worthwhile experiences may compensate for less worthwhile outcomes.

Experience values tend to be instrumental, while outcome values tend to be terminal (Rokeach, 1973). HCI research has looked at experience values more than outcome ones, but with diverse terms, e.g., experiential qualities (Löwgren, 2013) or interactivity attributes, with a preliminary set of seven dimensions to express the quality of interaction (Lim et al., 2011): concurrency, continuity, predictability, movement range, movement speed, approximativity, and responsivity. These apply to low-level interaction rather than affective experience, which is associated with much larger sets of attributes that can provided a basis for evaluation questionnaires. They can be positive or negative in specific contexts. A mix of valences may be sought for experience values. For example, Gaver's (2011) Prayer Device concept mixed intimacy and potential discomfort.

Hassenzahl (2004) developed four scales to evaluate user experience: two for hedonic quality (identification and stimulation); one for pragmatic quality; and one for evaluational constructs. The latter has two scales (ugly-beautiful and bad-good), and the others have seven, for example: complicated-simple (pragmatic quality); easy-challenging (hedonic quality-stimulation); and gaudy-classy (hedonic quality-identification). This formed the basis for the 28 scales of the Attrakdiff questionnaire, but translation into other languages cannot keep all scales distinct. For example, when translated to Icelandic, only 27 of the scales could be used (Ísleifsdóttir and Lárusdóttir, 2008). Even when axiological vocabularies do not need to be translated, wording can bring challenges. One way to maintain consensus and understanding in design teams is to use aliases (i.e., using synonyms for benefits, costs, and risks), until the interface from purpose to evaluation forces convergence.

Even with 28 scales, Attrakdiff is relatively concise. The Microsoft Desirability Toolkit (or Product Reaction Cards; Benedek and Milner, 2002) has 118 cards bearing single words or phrases that users can select to indicate how they feel when using a product. Examples include: stressful, gets in the way, patronizing, time-consuming, intimidating, inviting, confusing, sophisticated, frustrating, fun, and exciting. One hundred and eighteen may seem a lot to some, but they can be used quickly in evaluations with users.

Experience vocabularies are large. For example, dozens of values relevant to architectural design can be found in even a very short introductory text (Ballantyne, 2002).

- Privacy, serenity, anchor point, landmark, nationhood, show, extravagance, exuberance, pomp, civilisation, craft, beauty, mass, proportion, austerity, mystery, awe, magnificence, glamour, familiarity, visibility, atmosphere, originality, novelty, generosity, simplicity, openness, harmony, lavish, escapist, cultivated, hopeful, stable, authoritative, confrontational, challenging, ingratiating, dominating, comfortable, reverent, optimistic, theatrical, and cosmopolitan.

As noted above, axiological values for outcomes have even larger vocabularies: a search engine can currently indicate over 175 million hits for "lists of needs and wants" and over a billion for "lists of human values." We should avoid making assumptions about how many is too many. If you highlight all of the adjectives in reviews and adverts in a selection of car, fashion, or interior design magazines, you will soon reach 1,000 valenced words that may be relevant to Interaction Design. Reviewers and designers share these vocabularies. Creative designers routinely work with repertoires of hundreds of values for design purpose. Imagine design magazines that never use more than a few dozen valenced words and you will be imagining boring, unimaginative, mean, and repetitive publications that cannot communicate the qualities of designs to engaged audiences.

2.5   CHAPTER SUMMARY

BIG Design promotes Balance, Integration, and Generosity for all design activities. It is almost wholly agnostic about preferred research approaches, other than requiring equal respect in principle for primary research, secondary research, and personal knowledge and experiences. Generosity is not possible without personal ideas and insights from design teams. Generosity involves going beyond stated or discovered requirements with strategic vision from designers' "certainty of knowledge of something worthwhile" (Darke, 1979).

Balance and integration will combine generous purpose with appropriate work in other design arenas. A balance of experiences and outcomes and disciplines and sources is needed. Within each, further balance is needed, e.g., between individual and collective worth, across physical and mental phenomena, across stakeholder groups and social contexts, and across past, present, and future.

As Richard Banks noted early during the Family Archive project, ideas can come from anywhere. Few become "the right idea" or contribute directly to it, but the fortunes of any idea or insight in design are not known until integration crowns the right idea. Balance must be maintained until integration work prunes design arenas back to the insights and ideas that drive the successful design forward.

The best design combines innovative vision, creative craft excellence, and well-judged research and evaluation. HCI has focused on research excellence (not always well judged), with more recent acknowledgements of the importance of creative excellence. Strategic vision received less attention until the emergence of Lean UX (Gothelf with Seiden, 2013), although at least one IxD book at the start of the dotcom boom did address strategy (Mok, 1996).

There is much talk of value in agile software development (Beck et al., 2001), but little practical support for making it a design focus (Cockton, 2016a). Explicit informed Wo-Fo approaches fill this gap. We are just moving beyond the early stages of developing an understanding of purpose for IxD that is compatible with human-focused practices. There is still much to learn from the business world (e.g., Osterwalder et al., 2014; Kalbach, 2019), but little can be imported directly without adaptation.

Work on design purpose is largely about Darke's (1979) "fill[ing] boxes with concepts." The importance of this should not be underestimated. Data from contextual research and evaluations may be seen as more substantial, as may concrete craft work on apps, websites, appliances, kiosks and other IxD artefacts. However, with no clear sense of purpose, it is hard to plan evaluations and contextual research, and to weigh up artefact design alternatives. A focus on worth can direct focus in other arenas, which we consider next.

CHAPTER 3

Mixing Balance at All Scopes of Design

Design purpose is the most abstract design arena. In the other arenas, design teams interact "intimately with the concrete elements of the situation" (Carroll, 2000).

Chapter 2 covered Wo-Fo approaches and resources for filling out the purpose arena. This chapter takes a more general approach to the other arenas, since there are very extensive research and professional literatures on IxD and interactive technologies (a_tefacts arena) and on HCD (evaluation and anyficiaries arenas). These cannot be properly reviewed in the space available here to add much of consequence. The synthesis series on HCI, of which this book is part, provides many useful overviews of HCI, HCD, UX, and IxD approaches. This chapter augments these and other texts with additional BIG considerations for studying anyficiaries, and designing, developing, and evaluating interactive digital products. The main focus is on the complexity of balance in design work. This has largely been considered so far as balance of disciplines, qualities, perspectives, design arenas, and connections, of interfaces within design arenas, and of experiences and outcomes for the purpose arena. As we consider design work below the level of design arenas, complexity increases substantially, adding concerns over balance of approaches, resources, functions, sources, voices, power, forms, and content. These are considered as they arise below.

Balance in BIG Design is not measured by scales of justice, but by sliders on a sound mixer. A good balance is a good mix. Design work is like sound mixing in that at any time a slider can be pushed up (through more work) or down (though less work or by setting aside). Design work sliders operate at all scopes from major design paradigms through organisational palettes, playbooks, projects, episodes, activities, approaches, and resources down to single design moves. The current mix for any unit of design work can be appropriate or adverse. With apt tracking resources, reflection and deliberation, adverse balances can be spotted and addressed, and favourable ones celebrated.

In Chapter 4 (Cockton, 2020a), we focused on major design paradigms and design arenas, and in Chapter 5 (Cockton, 2020a) on progression, projects, episodes, connections, and interfaces. We now focus on balance:

- of design arenas in projects;

- within design arenas (approaches, resources, power); and

- within approaches and resources (functions, qualities, disciplines, content, sources, voices, forms, design arena scope).

The pervasiveness of Abstract Design Situation (ADS) structures across all scopes of design activities involves design arenas from the most abstract to the most concrete:

- major paradigms (Cockton, 2020a, Chapter 4);

- organisations' Strategic Design: playbooks, palettes, and processes (Chapters 5, Cockton, 2020a; Chapter 1–4);

- projects as a Sequence of MADS (SoMADS; Cockton, 2020a, Chapter 5);

- episodes (Cockton, 2020a, Chapter 5); and

- approaches and resources (Section 1.1).

Even design moves of several minutes or less have an ADS, which is a key part of a common theoretical basis for design work at all scopes: the Working to Choose (W2C) framework (Cockton, 2013b). W2C takes its name from the work needed to make design choices. Design options rarely come ready made. Design teams have to work to develop, commit to, make credible, and express options. Choices are more often made tacitly. For some time, there may be no favoured option, but as connections build and strengthen, options are side-lined by a Darwinian survivor, THE right idea (Davies and Talbot, 1987). If a fittest survivor weakens, side-lined options come back into play.

W2C systematically relates ADS to design work via: Meta-Principles for Designing (M-P4D; Cockton, 2009a), and a resources model of method use in design (Woolrych et al., 2011). W2C has a tongue in cheek formula (Cockton, 2012):

$$W2C = ADS+M\text{-}P4D+A/R$$

Working to Choose = Abstract Design Situations + Meta-Principles for Designing

+ Approaches divided into Resources

Meta-Principles for Designing co-evolved alongside Heskett's different choices of alternatives (a.k.a design arenas). Existing sets of IxD principles were not comprehensive. Four example sets focused on different arenas: artefacts (Direct Manipulation principles; Shneiderman, 1983); anyficiaries (Dourish, 2001); anyficiaries and evaluation (Gould and Lewis, 1985); or anyficiaries and a_tefacts in creative design contexts (Brown, 2009). Different disciplines underpinned each: design (Shneiderman, 1983; Brown, 2009), applied psychology (Gould and Lewis, 1985), and phenomenological social theory (Dourish, 2001).

A set of meta-principles was derived to cover all design arenas and more disciplines. In contrast to principle sets derived from *a posteriori* disciplinary analyses, four meta-principles were derived *a priori* using basic concepts from Choice Theory (Allingham, 2002). The first was *receptiveness* (Cockton, 2009a), which was implied by Heskett's (2005) choices from alternatives. Design teams must be receptive to possible options across arenas. However, only some options will converge into

THE right idea (Davies and Talbot, 1987), requiring additional meta-principles of *committedness* and *credibility*. The former assesses a design team's commitment (here, to an option) and the latter is a separate assessment of its viability. Credible options that are committed to must be manifested in some way, requiring a fourth meta-principle of *expressivity*.

The first two meta-principles are *virtues* in Aristotle's sense that risks must be avoided through "golden means" (Barnes, 2000). We can be either insufficiently or overly receptive or committed. The second two are potentials that are subject to something akin to Juran's misnamed *Pareto Principle* (80% of outputs result from the vital 20% of inputs; Juran, 1975). Whereas with virtues, excess can damage, potentials are subject to diminishing returns as benefits slow down while costs increase for additional inputs that are useful rather than vital.

Two further meta-principles each focused on one design arena. *Inclusiveness* was specific to anyficiaries, with its golden mean of having enough beneficiaries and acceptable maleficiaries. *Improvability* was specific to evaluations, with diminishing returns applying to evaluation effort. The arguments for each are in Cockton (2009a), but a short argument is that balance in BIG needs to support HCD through proper consideration of stakeholders in context (inclusiveness) and artefacts in use (improvability). These, respectively, broaden two of Gould and Lewis' (1985) key principles for usability: focus on users and tasks and empirical evaluation. A flaw in the argument in Cockton (2009a) is that it ignored the other two arenas, but there was no basis for excluding them *a priori*, so there are at least two missing meta-principles (Cockton, 2013a).

Meta-principles are more abstract than the four example sets (Brown, Dourish, Schneiderman, Gould, and Lewis). They cannot act as "principles" to provide rules or a code of conduct. Instead, they guide formation of rules or codes of conduct via *progressive instantiation*, which refines a meta-principle into project-specific directions for design activities. This turned out to be too simple for moving from abstract to concrete. Instead, a mix of design considerations at varying levels of abstraction will be continuously in play. W2C spans these considerations with more structure.

When meta-principles became part of W2C, their role shrank back to *evaluative* concepts to guide consideration of whether design quality is adequate, e.g., with regard to what has been considered (receptiveness), how seriously teams take this (committedness), how seriously others can take this (credibility), how well it is expressed (expressivity), and also whether enough thought has been given to inclusiveness and improvability.

As with all axiological constructs, there is no clear route from *ought* to do to *what* to do. It turned out that W2C's third element, the *resources model of method use* (Woolrych et al., 2011) enabled a more concrete account of design work. As argued in Section 1.1, design work starts with potential approaches and their incomplete sets of incomplete resources (approaches divided into resources). As resources get completed in projects (e.g., a test user recruitment plan), they assemble into a method that makes sense retrospectively in the rear-view mirror. Specific design actions mobilize reticent resources by coaxing functions from them.

While meta-principles are *evaluative*, functions are *descriptive*, e.g., *expressivity* vs. *expressive*. As new resources functions were identified, new meta-principles were associated with them, as they were with overlooked design arenas. For purpose, the related meta-principle is a virtue, *generousness*, rather than the ungenerous potential (*viability*) identified initially (Cockton, 2013a). A golden mean for generousness will not stifle creative strategy while avoiding paltriness and lavishness, as a lack and excess respectively of generosity.

W2C has moved progressive instantiation from meta-principles to ADS, with design arenas and connections progressively instantiated by approaches and resources, which are progressively instantiated by realising functions, W2C thus supports reasoning about balance at all extents of design work. Analyses below exploit ADS constructs and resource functions.

3.1   BALANCE ACROSS DESIGN ARENAS

Design work repeatedly zooms in and out. By zooming into an arena and through subarenas with ever-increasing detail, teams *progressively instantiate* arenas. However, this is not the stepwise refinement of rational software development, as teams also keep zooming out again to review, focus and reflect on the current big picture across a project's arenas. When zooming back in again, some existing work within an arena may be pushed to one side when its credibility diminishes and new considerations come into play. This may appear to be iterative for a single arena, but at project level, work is concurrent and new connections can bring changes to arenas.

A range of balances is called for by three subprinciples of the *improvability* meta-principle: evaluability, understandability, and responsiveness (Cockton, 2009a). *Evaluability* must involve a mix of arenas, assessing not just artefact qualities, but also achievement of intended purpose against targets for specific metrics. Grounded in usage, *understandability*, too, involves a mix of arenas as causal relationships between artefacts, purpose and beneficiaries. *Responsiveness* may require greater receptiveness, i.e., further questions, ideas, and insights across all arenas. The first two subprinciples are potentials (more can bring less, but without risks) and the third is a virtue (both too little or too much are risky).

Balance needs to be achieved *across* arenas by devoting sufficient effective effort to each and to their integration. Tracking with ADS (Cockton, 2020a, Chapter 5) has useful *adumbrative* and *protective* functions, indicating the cumulative scope of design work and exposing oversights to address, but the hard work gets done within arenas.

From a BIG perspective, combined work across design arenas should have an appropriate balance, but not an equal split. Design work is not a cake for cutting into equal shares. A hypothetical distribution of effort may devote half a project's time to the a_tefact arena (e.g., prototyping, IxD, media assets, coding, construction, and testing), one-fifth of the time each for the evaluation and anyficiaries arenas, and one-tenth on design purpose. As a comparison, a one-week Google

Ventures Design Sprint (Knapp et al., 2016) allocates 20% each to beneficiaries and evaluations and 60% to antefacts. With ten people in a sprint including one organiser, who spends a week preparing, there are 55 person days of effort. Two days spent preparing the challenge (design purpose) is 4% of total effort. The other three planning days, if split equally between beneficiaries and evaluations, will each get under 3% of total effort. This results in 21% of total effort each on beneficiaries and evaluations, 4% on purpose and 54% on antefacts, excluding effort from interviewed beneficiaries and user test participants. This is close to the hypothetical distribution. When sprints focus on problems with existing designs, less time will be spent on purpose (product strategy).

The mix of *effort* reflects a team's planned committedness. However, the mix of *achievement* is more important, and a team's committedness must flex to achieve an appropriate balance. George's (2016) use of PADS (Cockton, 2020a, Figure 5.4) revealed variable returns on planned effort. BIG practices recognise that effort needs to be adjusted to compensate for gaps between aims and achievements, unless aims are adjusted instead. Fixing effort per RILED phase up front is unrealistic.

3.2   BALANCE WITHIN A DESIGN ARENA

Balance extends beyond balance across design arenas (as visualised by PADS) to balance within them. Chapter 2 has already considered design purpose, so we will use its coverage to form an analysis framework for balance within arenas. This framework considers different forms of balance such as content or approaches, for which teams must zoom in and out to keep work on track.

3.2.1   BALANCING THE PURPOSE MIX

Wo-Fo approaches balance benefits against costs and risks, which can be regarded as three subarenas. Subarenas provide one basis for reflecting on balance of *content within* design arenas. A reasonable mix of effort needs to be spread across their identification and prioritisation. Appropriate coverage of subarenas results in good *balance of content*.

Chapter 2 argued for a balance of *sources* for worth elements: individuals' ideas, knowledge and experience, secondary and primary research, and critical reflection and deliberation. These sources may distinguish between morals and ethics. Morals apply to a general public, and are universally applicable within a spatially bounded community. Ethics are specific to communities of kind that cross spatial boundaries, such as professions, clients, customers, and groups based on age, faith, gender, sexuality, race, or impairment.

Chapter 2 surveyed a range of research approaches, e.g., focused analysis of ethnographic data, sentence completion questionnaires. A *balance of approaches* is important. For the purpose arena, a relevant balance is between DAN elements with origins in strategy and vision on the one hand, and ones grounded in anyficiaries research on the other. A design wholly based on the latter is not generous and is also less likely to be innovative. However, a balance skewed to the opposite extreme, with most intended purpose lacking empirical grounding, increases risks of product failure.

Another mix considered in Chapter 2 was how worth is expressed. As well as a DAF and DAN "verbal sketches" for design purpose, there were examples of worth boards in a slide deck format and a tabular DAN. The relevant balance here is *balance of form*, with different forms being considered for different audiences and uses. We next consider various balances for other design arenas.

3.2.2   BALANCING THE EVALUATION MIX

A balance of both content and approaches is also needed. Balance of content for evaluation is tightly coupled to balance of approaches through an appropriate mix of inspection, modelling, observed usage, analysis of usage logs, and questionnaires. Inspection includes applying heuristics, conducting walkthroughs, and checking conformance to guidelines and platform standards (Cockton et al., 2012). Modelling has tended to be restricted to high dependency systems such as healthcare, automotive interfaces, and air traffic control. Expertise and time requirements remain relatively high, but modelling is becoming more accessible (Oulasvirta, 2019). Observed usage such as user testing is one of the most common approaches, with evaluators present or via remote recording. Usage log analysis can be used for online platforms with massive user populations.

Questionnaires are common on websites, including cloud services. They range from the very simple net promoter score to more elaborate questionnaires. User testing may end with a debriefing questionnaire or interview. Social media and feedback capabilities on websites can provide substantial user feedback (Stickel et al., 2016; Qaed et al., 2016). Contextual inquiry (Holtzblatt and Beyer, 2014) combines interviews with observed usage. Focus groups (Rosenbaum et al., 2002) are also used in some evaluation contexts. Hostile or destructive testing is used in areas such as security, and has been used in usability evaluation (Hewett, 1986).

In all cases, an approach's effectiveness impacts balance of content (as evaluation data and analysis). Each approach brings its own costs and risks, although costs can range over four orders of magnitude from very low (Kjeldskov et al., 2004) to very high (Hey, 2006) for user testing. Low costs do not automatically translate into high risks.

An approach mix results in a balance of *qualities* (e.g., rigour, innovation, breadth). Qualities for approaches and resources are typically associated with disciplinary values. Scientific quality matters, but evaluation can also benefit from creative practices (Cockton, 2014). Innovative approaches such as Creative Sprints (Garnik et al., 2014) emerge when evaluators respond constructively to surprises. An important aspect of teams working to choose is their *working to balance* that is both multidisciplinary and multi-imaginary. HCI has had a strong focus on multidisciplinarity, but will only have *multi-imagination* when it gives full play to ideative disciplines to draw on multiple forms of imagination. Creative practices must extend beyond the a_tefact arena (Cockton, 2014).

3.2.3   BALANCING THE ANYFICIARIES MIX

First-wave HCI had an Human Factors engineering focus on universals rather than individual differences. An anyficiary here was literally any human, with presumed universals of perception, cognition, and other psychological and biological factors. This could be well applied in approaches such as Claims (Carroll, 1990). However, the knowledge provided by much early human factors was not inclusive, reflecting the young American males (often military) from whom measures were taken. Thus, when UK public transport interiors were being redesigned to reduce accidents, with a focus on the elderly, existing anthropometric data was unsuitable. Custom measuring instruments and rigs had to be improvised (Brooks, 1981) to establish parameters for seat heights, grab pole diameters and other interior features. The inclusiveness meta-principle for anyficiaries needs a third-wave HCI focus that embraces diversity in all usage contexts.

Second-wave HCI directs design teams toward appropriate adumbration of stakeholders. Strategic Design (Stevens and Moultrie, 2011) involves both customer advocacy and long-term trends, with foresight teams considering many possible social, geopolitical, and environmental futures. However, commercial innovation can also focus on "off-trend" individuals, such as lead users (Von Hippel, 1986; Convertino and Frishberg, 2020). For social innovation, both individual inequality trends and their intersection must be considered (Romero, 2018), so that a good cross section of existing maleficiaries become beneficiaries.

There are thus a range of approaches to balancing content for the anyficiaries arena, which can be informed by subarenas that span the social structures within which stakeholders have roles and responsibilities, as can be seen from a comparison of the L-ERG-IKK model (Cockton, 2009a) with Shneiderman's (2003) framework for designing for people.

L-ERG-IKK subarenas focus attention on collective worth for *Institutions*, communities (*Kind*), and family (*Kin*). When understanding stakeholder roles and responsibilities, it is important to distinguish formalised social entities (i.e., legally incorporated institutions) from informal ones (i.e., open communities of interest or *kind*). L-ERG-IKK replaced an earlier MILKK group of anyficiary subarenas (Cockton, 2006): Markets, Institutions, Locales, Kin, Kind. L-ERG-IKK retained locales as a spatial aggregator. Markets were dropped as they are complex hybrid social structures that integrate institutions (producers, intermediaries, retailers, regulators) with market segments (kin and kind). Similarly, political structures such as countries are also hybrid structures that are best separated into separate stakeholders, as are religious faiths that combine legal institutions with communities of "kind" (identity, practice). It is important to see through hybrid structures to their constituent parts.

Shneiderman (2003) proposed two structures for anyficiary arenas. One has nested locales centred on the self and moves out to family, colleagues and neighbours, citizens of a country, and participants in a market. The other has four human needs as motivators: living, loving, learning, and leaving a legacy. This overlaps with the later L-ERG-IKK structure, but notable differences include his:

- fusing locales (e.g., neighbourhoods) with their dynamic constituent social groupings;

- mix of basic (family, colleagues, neighbours) and hybrid (markets, countries) structures; and

- lack of broad motivators such as Existence, Relatedness and Growth (Alderfer, 1972) and their relation to Mind, Body and Spirit (L-ERG-IKK+, Figure 2.1).

L-ERG-IKK+ exposes the hybrid nature of "living, loving, learning, leaving a legacy": Alderfer's growth subsumes learning; leaving a legacy involves relatedness across mind and spirit; as does loving (with body too). Living covers everything else. Combined with nested locales of self, family, colleagues, neighbours, countries, and markets, Shneiderman's model spans less with more than L-ERG-IKK+. Nevertheless, Shneiderman (2003) is one of the earliest HCI attempts to cover both individual and collective value. Its main limitation is a lack of disciplinary balance, preferring Covey et al.'s (1994) pop psychology to a mix of broader established psychological and sociological constructs. Even so, following its direction would give a wider scope for anyficiaries than established mainstream HCI approaches in use at the time. It would have improved balance of content, but more was possible.

Even so, L-ERG-IKK+ needs support from additional directive and informative resources. For example, for sustainable design, design teams can think of our planet as the locale within which all others nest, from rooms in our homes through neighbourhoods, cities, countries, and regions. A good grasp of varieties of institutions and communities of kind is needed to make best use of L-ERG-IKK+. As ever, this must come from the team, but some informative lists can provide support.

- Institutions include governments, and religious, commercial, charitable, educational, healthcare, law enforcement, professional, and scientific organisations.

- Kind spans spatially coherent communities such as neighbourhoods, and also communities of: identity such as interest, impairment, issues, gender, sexuality, age, faith/belief, class, and language/ethnicity. All are more focused on collective than individual experiences.

Ignoring any community of kind within target locales risks creating maleficiaries through a lack of universal design. For example, if groups with impairments are not properly considered, accessible designs are unlikely to result. Intersections matter too (Romero, 2018).

L-ERG-IKK+ is simple enough to create a broad focus on who matters and what matters about them. It is easy to inform with expertise about spatial locales, motivators (ERG), individuals

(Mind, Body, and Spirit), and collectives (IKK). Some existing canvases for anyficiaries are very limited in this respect. For example, *empathy maps* (Siegel and Dray, 2019) use low-level data coding constructs rather than psychological and sociological fundamentals to gather insights and information from project teams. There is variation in the content of empathy maps, but they commonly include areas for *pains and gains* (as in Value Proposition Canvases) and what *users hear, think and feel, and see and do*. However, this lacks the collective *Jobs to be Done* focus in a Value Proposition Canvas. While it is possible to have an empathy canvas for each stakeholder, Empathy Maps lack resources to support their identification, unlike the locales focus in L-ERG-IKK+.

Overall, the concern addressed by L-ERG-IKK+, Shneiderman (2003) and similar conceptual structures is with balance of *content*. Inclusiveness requires a broad range of beneficiaries with only intended maleficiaries, not accidental ones. Trade-offs between anyficiaries must be explicit. They apply to benefits, risks, and costs, and the resulting balance of worth for each included stakeholder.

As design resources, conceptual frameworks for subarenas such as worth, improvability, and L-ERG-IKK+ are largely adumbrative with some inquisitive and directive potential. Appropriate direction and information depends on balance of approaches. As with evaluations, creative approaches are needed when researching anyficiaries, especially when respondents and participants do not come from demographics typically associated with psychology experiments. Existing human science research approaches from psychology, ethnography, cultural studies, and other HCI disciplines may have to creatively adapted to work with anyficiaries who are new to participative design work.

Disciplinary positions for anyficiaries are unfortunately associated with attempts to oust rival approaches. Crabtree et al. (2009) argued against a cultural turn in social research practices, motivated by their preference for the ethnomethodological approaches that were dominating social research in HCI. A less confrontational approach warps approaches to fit disciplinary values. For example, Cultural Probes' roots are in creative arts and design practices, but have been appropriated by imposing quantitative and qualitative practices from human sciences (Boehner et al., 2007).

Both proscription and appropriation adversely impact balance. Cutting back research approaches for anyficiaries to a pure human science focus reduces their ADS to a single design arena with few useful interfaces. Implications for design get stifled. The ADS for "true" cultural probes spans anyficiaries, antefacts, and connections between the two. Cultural probes were crafted to support ideation, resulting in a balance of *qualities* that combines research rigour with creative practices.

Participative design approaches improve the balance of content, sources, interfaces, approaches, and qualities, since collaborators can add their own knowledge, perspectives, and practices to those of researchers and professionals in design teams. As with user participants in evaluations, additional individuals contributing to a project adds are sources of additional voices and perspectives.

Overall the anyficiaries arena needs a broad mix. Ease of integration is eased when Lean UX approaches (Gothelf with Seiden, 2013) direct primary research on anyficiaries and for evaluations. Lean's "just-in-time" approach to content and qualities delays primary research until it is needed, with eye on value to projects and not what is expected in academic research, which may be too time consuming for the actual value delivered. It can also lack relevance, as evidenced by a lack of interface details to support integration. Silos aren't worthwhile in design.

3.2.4   BALANCING THE A_TEFACTS MIX

All design work requires craft expertise. The a_tefacts arena is an obvious example, but Chapter 2 argued for the importance of personal resources for design purpose, which could be made explicit through resources such as L-ERG-IKK+. For evaluation too, craft expertise has been recognised in the use of experiential knowledge (Blandford et al., 2008). However, these important individual resources are complements to re-usable public approaches and resources. The reverse is true for the a_tefact arena, where craft expertise is the dominant resource. The final quality of a digital artefact depends on the craft expertise of many specialists: developers, software architects, software testers, infrastructure specialists, and visual, industrial, and interaction designers, who are guided by self-imposed constraints of established practices, as were architects in Darke's (1979) study.

Work within the a_tefact arena is initially progressed by inspiration driven individual sketching that is relatively independent of the design team, apart from some informal discussions (Gaver, 2011). Designers tend to derive guidance from specific examples of practice, often as themes, and not from theory (Gaver and Bowers, 2012).

The importance of personal resources is recognised in "design-aware" HCI research (e.g., Löwgren, 1995). Criticism, erudition, and scholarship are vital resources for creative work, as is knowledge of precedent such as Dynabook in IxD (Löwgren, 2013). In his analyses of structural failures, Petroski (1994) cites a range of authorities who stress the importance of precedent to have as wide and deep an acquaintance as possible with past failures: Christopher Alexander (1964) recommended that engineers reflect on them; and Lev Zettin (Browne, 1983) recommended imagination and fear as best engineering tools for preventing tragedy, since engineers cannot rely on handbooks and manuals.

There are of course approaches and resources beyond the individual for the a_tefact arena. There are re-usable guidelines and heuristics (Löwgren, 2013), some of which are based on robust guidance from engineering psychology. However, as Zettin noted, designers cannot rely on them 100%.

Balance of content is contributed to by a range of technologies (e.g., apps; web; Artificial Intelligence; Internet of Things/Ubicomp; Augmented, Virtual, and Mixed Reality) and architectural frameworks such as Elements of User Experience (Garrett, 2002). Garrett's "elements" are strategy (the design purpose arena) and four architectural artefact subarenas: surface, skeleton, structure, and scope. These correspond to the perceptual (surface and skeleton), temporal (dialogue or navigation structure), and conceptual (capabilities, scope) levels of a software design architecture that has taken various forms since the 1980s (Gram and Cockton, 1996).

Keeping abreast of new technical possibilities is also important (Stevens and Moultrie, 2011), but this may expose a need for research on usage contexts. For example, when considering new home technologies, the floor load capacity of domestic environments had to be considered (Gaver, 2011).

A mix of sources, perspectives, and content is thus important for the a_tefacts arena. A mix of *forms* must span from the antefacts of experience prototyping (Buchenau and Fulton Suri, 2000), via lo-fi and hi-fi prototyping, to fully engineered interactive digital artefacts. Written accounts are partial views at best onto artefacts (Gaver and Bowers, 2012). The image is primary, whether in two or three dimensions. However, annotations can improve collages. Physical objects can be combined as early prototypes, for example a snorkel and lamp as a critical prayer device (Gaver, 2011). Sketching is possible in a wide range of media, so there is no single definitive sketching medium (Vistisen, 2015).

Some sketches are prepared to support conversation within and beyond the core design team (Vistisen, 2015). Different forms of a_tefact representations suit different audiences. For a large organisation such as Autodesk, annotated prototypes using tools such as Invision are a workable alternative to sketches and other lo-fi formats (Convertino and Frishberg, 2020) in comparison to the bespoke formats in Section 5.8 of Cockton (2020a), some of which are for retrospective use.

A mix of forms must be complemented by a *mix of approaches*, including software development approaches from experimental programing through agile approaches to structured methods for high-dependency systems.

Software quality models such as ISO/IEC 25010 SQUARE (ISO/IEC, 2011) provide a framework for a *mix of qualities*. ISO/IEC 25010 takes a normative approach to software quality. It can direct and inform reflection and deliberation in software development, and provide a resource for reasoning about balance of qualities alongside expert craft judgement.

ISO/IEC 25010 hedges its bets on interaction quality, considering both intrinsic qualities of software artefacts and quality in use. Silos need to be avoided in all design arenas, so for a_tefacts this means accepting that quality extends beyond artefacts to axiofacts (Cockton, 2020a, Section 4.4.1). Empirically, only worthwhile use can provide evidence for *desirableness*, the meta-principle for the a_tefact arena. Although initially identified as a potential (desirability; Cockton, 2013a), it is a virtue with a golden mean between the vices of repulsion and addiction.

3.3   APPROACH AND RESOURCE INNOVATION IN DESIGN WORK

Approaches and resources can span design arenas, providing worth through a mix of functions.

3.3.1   BALANCING THE DESIGN ARENA MIX WITHIN APPROACHES AND RESOURCES

In RILED methodologies, design and evaluation approaches are typically associated with a single phase, and thus with only one design arena. For example: personas may be thought to be solely for beneficiaries, user testing only for evaluations, wire-frames only for antefacts, and value propositions only for purpose. However, tame problems apart, the concurrent realities of creative design work need approaches and resources that span a mix of design arenas.

To compare theory with practice, in 2011 I led a workshop on Fusing Design Paradigms at the annual German Design Research conference, DGTF (www.dgtf.de/tagungen/tagung2011). In one exercise (Cockton, 2013a), two groups completed MADS formed from four overlapping circles: evaluation (top), purpose (bottom), artefact (left), and beneficiaries (right). These Venn Diagrams were a form of a MADS, with their intersections (overlaps) corresponding to 2, 3, and 4 arena concourses (Figures 3.1 and 3.2). A merged list of 83 design and evaluation methods (from 3 sources) was provided. Groups were asked to select methods from it (or provide their own missed ones), write its name on a sticky note and then place that appropriately on the Venn diagram.

Figure 3.1 is fairly sparse and reflects the extent of Group A's discussion when placing each sticky note. They only associated one method, *detailed drawing*, with a single arena. All their others were in overlaps, indicating co-ordination of at least two arenas. Methods were sometimes placed to indicate their full potential, rather than typical usage. For example, Group A placed *brainstorming* in the intersection of all arenas (as with Cloudbook's brainwriting, Cockton 2020a, Chapter 3).

Some participants were surprised, expecting there to be a single arena for a method, but others participants had it provide complex support across arenas. This could typically only be achieved through local practices that extend simple approaches with additional comprehensive resources, confirming that what some design literature claims are complete methods are actually incomplete approaches that must be configured and extended in a local context.

Group B placed *personas* wholly within the *beneficiaries* arena, but Group A placed personas in the four arena concourse, which requires persona skeletons to be configured to support integration of information and insights about beneficiaries with other arenas (Chapter 4).

40 of Group B's methods were placed within a single arena. With no recordings of the discussions, it is not known why every method was placed where it was. What was clear from group discussions was that participants could explain their placings to each other, exposing differences in how methods are configured by different designers. This is a further example of the worth of the

ADS construct. The use of a MADS representation in this exercise prompted conversations with this tracking material through group deliberation and individual reflection.

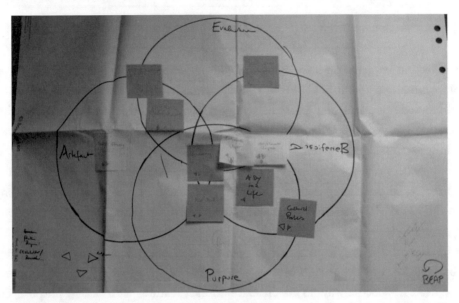

Figure 3.1: Group A's completed MADS Venn diagram.

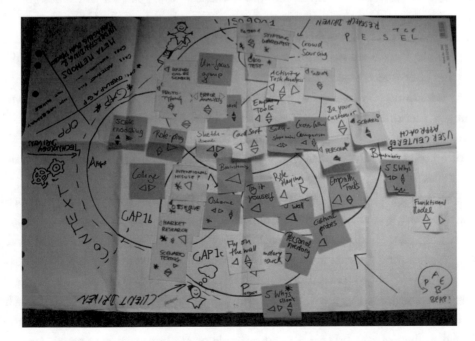

Figure 3.2: Group B's completed MADS Venn diagram.

Table 3.1: Gap analysis-based identification of method innovation opportunities		
Gap	Opportunity	Notes

For a second exercise on identifying and filling gaps in the provision of design methods, participants were asked to fill in Table 3.1. Group B made notes at the top-left of their MADS. Group A discussed opportunities, but made no notes. They identified a lack of methods for making choices about design purpose. Group B made a general observation on the lack of *meta-methods* for understanding and managing a design team's own practices. The evidence at the workshop however was that W2C provides such a meta-method. It supported insights on differences and gaps in design practices. Similar exercises were used a month later at a European Ph.D. training school (TwinTide DEVISE II), with similar outcomes in terms of supporting reflection on the scopes of design approaches.

Group B noted a gap in methods to connect artefacts and purpose, despite placing four methods in that concourse: scenario testing, market testing, observation, and intentional misuse. All must be used in specific ways to co-ordinate artefact features with design purpose, but this is straightforward. However, methods such as scenario testing and task specification and analysis are more typically used in ways that restrict purpose to the low-level goals for which designed artefacts provide support, rather than the higher-level motivating goals in focus for Cooper's Goal-Directed Design (Cooper et al., 2007). This focuses on what designs *can do* instead of what beneficiaries *want to do*. For example, I never wanted to program a video recorder, and I still do not want to program a central heating controller. Instead, I want to watch television programs when I choose (now much simpler with streaming services) and to have a warm enough house with no energy or money waste.

This gap identified by Group B is addressed by worth delivery scenarios and worth maps (see Chapter 4). Both were briefly presented in the closing section of the DGTF 2011 workshop as examples of method innovations that were designed to fill gaps identified through reflection using MADS.

Two further gaps identified by Group B were methods that *only* provided support for options for artefacts or evaluation, with the notes that these were, respectively, not necessary or not possible, although they had identified three such methods for artefacts and five for evaluations! This raises an interesting point as to whether single-arena methods are desirable. At some points in design work, it is efficient to let specialists focus on their arenas of expertise, for example IxD (for software and media specialists) and UX evaluation (for human-centred specialists). Risks, however, will arise if these activities are not co-ordinated through additional integrative approaches. Human science-based evaluations in IxD are a good example of methods that may poorly integrate with other design activities (Cockton, 2007). Nevertheless, to be able to integrate, there has to be something to integrate, and thus independent work focused within single arenas is essential.

Group B's positions here may reflect firstly, the HCD prejudice against design activities focused solely on artefacts, and secondly the reasonable belief that evaluation must be an evaluation of something. Even so, there are project-independent resources for evaluation such as re-usable measures or well-established data collection procedures. Also, some well-established approaches to accessibility evaluation can be applied with no or minimal specific adaptations.

3.3.2 BALANCING THE FUNCTION MIX FOR APPROACHES AND RESOURCES

The two workshop groups also annotated sticky notes with triangles indicating whether a method was informative (◀), directive (◆), or expressive (▶). Actually, a version of prior meta-principles was used: receptiveness for informative, credibility/tenacity for directive, and expressivity.

Group B did not just give Personas an expressive function, but also informative and directive ones, as in The Persona Lifecycle (Pruitt and Adlin, 2006), which provides broad support for design work. There is evidence here that for some designers, multi-arena multi-function approaches are well understood, while others still think in terms of narrower textbook versions for single arena phases. Personas can thus have one function (expressive) for a specific arena (beneficiaries), or three functions (informative, directive, and expressive) that support integration across all four arenas.

Overall, use of ADS and resource functions from W2C demonstrated variations in method use. W2C can be used to audit current design practices, with an emphasis on identifying gaps in method provision and opportunities for filling them through innovative approaches.

Innovative approaches benefit from productive interplays between potential functions of existing approaches and resources added by design settings. Such interplays have been recognised for some time. For example, for evaluation methods, Blandford et al. (2008) defined craft skill as:

> ...*the analyst using their experiential knowledge in conjunction with a method to achieve insights that are informed by the method or notation being used, but not directly derivable from it.*

This considers two arenas (evaluations, artefacts) and only analysts' declarative and procedural experiential knowledge (informative and directive functions). Even so, this leads to "chilling evaluator effects" that some HCI researchers find hard to accept, believing that the same method should produce the same results irrespective of who uses them and when and where (Hertzum and Jacobsen, 2003). Expectations that teams can be programmed to act the same way, even in radically different project contexts, are unrealistic given the nature of creative work (Cockton, 2013c).

Rationalist expectations for methods favour the three functions considered at the DGTF workshop. Methods are primarily expected to be *directive*, providing fool-proof procedures regardless of whether design teams are fools. Methods must also be *expressive* to communicate. They are also meant to be *informative*, providing objective valid knowledge for their failsafe procedures. However, design and evaluation approaches and resources are most effective when an appropriate balance of functions is realised.

Design work is not simply about working to choose (W2C), *but working to be able to choose* (W2BA2C!). Such work is, as Fallman (2003) noted, for a "specific design situation … that … locates the design process in a world which is already crammed with people, artifacts, and practices, each with their own histories, identities, goals, and plans." This situation provides, completes and realises resources that help with making choices (both explicit and tacit). Ideative functions inherently arise in Fallman's specific design situations of people, artefacts and practices. Social and affective functions can only be fully realised there, which often no re-usable approaches can provide. For example, for the emergence of Creative Sprints (Garnik et al., 2014), essential resources were:

- *team*: well-motivated knowledgeable lead users and IT experts, who could address management agendas; knowledge of UX and Agile development (and more as relevant, e.g., Service Design, customer experience, value chain analysis); openness to range of values;

- *process*: agility; creative responsiveness; collaborative mutual learning; coordination of emergent local resources; proactive risk management; constant focus on persuading key decision makers with well-evidenced credible proposals;

- *organisational*: management champions; crowd sourced list of (grouped) usability problems; and

- *physical resource*s: A suitable collaborative workspace.

This is a far broader range of resources than typically provided by textbook methods. A broad mix of functions needs resources beyond those provided by processes, phases or approaches, all of which are made or broken by Fallman's (2003) "specific design situations." BIG design projects thus must look beyond low-level cognitive functions (informative, directive, expressive) to: high-level holistic ones (adumbrative, ideative, inquisitive, integrative, reflective); affective (protective, invigorative); social (affiliative, deliberative, performative); and axiological ones (ameliorative).

Balance is required to best mobilise resources through extensive activation and realisation of their potential functions:

- informative functions require a mix of *sources* for a balance of *content*;

- directive functions require a balance of *disciplines*, *approaches*, and *qualities*;

- inquisitive, protective, and reflective functions require a balance of *perspectives*;

- ideative, invigorative, and deliberative functions require a balance of *voices*;

- affiliative functions require a balance of *power*;

- expressive functions require a balance of *forms*;

- ameliorative functions require a balance of *outcomes and experiences* (Section 2.4);

- adumbrative functions require balance across and with *arenas*; and

- integrative functions require a balance of *interfaces and connections* (Cockton, 2020a, Section 5.4).

Balance is thus a constant concern for design teams, starting with paradigms, playbooks, and palettes and continuing through work episodes, design arenas, approaches, and resources to functions. Teams can start projects with good support from re-usable practices, but constant awareness, imagination, openness, and vigilance and responsiveness are needed to make best use of whatever exists before project inception. New resources and approaches such as Creative Sprints may result, which can be used in a current or future design programme, adding to competitive advantage.

Achieving balance as appropriate mixes at all levels of design work introduces a risk of unrealistic extravagance. A further meta-principle of *assortedness* cautions against extremes of narrowness and extravagance. An appropriate mix avoids both extremes in all assortments of design work.

3.4   CHAPTER SUMMARY

Balance as an appropriate *mix* operates at all levels of design work. Due to the generality of ADS across paradigms, progressions, processes, projects, episodes, and approaches, balance *across* arenas impacts design outcomes. In addition, *within* design arenas, there are extensive balance factors:

- *content*: with support from subarenas and a mix of forms;

- *sources*: e.g., design team members and stakeholders, a mix of primary and secondary research, plus creative insights and ideas from a mix of voices within projects;

- *approaches*: a mix of disciplines, perspectives, qualities, resources, functions, and imaginations, with no adverse power distribution to impose unbalanced mixes; and

- *interfaces*: for connections to other arenas.

Achieving balance in so many ways may feel an impossible demand for mere mortals, but leading-edge design research has already embraced the need for "Renaissance" designers with extensive repertoires (Rodgers and Bremner, 2013). Whereas science controls its focus through reductionism, design work must be holistic. It must embrace whatever complexity is thrown at it. Good designers are skilled at handling complexity, and BIG Wo-Fo design exposes just how extreme this is, making explicit how the scope of designers' responsibilities has been steadily expanding for decades now (Young, 2008). While RILED methodologies would seek to control and constrain, CREAM ones are always open to ever expanding scopes of design and the consequent complexities.

Design work is not wholly cognitive. It is also social, embodied, axiological, and affective. Approaches and resources can exploit and enhance all facets of design work, but what appears on the page, physical or digital, can never fully script design work. By its very nature, creative collaborative design work has to be worked out as projects progress. No process can fully script design work, nor can any set of approaches and resources be complete enough to provide ready-made support for all design activities. This gap, and the risks associated with the critical creative practices that fill it, require vigilance, reflection, and correction throughout design work.

Balance must be worked at continually. *Progressive instantiation* is guided by reflection and deliberation on balances within design work, and thus helps teams to manage complexity. Although primarily focused on adding ever more detailed content to design arenas, progressive instantiation applies to all forms of balance. Design work should not only add content. It should add sources, approaches, qualities, and all other balance factors. However, what is added at one point may be set aside later. "Progressive" here is qualitative rather than quantitative. It is *design quality* that progresses, even if there is some quantifiable waste from a Lean perspective. The nature of creative work means that waste in the Lean sense cannot avoided. Careful tracking and re-planning within projects however can avoid excessive waste. A major source of excessive waste is failed integration. We next consider integration in design work.

CHAPTER 4

Integrating Across Design Arenas

To progress a project, a range of integrative resources is needed, which this chapter reviews. Much has already been covered in Book 1 (Cockton, 2020a) on the need for, and nature of, connections in BIG design.

- Chapter 4 (Cockton, 2020a) contrasted design paradigms with forms and mixes of connections in MADS.

- In Chapter 3's Cloudbooks fiction (Cockton, 2020a), brainwriting items were sorted into "work areas" using something like a design arena canvas, a tracking representation (Cockton, 2020a, Chapter 5), which places integration work straight on the agenda. Subsequent design work needs explicit connections. Section 5.6 (Cockton, 2020a) reviewed different forms of connections in BIG paradigms.

- Chapter 2 included posters developed by a TU/e Industrial Design Master's group. These *concourses* used a common advertising tactic of combining messages about outcomes (purpose) with support points (implicit antefact capabilities).

- Chapters 1, 2, and 3 all considered the importance of support for a *balance of interfaces* for connecting beyond an arena. Balance extends from across and within design arenas to balance across *connections* between them.

Concourse connections are implicit and undirected rather than explicit and directed, i.e., *between* arenas rather *than* from one *to* another. This chapter introduces some further concourses, but focuses mostly on explicit directed connections.

Integration work accumulates up to and beyond Davies and Talbot's (1987) *imago* moment. It caps off design work. There is much to explore here. The ADS construct is a useful resource for seeding methodological innovation in IxD (Cockton, 2010), providing a space of connections with a range of arities and structures. Some connections are already supported by existing UX and IxD approaches, or extensions of them. Other connections have hardly been explored in HCI, so below we consider possible approaches to fill gaps.

Connections exist in all design paradigms, but RILED ones fix them as arrows between phases. Figure 4.3 in Cockton (2020a) showed how RILED boxes and arrows can be swapped, with boxes containing co-products and arrows labelled with phases and their tasks that work on input co products to produce new ones. This aligns with Parnas and Clements (1986) faking rational design processes by ensuring that work products (i.e., co-products) are regularly revised to feign systematic development.

As snapshots, MADS and related representations track co-products at different stages of progression, including connections. Connections have an integrative function and, transformative loops aside, involve more than one arena. This can improve on RILED's lack of detail on how fixed phases in fixed orders transform inputs into outputs.

RILED processes assume that arrows in diagrams guarantee connections' existence. In BIG design, connections must be actively created and recognised. There is no fixed process to blame for lack of beneficiary implications for design, downstream utility of evaluation, or upstream futility before evaluation. Concurrent work on arenas replaces imagined RILED arrows with a range of connections ranging from implicit to explicit, latent to realised, and hinted to directed. Well directed concurrent design work invigorates reflection and deliberation on possible connections.

4.1   CONNECTING PAIRS OF DESIGN ARENAS

In RILED processes, most connections are binary, and directed from a phase to its successor. Exceptions include the V-model (Rook, 1986; Cockton, 2020a, Figure 5.6) and ISO 9241-210 (2019). Both have a few binary connections between non-adjacent phases. The V-model adds three for verification from early phases to later ones, but all its phases from specification onwards are in the a_tefact arena, which simplifies interfaces (e.g., a Design Structure Chart can guide Software Integration). ISO 9241-210 adds three for iteration (evaluation to a_tefact, purpose, and anyficiaries). In a concurrent progression, connections are far more extensive. We first consider binary connections in both directions for six possible arena pairs, as framed in Figure 5.10, from Cockton (2020a) (Figure 5.10:x below means connection *x* in Figure 5.10, e.g., Figure 5.10:5 *Fit with*). We follow ISO9241-210's RILED order, with requirements framed as worthwhile purpose. We consider standard connections first (anyficiaries to purpose, purpose to a_tefact, a_tefact to evaluation, in both directions (*from … to …* and *to … from …*), and then iteration ones.

4.1.1   CONNECTING BETWEEN ANYFICIARIES AND PURPOSE

We first review connections to purpose *from* anyficiaries (Figure 5.10:12 *Desires for*), using examples from Wo-Fo design and Design against Crime. Section 2.3.3 presented two primary research approaches for connecting *to* purpose *from* anyficiaries: field research revisited with a Wo-Fo (Cockton et al., 2009a); and collaborative analysis of sentence completion data (Cockton et al., 2009b). Any primary research that can identify anything with a positive or negative valence (e.g., needs, wants, pains, gains, motivators, demotivators) can connect *from* anyficiaries *to* purpose. These Wo-Fo practices begin by developing understandings of anyficiaries. The sentence completion approach compared two user demographics for an online gambling site.

1. Actual worth to
2. Assessment of
3. Achievement of
4. Target for
5. Fit with
6. Enablement of
7. Participate in
8. Preferences for
9. Reasons for
10. Focus for
11. Intended Worth for
12. Desires for

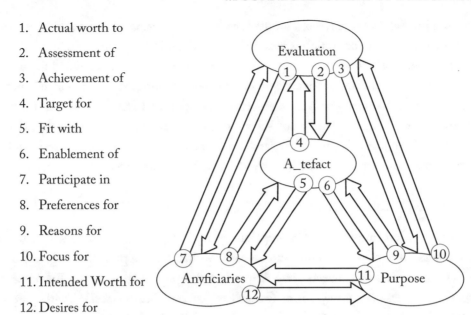

From Cockton (2020a): Figure 5.10: Generic framings of directed binary connections in BIG paradigms.

Primary research on anyficiaries can be *realised* as elements of purpose through data coding (using values), followed by curation (i.e., choosing which value codes to use for purpose). However, this may not be wholly a user-centred practice. For example, sentence completions needed to address inappropriate gambling for business and regulatory considerations as well as user ones. Realisation is not translation as it is not reversible. It realises something from one design arena in a form specific to another one. It can involve elaboration or condensation. It always involves judgment.

Design against cybercrime has developed anti-spam and anti-phishing capabilities to intentionally stop crime. If cybercrime is not considered where likely threats exist, then wilful maleficiaries can create unintended maleficiaries. Empirical research on criminal practices inform connections here from anyficiaries to purpose, but as with gambling, the focus is not wholly user-centred, but involves *direct transfer* from general ethics to design purpose, i.e., to design *against crime*. Direct transfer is a second form of connection. Realisation, above, was the first.

The reverse connection *to* Anyficiaries *from* Purpose (Figure 5.10:11 *Intended Worth for*) would be business strategy-led, not user-centred. It would begin by identifying new possibilities for worth and look to link to possible anyficiaries. For example, secondary research resources (Section 2.3.1) and critical and reflective resources (Section 2.3.2) can be reviewed to identify potential beneficiaries for forms of worth that have hardly been considered in IxD. Value- and values-focused approaches can start with existing value frameworks rather than with primary user research (van de Poel, 2013; Winkler and Spiekermann, 2019). New promising connections can spawn inception of a market-focused project. In some cases, a product marketed to existing groups could be repositioned for others. Much disruptive innovation works this way, with radical adaptations of existing products such as air travel for sale at low prices to groups who rarely or never use scheduled flights. A third connection form here, ideation, creatively connects purpose opportunities to possible beneficiaries.

Desires for and *Intended Worth for* connections are rare in RILED processes, because they need a separate purpose arena that is not subsumed within anyficiaries or a_tefacts. Grounding purpose in a mix of product strategy and research on anyficiaries moves the "implications for design" challenge to connections from purpose to a_tefacts, which we next consider.

4.1.2   CONNECTING BETWEEN PURPOSE AND A_TEFACTS

RILED processes often simplify these connections by replacing design purpose with artefact-centred requirements, and thus turn ends into means, which BIG approaches keep separate. For example, a Wo-Fo approach connects *from* Artefacts *to* Purpose (Figure 5.10:6 *Enablement of*) by annotating wireframes, with arrows from features to "callout" boxes (labelled with purpose elements). Wireframes become *why-frames*. Connections will be *implied* when there is little detail in the callout and *argued* when a connection is more detailed, a fourth form of explicit connection.

Usage connects *from* artefacts *to* achieved purpose. A coherent unit of interaction such as a task achieves purposes by using a sequence of artefact capabilities. Connections can be expressed as explicit task sequences, use cases, or other representations of user experiences. These are a fifth *articulated* form of explicit connection. Section 4.3 looks at two articulated connections in detail: *UX Cases* and *worth* maps.

Approaches to connecting *from* Purpose *to* Artefacts (Figure 5.10:9 *Reasons for*) are often inspired by appropriation, where users find ways to achieve unanticipated purpose. Awareness of appropriation can add new purposes to design intentions, or it can spawn new projects. For example, one young child's use of a digital Family Archive (Kirk et al., 2010) inspired a similar more specialised TellTable system for children's story telling (Cao et al., 2010). The young child's appropriation was not anticipated, so the first design team can claim limited credit for it. However, once an appropriation is explicitly adopted for a new artefact, then a project team does explicitly design it. This is another example of the second *direct transfer* form of connection, which can proactively add value to existing products or create new ones. This has been very effective with aids for impairments such as improved styling (demedicalising) of wheelchairs and mobility scooters, and sports glasses for people with visual impairments.

Connecting *from* Purpose *to* Artefacts involves creative as well as opportunistic practices. "How Might We?" questions (Dam and Siang, 2017) can be chosen to direct brainstorming to focus on connections between possible new purposes and digital capabilities to achieve them. Work here may progress to a prototype to better communicate a novel product strategy (Stevens and Moultrie,

2011). This is another example of the third ideation form of explicit connection, which can develop into other forms of connection through constructive rigour.

4.1.3   CONNECTING BETWEEN EVALUATION AND A_TEFACTS

This is the only connection that exists in both directions in ISO9241-210. HCD and IxD have developed many approaches to connecting *between* a_tefacts and evaluation. For example, walkthroughs, heuristics, design principles, platform guidance and styles, and accessibility check lists can be applied to antefacts in early evaluation before committing extensive resources to implementation. These connect *from* evaluation *to* artefacts (Figure 5.10:2 *Assessment of*). This is an example of a sixth *fit/misfit* form of explicit connection. Inspection reveals whether elements of an a_tefact do or do not fit guidance or meet requirements, supporting reflection in action during design, and thus interleaving evaluation with it. Alexander (1964) saw misfit as more natural to recognise than meeting requirements.

Design Rationales based on Questions, Options, and Criteria (QOC; Maclean et al., 1991) connect *from* Questions and Options (a_tefact) *to* Criteria (evaluation). In contrast to secondary sources for inspections, QOC primarily draws on the knowledge, expertise, and experience of design teams. It is a rare example of an HCD practice that forges *explicit* connections, albeit within a simpler design space than BIG's four multiply connected arenas. This is another example of the fourth *argued* form of connection. In QOC, criteria are used to argue for one option over others. Ternary and Quaternary connections are also possible when Questions reflect purpose and Criteria link to Beneficiaries.

As with *Enablement of* (Figure 5.10:6) connections *from* A_tefacts *to* Purpose, *usage* also mediates *from* A_tefacts *to* Evaluation (Figure 5.10:4 *Target for*), as in inspection methods such as Cognitive Walkthrough (Cockton et al., 2012), which bases evaluation on a task. This is another example of the fifth *articulated* form of connection (Section 4.3). Connections can combine more than one form. Walkthroughs and similar usage-based connections combine *articulation* (via usage) with *argument* (e.g., success or failure cases in Cognitive Walkthrough).

Software instrumentation connects *from* a_tefacts *to* evaluation by collecting evaluation data during use. A:B tests of alternative web page designs are a common approach here, with a current and new page design compared against key metrics. For e-commerce sites, sales and engagement with promotions and communications are common metrics. To instrument software for evaluation, metrics must be in place before implementation, resulting in connections in both directions, to A_tefacts *from* Evaluation (Assessment of) as well *from* A_tefacts *to* Evaluation (Target for). The former goes beyond a *direct transfer* connection when it requires *realisation* of metrics as additional instrumentation capabilities.

For example, a key purpose of a university website is to recruit students, staff, and collaborative partners. However, to evaluate achievement of purpose here, "sales pipelines" or similar features must be added to track prospective students, staff and partners. This is a digital variant of the *observer effect* in physics, but more welcome creatively. Just as attempts to measure some physical phenomena change what is observed, so instrumentation can need extra capabilities. Whereas in physics, the observer effect can give rise to dilemmas or undesirable phenomena, *Direct Worth Instrumentation* (Cockton, 2008c) can add value through additional beneficial capabilities.

Creative work may recognise a need for evaluation, but metrics may not be in place. Darke (1979) observed that where performance was not specified in advance, detailed requirements would be argued for in co-evolution with detailed design, connecting evaluation and a_tefacts both ways.

Connections above correspond to two of ISO9241-210's six arrows: a forward "standard" one from a_tefacts to evaluation (Figure 5.10:4 *Target for*) and the reverse (Figure 5.10:2 *Assessment of*), one of ISO9241-210's three iterative connections, all *from* evaluation, not *to* it. The other two are considered next.

4.1.4   CONNECTING BETWEEN PURPOSE AND EVALUATION

HCD evaluation measures tend to be associated with *quality in use* rather than *outcomes* of use (Cockton, 2007), which should overlap enough with the intended purpose for a digital product. To measure achievement of intended purpose, we need to connect *from* Purpose *to* Evaluation (Figure 5.10:10 *Focus for*). Measures can be associated with purpose elements (i.e., specific target benefits, reduced/removed costs, and risks). Targets can then be set for each measure. George (2016) formed such an *Element Measurement Strategy* (Cockton, 2008c), contributing to the evaluation plan for her *MyCareCircle* system. This is another example of the fourth *argued* form of connection.

A weaker *Focus* for connection is van de Poel's (2013) "translation" from values via "norms" to "specified design requirements." His example relies on a European animal welfare standard, for which no arguments are presented. His connections thus appear to be more *ideative* than argued.

Focus for connections are rare in RILED processes due to the absence of a separate purpose arena, as are *Achievement of* (Figure 5.10:3) connections. Implementation of an Element Measurement Strategy (EMS) within a Wo-Fo evaluation would form such a connection. Generally, connections *to* evaluation result in plans, whereas connections *from* them yield evaluation results for arenas.

4.1.5   CONNECTING BETWEEN ANYFICIARIES AND EVALUATION

As connections between the two core HCD design arenas, approaches to integration here are well established. One long established connection *from* beneficiaries *to* evaluation (Figure 5.10:7 *Participates in*) creates *user profiles* for recruiting and screening evaluation participants. This jumps over two intermediate phases (requirements, design) and is not diagrammed in ISO9241-210, unlike the iteration connection *from* evaluation *to* beneficiaries. It is like a V-model connection from an early design phase to a later evaluation one. It is a further example of a *(mis)fit* connection, with (mis) match between a profile and possible participants.

More recently, the role of anyficiaries in evaluation has become more proactively independent with users providing feedback via web channels or social media (Stickel et al. ,2016; Qaed et al., 2016). Users may also provide and organise evaluation data independently, as in the novel practice of *Creative Sprints* (Garnik et al., 2014). These practices, channels and media reduce the chances of unintentionally creating maleficiaries by unknowingly excluding specific groups from evaluations, and thus being unaware of usage difficulties. Crowd-sourced dislikes (likes are possible too) connect *from* anyficiaries *to* evaluation, so here the typical directions for evaluation planning (*to*) and results (*from*) do not apply, since there is no planning for spontaneous or reactive reporting. Users take on the role of evaluators and directly transfer their "results," which can be analysed subsequently by UX specialists or designers to identify artefact features as possible causes as part of a formal evaluation (Figure 4.20). If users do identify potential causes (artefact), impacts (purpose), or both, then ternary or quaternary connections result.

Binary connections to anyficiaries *from* evaluations (Figure 5.10:1 *Actual Worth to*) can be encountered where there is a sizeable sample of evaluation participants. Here it may be possible to identify demographic or psychographic differences that reduce artefact inclusiveness. More recently, "Big Data" analysis of online behaviours can target users for advertising and promotional communication, but similar approaches could be used to reduce users' addictive behaviours. This goes beyond evaluation in the original narrow sense of quality in use (ISO/IEC, 2011) with evaluations of collective usage that organise data by anyficiary subarenas rather than usage problems. This adds a seventh form of explicit connection, the familiar use of *statistical inference*.

Connections between anyficiaries and evaluations are thus currently limited, with the best established *from* anyficiaries *to* evaluations (Figure 5.10:7 *Participates in*). However, as big data practices increase, we can expect analyses of usage data to segment user populations on the basis of their user experiences, content preferences or feature usage (Figure 5.10:1 *Actual Worth to*).

4.1.6   CONNECTING BETWEEN ANYFICIARIES AND A_TEFACTS

This phase jumping connection is absent in both directions from ISO9241-210, but as with the arrow of hope from analysis to requirements (Section 4.1.1), connections *from* anyficiaries *to* antefacts (Figure 5.10:8 *Preferences for*) are *implications for design* (Dourish, 2006). The debate here mixes expectations and doubts on the ability to derive or otherwise generate design requirements from contextual research. For Fallman (2003), there is no "one-to-one correspondence between … fieldwork findings and resulting artefact." This is less of an issue in media fields, where creating specific content for audiences is well established and less contentious.

There are also fewer issues in requirements engineering, where Domain Analysis connects to artefacts *from* analyses of the language of problem specifications and similar anyficiary documents (Figure 5.10:5 *Fit with*). Nouns and verbs in such documents, combined with domain experts' knowledge, can be *directly transferred* from stakeholder needs to the object classes of a software artefact (Song et al., 2004). Clarke (1997) in an early study of explicit connections in HCD work replicated this second *direct transfer* form of connection from contextual scenarios to antefact object models.

Similar direct transfers can result from field research. For example, Goldsmith's Photostroller (Gaver and Bowers, 2012) developed from web-browsing sessions with care-home residents, who had shown interest in Flickr photographs. This guided a lo-fi prototyping session with photographs collected to show the residents, who gave them an enthusiastic reception. However, existing designs such as Goldsmith's Local Barometer, which reframed web content, also influenced this prototype and subsequent development of the Photostroller.

An often-contentious area of HCI that connects *from* anyficiaries *to* artefacts is guidance on cultural differences in design preferences (Choi et al., 2005). Expectations and doubts in the implications for design debate are replaced by confident recommendations on user interface and experience preferences of different territorial cultures (EL-Qirem and Cockton, 2011). Disciplinary differences may be at work here, with cultural recommendations based on formal experiments, and well-grounded reluctance to generalise from ethnographic research. Design resources here come from secondary rather than primary research. Similar resources exist for designing for impairments and age (children, teens, elderly). If any demographic group with specific needs is excluded from consideration during design and evaluation, then unintended maleficiaries can result.

Early HCI did not distinguish between user groups or consider individual differences (Cockton, 2004a). The Human Factors tradition made design recommendations for a single universal beneficiary: "the operator." Such *universal* connections support general IxD guidance on designing for people. They can still be informative if design teams protect against unwarranted generalisations. Generally, *Fit with* connections (Figure 5.10:5) *to* anyficiaries *from* a_tefacts are informative, applying knowledge, for example, to check fit between user competences, preferences or digital ecosystems on the one hand, and an a_tefact's demands, features, capabilities, and technological contexts on the other. This information can be incorporated into holistic personas (Section 4.5).

Connections between anyficiaries and a_tefacts have roots in several disciplinary practices, and can be contested across them, with social contexts and cultural differences eroding the universals of human factors. Established binary connections unsurprisingly have a *from-to* RILED order, but the reverse direction explicit in lean approaches such as MVP experiments (Section 4.5).

4.1.7   MODES OF CONNECTION

We have seen seven modes of explicit connection so far.

1. *Realisation*: elements from one arena are recast as elements in another, employing judgement in, e.g., interpretation (coding), selection (curation), condensation, or elaboration.

2. *Direct transfer*: elements in one arena become elements of another with no reframing.

3. *Ideative*: elements in one arena inspire ideas for another.

4. *Argued*: reasons are given for associating elements in one arena with elements in another.

5. *Articulated*: elements in one arena are combined (e.g., in some usage sequence) to connect with elements in another arena.

6. *(Mis)Fit*: elements in one arena (do not) fit criteria from another.

7. *Statistical inference*: subarenas of elements in one arena formed by statistical analysis of their interactions with elements of another arena.

In addition, concourse connections can be *latent* or *implicit*. The FCM's second *Core Paradox* step (Cockton, 2020a, Section 5.1.2) was modelled as a ternary concourse. This simplest form of connection is the most opaque due to its latent or implied nature. Additional work is required to expose connections, which can be one of the forms above. We can associate the nine forms identified with design paradigms:

- CREAM: latent, implicit, ideative;

- Hybrid: argued, articulated, realised; and

- RILED: direct transfer, fit/misfit, statistical inference.

Three forms of connection are common in CREAM practices that accept "felt" tacit associations and creative leaps. Three forms of connection can meet RILED standards. Direct transfer involves no subjective interpretation, (mis)fit can be judged objectively, and statistical inference underpins much science. The other three can range between RILED and CREAM practices, blending aspects of both, depending on how arguments, articulations, and realisations are formed.

Rejection of fixed rational linear processes and repeatable complete public methods does not plunge design into irrational anarchic practices that make rigorous systematic work impossible. Just as the final version of a mathematical proof is a systematic derivation of each point from the previous one, so the final version of a BIG design could systematically connect between arenas. However, such formal structures are means to ends, and not ends in themselves. There is no automatic causal connection between any notion of process quality and actual design outcomes in terms of achieved worth. Some connections may never progress beyond CREAM's tacit creative associations. Hybrid connections may be more CREAM than RILED. However, if they instead come close to meeting RILED standards without jeopardising design outcomes, then the *balance as mix* of BIG design would value this, as well as extensive use of standard RILED connections.

Systematic rigour in design is achieved through connections that must be forged in specific project practices. They cannot be preformed as generic resources for re-use without adaptation. This closes the remaining unaddressed third point of Chapter 3's (Cockton, 2020a) manifesto: *connections between work areas* [design arenas] are *created*, not preformed. Nine forms of connection have been identified so far, thus answering Chapter 3's (Cockton, 2020a) fifth question: *What sort of connections and interfaces would be in a comprehensive model of design work?*

4.2   CONCOURSES AS LATENT AND IMPLIED CONNECTIONS

A concourse is an implied or latent set of undirected connections between design arenas. Concourses are shown as clouds in MADS diagrams (Cockton, 2020a, Figures 4.1 and 4.3). Sketch sequences can be considered as concourses when they expose the relationship between problem setting and a solution to the problem (Vistisen, 2015), through designers getting "to know the materials of the design situation" through which "*a parti* [see below] comes to materialise" (Fallman, 2003). In IxD, prototypes take on much of the role of sketches, adding users or usage as essential "materials of the design situation" rather than being some form of test (Fallman, 2003). Nelson and Stolterman's (2003) forms of design judgement are also concourses. Six of these were applied when rationalising the design research progression for the Rendezvous Project (Wolf et al., 2006).

Concourses often precede specification of design arena elements, hence Darke (1979) called hers *primary generators* for subsequent conjectures and analyses of co-evolving creative design work. Part of the work when using a concourse to seed DANs is to establish which arenas are involved. For example, in Darke's analysis of the Dawson Heights housing project, she identified a primary generator that combined respect for the scale of neighbourhood and neutrality on housing densities ("lack of presumption about flats" [apartments]). This combined purpose (respect) with an antefact framing of "stepping down" to cascade housing down a hill. Arguably, this also connects to beneficiaries as both existing human neighbours and the hillside locale itself. In architecture, human benefits are mediated by built environments, and thus neighbourhoods broadly can be understood as beneficiaries (just as sustainable design benefits local to global environments). Darke's primary generator for the Marquess Road development respected the area's traditional visual and social patterns, connecting purpose (respect) and beneficiaries (existing social patterns) with the antefact (retain existing features and qualities).

A later example of a complex primary generator in architecture relates to the Byker Wall in Newcastle (Abrams, 2003). The local community, whose homes were to be demolished, participated in the design of new housing for them, which would cascade down from a new noisy busy road. One purpose was to shield (purpose) re-co-located residents (beneficiaries) from the noise and traffic with a housing "wall" (artefact) that would span the top of the neighbourhood, with pedestrian and road access through shared spaces (artefact) dropping down toward the River Tyne. The concourse here is ternary, spanning purpose, beneficiaries and artefacts in a co-designed peaceful walkable development with shared spaces shielding re-co-located neighbours from noise and traffic.

Concourses as loosely structured undifferentiated broad ideas spanning design arenas are implicit in older design research concepts of *codes* (Hillier et al., 1972) and *partis* (Stolterman, 1999). The latter, short for *parti pris*, a departure point, may not extend much beyond a_tefacts, but is not restricted to it. Uncertainty over the arenas covered by a concourse disappears with subsequent DANs, which make it clear which arenas were involved.

After Charles Eames' "everything eventually connects," Hillier et al.'s (1972) codes are one of the earliest examples of recognising the critical role of links in creative design work. As architecture moved away from established forms to "one-off kinds" of design progressions, the result was "a much freer, more indeterminate situation." This indeterminacy or "deficiency":

> *…is made up in terms of information which is expressed in terms of the users rather than in terms of buildings, and the designer operates a kind of informal code for linking one to the other* (Hillier et al., 1972).

Codes pre-exist specific projects, giving them a similar role to patterns (Alexander et al., 1977). Codes combine with project-specific information to form more specific conjectures, which do not:

> *arise out of … information although it may contribute heuristically. By and large they come from … knowledge of the instrumental sets [i.e., technologies], solution types … informal codes, and occasionally from right outside - an analogy perhaps, or a metaphor, or simply what is called inspiration* (Hillier et al., 1972).

Codes and patterns are preformal pre-structuring devices. The latter have a more explicit structure, but remain concourses because connections between arenas are implied or latent. All are

> *hypotheses, all 253 of them—and are, therefore, all tentative, all free to evolve under the impact of new experience and observation* (Alexander et al., 1977).

Patterns have a *name* that is "usually more indicative of the solution than of" two other elements: *problem* and *context*. The problem should be expressed as constraints and a balance of forces. Context covers "situations under which the pattern applies" which "often includes background, discussions of why this pattern exists, and evidence for generality" (Alexander et al., 1977). These tend to be intertwined. For example, Pattern 159 *LIGHT ON TWO SIDES OF EVERY ROOM* is 1,295 words long with 3 photos and 2 diagrams. Within it, the focus moves between artefacts, purpose, beneficiaries, and evaluations, with varying clarity on connections between them. Solutions within patterns combine static relationships (including referencing and relating other higher-and lower-level patterns) and dynamic rules ("microprocess") that describe "how to construct artifacts in accord with the pattern, often listing several variants and/or ways to adjust to circumstances."

Three decades later, agile software development produced its own concourse form, the Connextra format for user stories (Cohn, 2004), which has more clear structure than Alexander's patterns.

As a (who wants to accomplish something)

I want to (what they want to accomplish)

So that (why they want to accomplish that thing)

This is often simplified to: *role needs feature for reason*. "What they want to accomplish" is an instrumental goal and "why they want to accomplish that thing" is a terminal one (purpose).

More recently, many concourses in design work have taken the form of a canvas. For example, the *Business Model Canvas* (Osterwalder and Pigneur, 2010) focuses on the project sponsor as the main beneficiary for a commercial product, but a spread of beneficiaries is considered: customers (relationships, channels, and segments) and key partners who can provide key resources, including technology components (artefact materials subarea). A Value Propositions section covers design purpose. The canvas would typically be filled in at project inception, with content added concurrently in any order.

Current canvases have rapidly evolved as part of new approaches to innovation. They have greater breadth and depth than older resources such as feature-benefit charts or tables (Douglas, 2000), where arbitrary links between a_tefact features and design purpose are possible, but as a complementary resource, they can be useful. For example, George (2016) created simple two column *Artefact Connection Tables* (from Purpose to Antefacts) from more extensive five column Worth Integration Tables (Figure 4.3).

The long-established concourses construct in design research is obscured by multiple names: codes, patterns, primary generators, partis, frames, canvases, user stories, and feature-benefit charts/tables. They all foreground connections and background the connected. This contrasts with the representations and records reviewed in Section 5.8 of Cockton (2020a). For example, Gaver's (2011) workbooks rely on a community of practice for interpretation who are familiar with the "inexplicable imaginative leaps" there. There is a span of forms of connections within workbooks and annotated portfolios (Gaver and Bowers, 2012), and aptly so because they reflect the range of forms reviewed above. This recognizes and builds "upon practices already in use within the field" making "careful articulation of their existing approaches in a way that is legible to those from other disciplines" (Gaver and Bowers, 2012). While they do not "prescribe a series of categories to be employed, or advocate an elaborate ontology of entities and relationships," most annotations can be modelled with a MADS, which embody "practices already in use within" creative design.

There are many ways to make connections, from "inexplicable imaginative leaps" (Gaver, 2011) to the systematically articulated links reviewed below. If the choice is to foreground artefacts, then links within workbooks and annotated portfolios will not "occlude the potency of unique, embodied artefacts in a cloud of words and diagrams," but instead achieve "sense and relevance by virtue of ... indexical connection with an artefact" (Gaver and Bowers, 2012). Similarly, if purpose is not managed as a separate design arena, a concourse will result for approaches such as Cultural Probes (Gaver et al., 1999), which combine insights about anyficiaries and purpose.

Annotations that are "extremely succinct" can best suggest direct transfer or (mis)fit. For example, there is direct transfer from the accessibility literature on the variably abled to its "concretely exemplified" influence on the Photostroller (Gaver and Bowers, 2012). Each instance of these "traceable connections" has a specific sense and thus moves beyond Hillier et al.'s (1972) codes to a project specific realisation.

Design workbooks (Gaver, 2011) can be understood as form of design method. Connections can be explicit, e.g., seeing a design idea "in an external context, whether literally against a setting used in depicting the proposal or implicitly in its relationship to other products, prototypes and proposals that surround it" but, unlike much use of scenarios not diverting "attention from potential problems or overlooked issues, some of which may even lead to new and more promising ideas." This needs to be borne in mind when considering articulated connections in the next section. A design workbook's loose concourse indicates:

> *what a system might do and establish, often implicitly, the 'needs' it might address, usually without including details of how this would be achieved technically or accessed by an interface. In their reticence, they invite viewers to speculate about these prospects themselves.*

This enables inquisitive and ideative functions, prompting consideration of plausibility, desirability (and thus anyficiaries), experiences and impact (and thus purpose), and preferred technologies (and thus a_tefact and evaluation arenas).

Wolf et al.'s (2006) progression visualisations can also be understood as concourses that arrange glimpses of design arenas around their interstices. As visualisations, their span across arenas is clearer than Darke's (1979) textual accounts of primary generators, which led George (2016) to understand a primary generator narrowly as antefact only, but she did extend its role beyond inception into all subsequent episodes.

Darke's primary generators have much in common with Dorst's pragmatic senses of frames (organising principle, a coherent set of statements, or both), which can have strong inquisitive, ideative, and informative functions by triggering "mini-stories" that open up shared experiences across a design team. Dorst's logical sense of frames limits initial consideration of anyficiaries and a_tefact arenas (his "WHAT") through a strong focus on evaluation and purpose in *HOW leads to OUTCOMES*. Dorst's logical sense of frames structures (Cockton, 2020a, Figure 5.3), transforms a concourse into a composite of more explicit connections, to which we now return.

4.3   ARTICULATED BINARY LINKS: PLAITING, NETTING, WEAVING, AND TWISTING

We noted seven forms of explicit connection in Section 4.1, and implied and latent ones for concourses in Section 4.2. A partial concourse results once any pair of its arenas is explicitly connected. Connections vary in their underlying rigour. Implicit, latent, and ideation connections are difficult to rationalise, but direct transfer, (mis)fit, statistical inference, argument, realisation, and articulation all allow clear rationalisations of connections. In this section we look in more detail at articulated connections, which draw on long established HCD and SE approaches to provide a strong contrast to the creative connections of concourses.

4.3.1   USER EXPERIENCE CASES

The first example of an articulated connection is the UX Case, a novel merger of usage and experience representations that combine Use Cases (Adolf et al., 2002), Cognitive Task specifications (Casner, 1991), and UX considerations. For a detailed account of the rationale and tactics for UX Cases, see Cockton (2009b), where they were called "User Experience Frames."

Carroll (1990) finessed the infinite detail of the a_tefact and anyficiaries arenas with a focus on tasks and how a_tefacts support them. Co-evolution was recognised:

A task implicitly sets requirements for the development of artifacts, and the use of an artifact often redefines the task for which the artifact was originally developed.

However, as with all task-based approaches, there can be a large gap between task goals and design purpose. A separate purpose arena can avoid this by shifting attention away from what can be done with a_tefacts to desirable experiences and outcomes. Winkler and Spiekerman (2019) argue that values must be examined in the intended operational context of a planned system, which entails consideration of *usage*, which is the appropriate generic concept here. There should be no exclusive commitment to tasks, activities, user journeys, or any other usage span as the sole focus. A UX Case (UXC) supports broad consideration of usage. A UXC's spine is a two-column use case as in Table 4.1. The left column mostly shows user input actions, and some cognitive operations (i.e., not users' inputs, Cell 27: review, determine that like, choose to add). The right column shows system actions. Extra columns can support focuses on usage or experience. UXCs are flexible tabular resources that can be adapted for different design and research purposes Project teams can decide on which columns they need to express and analyse envisaged UXs, but it is likely that the twin use case columns (user input actions and system actions or responses) will always be there. A column type can have more than one instance, e.g., there were user input columns for both browsing and searching actions for work on the Family Archive system (Cockton, 2009a).

Table 4.1: e-commerce transaction use case excerpt (Cockburn 2000, p.95)	
20. Shopper will select a product model	21. System will determine standard product model options, and then present the first question about determining major product options.
22. While questions exist to determine product option recommendations	24. System will prompt with questions that vary based on previous answers to determine the Shopper's needs and interests related to major product options, along with pertinent information such as production information, features & benefits, comparison information, and pricing.
23. Shopper will answer questions	
25. Shopper answers last question	26. At the last question about major product option desires, the system will present the selected model and selected options for shopper validation.
27. Shopper reviews their product selection, determines they like it, and chooses to add the product selection to their shopping cart.	28. System will add product selection and storyboard information (navigation and answers) to the shopping cart.
	29. The system presents a view of the shopping cart and all of the product selections within it.

In first-wave HCI, there was a focus on specifying cognitive operations for interaction steps. Casner (1991) used this to identify hard cognitive operations in decision support for replacement by simpler perceptual ones through use of visualisations. While a first-wave HCI column for cognitive operations could be added, in practice a higher level of abstraction is more useful, i.e., how users form (cognitive) *beliefs* about system capabilities, task status, and other usage aspects. Second-wave HCI columns can be added for its "turn to the social" (Rogers et al., 1994), e.g., expressing social interactions between co-present users and observers. Lastly, third-wave columns can be added for emotion and physical actions, respectively: feelings as they emerge to be shaped during interaction; and any actions in the physical world, e.g., printing out and pinning up. UXC columns can thus cover a range of design arenas, HCI waves, and disciplines.

- User actions (via a_tefact features, SE)

- System responses (from a_tefact features, SE)

- Beliefs (about user/system capabilities, anyficiaries, first-wave HCI)

- Social interactions (in the world, anyficiaries, second-wave HCI)

- Physical actions (in the world, anyficiaries, third-wave HCI)

- Feelings (sensual, emotional, interpretative, evaluative, anyficiaries, third-wave HCI)

Feelings and impressions matter positively when they propel worthwhile experiences and avert adverse ones, but also matter negatively when they make interaction unpleasant, inefficient, or even prematurely end it unsatisfactorily. Designers must expose and assess the likely path of a UX. UXCs let designers indicate how feelings, beliefs, and social and physical actions are expected to arise and steer subsequent interaction. Table 4.2 shows a UXC for booking a van via the imaginary lovelyvan.com website. The right-most "Actions in the World" column combines social and physical actions. A dotted arrow traces the van booking experience from top to bottom.

UXCs connect a_tefacts to purpose via usage experiences. They articulate how artefact use achieves instrumental goals, connecting between beneficiaries (who want to accomplish something), purpose (why they want to), and artefacts (capabilities). Content for the two-core use case columns comes from the a_tefact arena. The other columns add purpose and human dynamics from anyficiaries.

4.3.2   WORTH MAPS

UXCs were created to simplify *worth maps* (Cockton, 2009a). A single UX box replaces a previous rambling network of elements, with "inputs" from the a_tefact arena and "outputs" to purpose. UXCs provide "internal details" for worth map UX boxes. Since different UXs can share inputs and outputs' a worth map relates UXCs diagrammatically, linking a_tefact elements via UXs to purpose.

Worth maps express how designed means (a_tefacts) can be used to achieve design's ends. Means-end chains (MECs) are represented in worth maps as paths of arrows from a_tefact (sub) arenas via UXs to worthwhile outcomes (benefits). Figure 4.1 shows a worth map for a van hire website, mostly from a customer perspective. Element colours are: yellow for benefits, pink for UXs, light blue for a_tefact qualities, grey for a_tefact features, white for a_tefact materials, and red edged for costs/risks. An example MEC is highlighted in red. Purpose elements are ends. All other elements are means. Simpler forms of worth map are possible by replacing a_tefact subarenas with a flat set of product attributes (Cockton et al., 2009b).

This worth map indicates an imaginary design team's hope, i.e., they can make use of image capabilities for webpages (*materials*, white) to implement features that support directions to a van hire depot with maps and related content (*feature*, grey). The expectation is that these features will be perceived as helpful and considerate (*qualities*, blue).

Table 4.2: Good plan for van hire UXC (Cockton, 2009b). Numbers in brackets correspond to scenario paragraphs in Figure 4.18 below

Feelings	Beliefs	User Action	System Response	Actions in the World
(1) Worth a try		Open lovelyvan.com	Display Home	
Not a good place to start	(2) Can find prices and availability			
				Sally persuades Harry
		Enter Post Code		
			Show depots map	
	Nearest depot is on ring road	Sally sees nearest depot		
		Select depot on ring road	Display depot and van info	
(3) That's cool				
	Can find right van	Select appropriate van	Display book this van page	
				Sally checks details
		(4) Book and pay for van		
			Display and email confirmation	
Feels great, all well planned		(5) Save and print confirmation page		
	Booked right van for right time period			
		(6) Read email, follow link to info pdf	Display pdf	
That looks very smart				
		Print info and instructions pdf		Staple and pin up info and instructions
(7) Looking forward to getting van	Have all necessary details			

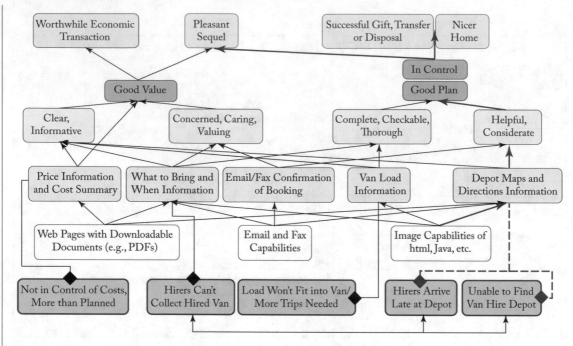

Figure 4.1: Worth map for a hypothetical van hire site.

Well-designed web pages can produce immediate feelings of helpfulness and consideration, but that has limited value if it does not follow through into worthwhile outcomes. When booking a van for hire, such outcomes include:

- making a worthwhile economic transaction;

- having a pleasant sequel after completing a van hire (i.e., not left so frustrated and exhausted that it ruins the rest of your day);

- successfully transferring something as a gift, purchase, sale or disposal; and/or

- improving one's home (by removing something old or bringing in something new).

Such worthwhile outcomes are indicated by yellow elements at the top of Figure 4.1. The two right-hand outcome elements are complementary: a "nicer home" potentially results from a "successful gift, transfer or disposal." This is one of two pairs of closely adjacent elements without connecting arrows. Non exclusive alternatives are horizontally adjacent. Sequenced UXs are vertically adjacent. Both are instrumental, but the upper one connects to a terminal outcome.

There are three main envisaged UXs for the van hire website. One develops and maintains the feeling that a booked van is good value. Another develops the feeling that a good plan is falling into place for collecting the van, transporting some goods, and then returning the van to the depot (the UXC for this is in Table 4.2). The "goodness" of the plan will be later revealed by how in control the hirer feels during the UX of collecting, using and returning a van. This third UX is vertically above "good plan" to indicate the typical time delay between on-line service purchases and their consumption (e.g., flight, theatre or theme park tickets, airport car parking bookings). Purchasers buy and/or book services that will be consumed later, requiring service UX to build confidence and trust, since the appropriateness of the purchased service is only known later.

Positive MECs indicate expectations that an a_tefact can enable UXs that deliver benefits. Such outcomes will not only be worthwhile because of achieved benefits, but also because of acceptable costs and risks. Dashed red lines ending with diamonds in Figure 4.1 are *aversion blocks*, indicating expectations that web site features will avoid adverse costs of being unable to find, or arriving late at, a van hire depot, which could destroy the worth of an intended transaction and/or result in an unpleasant sequel of a ruined day (or even longer). Adverse outcome elements are shown in orange with red edges. Full MECs are not shown for aversion blocks as Figure 4.1 omits a_tefact defects (negative qualities) and the adverse UXs that result and may lead to adverse outcomes.

Worth mapping (Cockton et al., 2009a) connects means to ends via:

- BIG's *ameliorative paradigm* of designing as connecting;

- the *informative concepts* of MECs and aversion blocks;

- a *directive* set of a_tefact subarenas (materials, features, qualities in Figure 4.1);

- a *directive* set of purpose subarenas (benefits and cost/risks in Figure 4.1);

- *protective* '"black boxing" of UXCs into simple UX elements;

- an *expressive* worth map with several participative, interactive and other formats; and

- a set of *directive* practices that configure and combine the other resources.

Worth maps indicate how a_tefact capabilities and features contribute to intended worth. Software development can prioritise implementation to achieve the most worth most quickly. It is common in worth maps to see features and UXs that are more connected than others. This is visually salient and draws attention (Kress and Van Leeuwen, 2006), which can support agile development. In Scrum, prioritisation by core purpose or connection density offers bases for selecting user stories from a backlog for the next sprint. The minimal viability of a Minimal Viable Product in Lean UX (Gothelf with Seiden, 2013) can be based on essential worth, and would thus have its artefact features and qualities in the MECs that end with essential worth elements.

Worth Maps can deliver on the Agile Manifesto's first principle (Beck et al., 2001):

> *Our highest priority is to satisfy the customer through early and continuous delivery of valuable software.*

It took over a decade for systematic approaches to value to mature for digital products and services (e.g., Osterwalder et al., 2014). Worth Maps communicate how software and other artefacts deliver value as worth. They adapt Hierarchical Value Maps (HVMs), developed for market research and advertising (Cockton et al., 2009a). The use of black box UXs (modularised as UXCs) overcame problems of complex cyclic consequence networks in HVMs by SE that extends readily for UX considerations.

Worth maps can get very large, so for practical projects they must be modularised. In the Family Archive work (Cockton et al., 2009a), there were five worth maps, one for each stage of an envisaged life cycle for archived objects: *enticing*, *capture*, *processing*, *creating*, and *consumption*. In an enticing stage, the Family Archive would attract interest. Objects would be digitised or imported in a capture stage, edited and curated in a processing stage, repurposed in a creating stage, and shared in a consumption stage. Each stage differs in intended purposes (with some overlap), with stages achieving different worth, moving from mostly instrumental toward terminal values.

In the VALU project (Cockton et al., 2009b), worth maps were modularised in the Visio drawing editor by creating separate layers for each UX and its connections. This simplified worth maps for focus during presentations and discussions. In Camara's (2012) Ph.D., worth maps for a mobile application developed in Orange Labs Lannion were modularised by coherent groups of materials on a mobile phone (e.g., GPS, aerial, screen, keyboard, camera).

Figure 4.2: A completed worth sketch for a family archive.

Worth maps can thus be split up in the basis of purpose elements, a_tefact elements (materials or features, and possibly qualities), or UXs to create more manageable submaps for group work and presentation. Modularisations can reflect a project sponsor's interests. The sociodigital research group at Microsoft Research Cambridge were interested in designing for human values (Harper et al., 2008), so modularisation was based on purpose variations across a lifecycle of archived objects. The online gambling company in the VALU project case study had a focus on UX, so UXs were a good basis for modularisation. Orange Labs Lannion were interested in exploiting the capabilities of smartphones, and thus modularised around a_tefact materials.

Worth mapping can be invigorated by omitting explicit connections, leaving them *implied* by position. Worth map elements (a_tefact, purpose, UX) can be printed onto cards or written on sticky notes and then (re-)positioned on a (large) table during design team deliberations. Figure 4.2 shows such a *worth sketch* at the end of a design workshop. Red lines have been drawn to allow the sketch to be reassembled, with the help of the photo, in the researcher's office. Regardless of how worth maps are represented, or whether only a worth sketch is used, the articulation involved is more explicit than in concourses.

4.4   DIRECTED TERNARY CONNECTIONS

Figure 5.9 in Book 1(Cockton, 2020a) showed basic connection forms, based on analysis (Cockton, 2010) that expected ternary and quaternary connections to be simple fans (i.e., 1:2, 2:1, 1:3, 2:2, 3:1). However, SoMADS modelling of Dorst's (2015) Frame Creation Model (FCM; Cockton, 2020a, Figure 5.3) mixed unary, binary, ternary, and grafted connections. Grafts can form ternary connections from binary ones. Two binary connections may also *chain* via a common arena, and perhaps close into a *ring* (i.e., three binary connections from one arena via two others and back to first). To not be just two binary connections, ternary chains and rings must be formed using one approach and expressed using one resource.

Figure 5.9 of Cockton (2020a) contains one grafted connection: a binary connection with a graft, similar to Dorst's *Themes* FCM step (Cockton, 2020a, Figure 5.3). There are many other forms of grafts, e.g. a binary connection grafted onto a ternary connection for the *Frames, Futures, and Transformation* FCM steps. A binary connection can also be grafted onto another binary one (e.g., extending worth maps with connections to anyficiaries; Figure 4.6). These, however, are only scratching the surface, because with grafts to grafts and so on, the number of possible connection forms is infinite (Cockton, 2010).

While Figure 5.10 of Cockton (2020a) fully enumerates and names binary connections, this is not possible for ternary or quaternary connections, due to infinite possibilities arising from complex grafts, chains, and rings. To simplify analysis, we group ternary connections by the arena that begins or ends them. We consider connections from and to this. We then identify gaps in coverage relative to six basic ternary connections for each arena: from the arena to three different pairs, and from these three to it. No gaps were identified for binary connections (Section 4.1), with all generic framings in Figure 5.10 (Cockton, 2020a) covered. Where gaps are identified for ternary connections, these could be filled by novel approaches, but often use of existing binary or quaternary connections is more advisable.

4.4.1   TERNARY CONNECTIONS BY A_TEFACTS

We first consider ternary connections that start or end with an a_tefact arena (bold edged in figures). For example, George's (2016) Worth Integration Tables are a ternary alternative to an augmented worth map (Figure 4.6). They have five columns:

- antefact capabilities under consideration;

- related purpose (benefits);

- potential beneficiaries;

- risks of increased costs or adverse consequences; and

- the number of the activity in the progression (as in Cockton, 2020a, Figure 5.4) that formed the integration.

The second and fourth columns, respectively, cover purpose as positive and negative aspects of intended worth. A table's rows can be read in different directions, i.e., from/to antefacts to/from purpose and beneficiaries. However, there is direction, so these connections are not concourses (Figure 4.3). In all cases, the type of each binary connection is ideative.

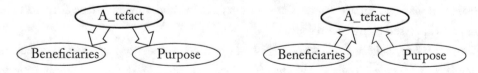

Figure 4.3: Worth integration tables as ternary connections starting/ending with a_tefacts.

In Section 4.1.3, QOC (Questions, Options, and Criteria) was introduced as a binary connection between evaluation (Criteria) and a_tefacts (Options). As noted, questions can be in the a_tefact or purpose arena, and criteria may connect to anyficiaries, forming a chain (Figure 4.4), in which the type of both connections is argued. Note that the evaluation here is analytical, and empirical evaluation may be better. Delaying decisions until after user evaluation defused tensions in one of Löwgren's (1995) case studies. If questions are also in the purpose arena, a quaternary connection results with an added Focus for connection to evaluation (Figure 5.10:10). However, augmented worth maps (Figure 4.13) provide a better basis for linking to evaluation from other design arenas.

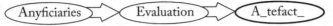

Figure 4.4: Design rationale as a ternary connection to a_tefacts.

A third approach with a ternary connection, *competitor analysis*, starts with existing competitor products (artefacts). A very simple structure is possible, where capabilities or features of competitor products are simply compared with a proposed new product, but this cannot establish the worth of capabilities and features.

A more useful approach to competitor analysis assesses the worth of capabilities and features in use (Figure 4.5). The articulated rootstock (grey fill) is a binary connection from artefact to purpose (Figure 5.10:6 *Enablement of*). It has two argued grafted binary connections from/ to evaluation (planned evaluation from/evaluation results to). There are two more argued grafted connections from Evaluation to loops on both Artefact (Figure 5.10:2 *Assessment of*) and Purpose (Figure 5.10:3 *Achievement of*). These transformative loops capture potential improvements to the evaluated competitor and its achievable purpose as possible elements for a_tefact and purpose of a proposed new product.

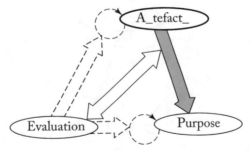

Figure 4.5: Competitor analysis as a ternary connection from and to a_tefacts.

Competitor analysis transfers insights into what existing products could become to new proposed products. There is an implied order within this approach, with valorisation (dashed) connections to artefact and purpose dependent on prior evaluation results. However, this is not an order within a whole design progression, but within a single activity (Alexander's "microprocess").

Five of the six possible basic ternary connection forms are covered above. Competitor artefacts are independent, but product understandings are dependent, so two basic forms are covered by competitor analysis (from *existing* and to *envisaged* a_tefacts). Worth Integration Tables cover two more basic forms (from/to antefacts) and Design Rationale covers a fifth (to a_tefacts). We need to imagine an approach for the sixth basic form *from* a_tefacts *to* anyficiaries and evaluation. For example, for a design-led experimental independent artefact (with no clear purpose), brainstorming could fan out (1:2) to identify possible beneficiaries (Figure 5.10:5 *Fit with*) and then plan to evaluate (Figure 5.10:4 *Target for*) suitability for them (Figure 5.10:5 *Fit with*). The connection to beneficiaries is (mis)fit and argued for the Target for connection. There is thus no unavoidable lacunation (Cockton, 2020a, Chapter 4) for ternary connections to and from a_tefacts, but the imagined approach here is a reduced version of MVP experiment planning (Section 4.5, quaternary), and may be inferior.

4.4.2   TERNARY CONNECTIONS BY ANYFICIARIES

We next consider connections between anyficiaries and two other arenas. For example, Worth Maps connect from A_tefacts to Purpose, but can be extended to also connect to either Evaluations, Anyficiaries, or both (quaternary connection). Anyficiaries become associated with specific UXs in a worth map when the logic of a corresponding UXC depends on specific considerations about them (otherwise a UX is generic and does not depend on knowledge of specific anyficiaries). Figure 4.6 grafts a connection from anyficiaries onto the articulated worth map connection (grey fill, Figure 5.10:6 *Enablement of*). The graft does not change the connection type, which remains articulated. A similar extension can be made to have UXCs (Cockton, 2020a, Section 5.3.1) for specific anyficiaries, with the same MADS.

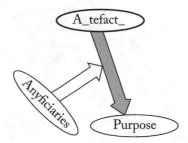

Figure 4.6: Augmented worth map as a ternary connection from anyficiaries.

The same three design arenas are also involved in an approach to questionnaires (George, 2016) that tests design assumptions about artefacts, beneficiaries, and purpose. Two questionnaires were designed, piloted and fielded to systematically address assumptions about three arenas: one for families of children with major motor impairments, one for professionals in their care circles. Questions were designed to cover six areas of missing or incomplete information. Results transferred directly in connections from anyficiaries to purpose, antefact and anyficiaries via transformative loops (Figure 4.7).

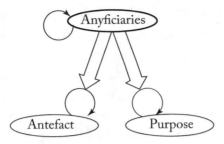

Figure 4.7: Assumption checking questionnaires as a ternary connection from anyficiaries.

The MADS for Von Hippel's (1986) *lead users* approach is very similar to Figure 4.7, but with no loop on anyficiaries (Figure 4.8). Lead users innovatively adapt products such as kite-surfing harnesses for specific purposes, creating a more competitive product. Companies can work with lead users to plan future product versions (left loop in Figure 4.8), using lead user modifications and experiences as evidence for the worth (right loop) of user innovations.

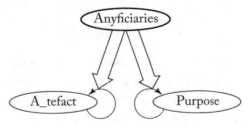

Figure 4.8: Lead user approaches as a ternary connection from anyficiaries.

The MADS for a *Value Proposition Canvas* (Osterwalder et al., 2014) is simpler than Figures 4.7 and 4.8. Three binary connections combine into a ternary one within a single canvas (Figure 4.9). This identifies current pains and gains of beneficiaries (from responsibilities from their "jobs to be done") and directly transfers them to purpose (Figure 5.10:12 *Desires for*). An ideative connection also connects these pains and gains to pain relievers and gain creators as features of an envisaged product (Figure 5.10:8 *Preferences for*), which creates a partial concourse. There is no articulation of any Intended Worth for connection (Figure 5.10:11) from a_tefact to purpose. The link here is at best implicit.

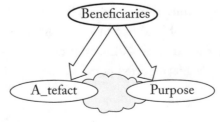

Figure 4.9: Value proposition canvas as a ternary connection from beneficiaries.

The three approaches above (Figures 4.7, 4.8, and 4. 9) are the same basic form from any-ficiaries to a_tefacts and purpose (1:2 fan outs; Cockton, 2020a, Figure 5.9), but involve different concrete connections. Reversed connections to anyficiaries from a_tefacts and purpose are possible. For example, analysis of articulated connections from artefact to purpose (Figure 5.10:6 *Enablement of*) as expected usage can identify assumptions about users, and thus graft to anyficiaries (i.e., not a fan in). These assumptions may be general (i.e., about any possible user) or specific (e.g., market segment). This could contribute to the planning of a MVP experiment (Figure 4.17).

Considering gaps in the ternary connections covered above, there are four: two connecting from/to a_tefacts and evaluations and two from/to purpose and evaluations. Rather than fill these gaps with ternary connections, all four are better filled by quaternary ones: the first two are not guided by purpose; the second two consider evaluation with nothing to evaluate. In addition, while design-led experimental testing of a speculative a_tefact may be revealing about anyficiaries, it is highly likely to also be revealing about purpose and thus be quaternary (2:2 fan). More gaps exist for ternary connections to/from anyficiaries than are filled, but there are better quaternary ones.

4.4.3   TERNARY CONNECTIONS BY PURPOSE

Section 4.1.3 presented *Direct Worth Instrumentation* (Cockton, 2008c) as a binary connection from Purpose to Evaluation. However, existing infrastructure for instrumentation is not enough (e.g., webserver logs), additional artefact capabilities will be needed (in general, custom instrumentation within a digital artefact is much more effective than generic logging capabilities). A ternary chain (Figure 4.10) extends the argued connection from Purpose to Evaluation (Figure 5.10:10 *Focus for*) onto a_tefacts with a realising one (Figure 5.10:2: *Assessment of*).

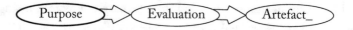

Figure 4.10: Direct worth instrumentation as a ternary connection from purpose.

UIE's Inherent Value Testing (Spool, 2004) compares experienced users' value perceptions with those of new website users. Instead of evaluating quality in use, it compares overlap between achievable and first use value. Figure 4.11 depicts this as a fuse of two MADS (left for experienced, right for new users) with grafted connections from anyficiaries to enablement of purpose (Figure 5.10:6). Usage of the same artefact enables different actual outcomes (purpose, grey arrows, articu-lated) and perceived value (UX, dashed arrows, direct transfer). A cross MADS (mis)fit connection can compare observable achieved value, reported perceived value, or both.

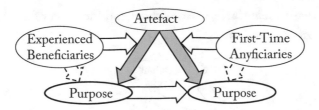

Figure 4.11: Inherent value testing as ternary connections to purpose.

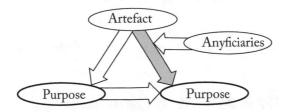

Figure 4.12: Intended and achieved worth comparison as ternary connections to purpose.

Camara (2012) developed a similar approach to inherent value testing that compared the design team's worth map for intended purpose with one for achieved purpose, based on usage data. The ternary connection is simpler than Figure 4.11. Only one group of anyficiaries is involved (Figure 4.12) and only achieved worth was considered, not perceived worth too. However, both articulated connections from artefact to purpose were worth maps, one created during design and another created from usage data. As well as showing differences between intended and achieved purpose, Camara could also show differences between expected and actual MECs. She could see how some intended worth was not achieved in the context of observed MECs, but also how unexpected worth was achieved within it. There are similarities here to lead user studies (Figure 4.8), with unexpected appropriations in focus for both approaches.

Considering gaps in the ternary connections covered above, there are again four. Only connections from purpose to evaluation and artefacts (Figure 4.10) and to purpose from anyficiaries and artefacts are covered (Figures 4.11 and 4.12). We need to imagine approaches to fill the gap or identify better quaternary or paired binary connections.

A loose reverse of the right MADS in Figure 4.11, connecting ideatively *from* purpose (1:2 fan out), could be an inception brainstorming approach to gather ideas on possible artefacts and beneficiaries, using value lists (Section 2.3.1) and/or L ERG-IKK (Section 2.3.2). A formal appropriation study could reverse Figure 4.10's chain (to purpose), but Lead User approaches (Figure 4.8) are better, because modified artefacts in demonstrable usage will provide more evidence of appropriation than a formal study. Once again, rather than fill a connections gap, it is better to use another one. Similarly, for connections between purpose and evaluations plus anyficiaries, a quaternary approach again seems more viable, since without consideration of a_tefacts, it is hard to see how worthwhile connections can form.

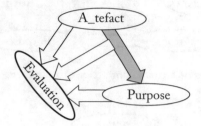

Figure 4.13: An annotated worth map as a ternary connection to evaluation.

4.4.4   TERNARY CONNECTIONS BY EVALUATIONS

The last ternary group focuses on evaluation. For example, each a_tefact, UX and purpose element in a worth map can have associated evaluation targets. A ternary connection to evaluation combines 3 binary connections and a graft: the articulated worth map connection (Figure 5.10:6 *Enablement of*), argued inspection connections (Figure 5.10:4 *Target for*), and argued measurement/ target connections (Figure 5.10:10 *Focus for*). For UX elements, there is an articulated graft from the *Enablement* of connection (Figure 4.13). These connections reflect human science approaches in evaluation, which direct evaluation plans for subsequent implementation.

Evaluation annotations on worth maps integrate several plans within a single representation. They allow checks for completeness: Do all elements have sufficient evaluation criteria? Are all envisaged evaluation approaches being applied to the appropriate elements?

The integration is wholly expressive, via annotations for each worth map element. For a_tefact elements, these can be targets for technical performance, or compliance with design guidance or platform standards.

Inspection methods are common approaches too. For UX elements, there can be subjective assessments by users or design team members. For purpose elements, measures and targets can form homogeneous connections, unlike ones from a_tefact to evaluation, which can connect to multiple evaluation subarenas (e.g., performance, platform compliance, compliance with heuristics, guidelines, accessibility, etc.), with one element being evaluated against several criteria.

A simpler MADS applies for HCD approaches to user evaluation, where plans are drawn for a_tefact use by anyficiary participants (Figure 4.14). Two binary connections combine to form an evaluation plan for tests by users: *Participate in* (Figure 5.10:7, articulated) and *Target for* (Figure 5.10:4, direct transfer). The ternary connection takes the form of a test plan.

Figure 4.14: Planning testing with target users as a ternary connection to evaluation.

There are again four gaps in the ternary connections above. One is for connections to evaluation from anyficiaries and purpose. This could be used to develop Wo-Fo evaluation plans for specific anyficiary groups. A chain is logically possible here, from anyficiaries via purpose to evaluation. However, this would not take an a_tefact into account. This gap is not worth filling with a ternary connection, nor are the other gaps for connections *from* evaluation. These all correspond to carrying out an evaluation and following it through. However, it cannot be known in advance which design arenas will need to change in response to an evaluation, hence ISO9241-120's three iteration transitions to three stages from evaluation. Any, and often all, of them will change in response to an evaluation. It is better to consider the quaternary connection from evaluation here (Figure 4.20), because it will subsume all possible ternary connections from evaluation, rather than plug three gaps separately. We now consider quaternary connections, which have been argued above to be better options than filling several ternary gaps. Only connections with a_tefacts cover all six basic ternary forms. As argued earlier, if design has any centre at all, it is a_tefacts and not humans, and the above analysis supports this argument further.

4.5   QUATERNARY CONNECTIONS

We again group considerations of quaternary ones by the design arenas that the basic connections fan out from and in to, following the same order as for ternary connections above.

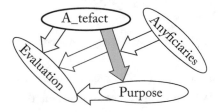

Figure 4.15: An augmented and annotated worth map as a quaternary connection.

For one quaternary connection from a_tefacts, the augmentation of worth maps in Figure 4.6 and their annotations in Figure 4.13 can be combined (Figure 4.15), as indicated in Section 4.3.1. The integration is wholly expressive, via annotations for each worth map element (UX elements are annotated for anyficiaries and evaluation, other elements for evaluation only). The three connections to evaluation planning are argued and the other connection and graft are articulated.

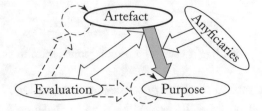

Figure 4.16: Anyficiary-dependent competitor analysis as a quaternary connection.

Similarly, *competitor analysis* (Figure 4.5) can become quaternary by grafting anyficiaries to an articulated connection from artefact to purpose (Figure 4.16), bringing in some aspects of Inherent Value Testing (Figure 4.11) by considering achieved worth for specific user groups and new potential worth (loop), as well as features and capabilities for a planned new product.

Lean UX (Gothelf with Seiden, 2013) is inherently quaternary. Lean UX's MVP experiments test hypotheses of the form: use of this *feature* for this *persona* (beneficiary) will achieve this *outcome*. As with all formal studies, these are first planned, then implemented. Figure 4.17 shows connections for an MVP experiment evaluation plan, which involves anyficiaries using a MVP (antefact) for the purposes for which it was designed. The graft to evaluation is argued and the other connection and graft are articulated.

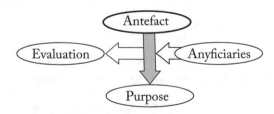

Figure 4.17: An MVP experiment plan as a quaternary connection.

MVP work follows Hillier et al.'s (1972) creative order of conjecture-analysis rather than RILED's analysis-synthesis. MVP experiment results reveal the truth of Lean UX hypotheses. When hypotheses fail to some extent, the evaluation is set up to link failures to antefact features, as well as exposing incorrect assumptions about anyficiaries and purpose. The corresponding quaternary connection for implementing the evaluation here is the broadest generic one (Figure 4.20). However, as with all evaluations, careful planning and dynamic adjustments are needed to be open to new information and direction, so evaluation planning and implementation may co-evolve.

A quaternary *fan in* connection to a_tefacts is unlikely to occur in practice. It would combine two problematic connections in HCI: implications for design from anyficiaries (and also from purpose) and downstream utility from evaluation. Such a connection has immense rational appeal, allowing designs to be derived from contextual research and empirical evaluation, but there is little chance of an a_tefact being simultaneously informed by insights on purpose and anyficiaries and from evaluation. However, it is not impossible, and could occur at the end of a design episode during critical and creative reflection on and for action.

For a quaternary fan out from *anyficiaries*, personas can be made broad enough, as seen in Section 3.3.1, which contrasted two DGTF workshop groups' understandings of personas (Pruit and Adlin, 2006): solely an expressive resource for informative research on beneficiaries; spanning all four arenas in the centre of their Venn diagram. An example of the latter are worth-oriented personas (WoPS; Cockton, 2010) that express three binary connections within one quaternary resource:

- *purpose*: personas are a key part of Cooper's Goal-Directed Design (Cooper et al., 2007), and can provide anchors for design purpose when used as intended with elements of persona skeletons that capture key goals and aversions (Figure 5.10:12 *Desires for*);

- *a_tefacts*: persona skeletons for interaction and service design often include information such as levels of IT familiarity, skills, preferences, and usage patterns, which can all guide and constrain desirable features. More generally, persona skeletons can express preferences for, as well as aversions to, specific artefact features and qualities (Figure 5.10:8 *Preferences for*); and

- *evaluations*: persona skeletons can contain elements that can be used directly to target user test participants and screen volunteers for suitability (Figure 5.10:7 *Participate in*).

A quaternary 3:1 *fan in* to anyficiaries is unlikely to occur in practice, but a 2:2 fan in-out to purpose and anyficiaries from a_tefact and evaluation is possible, but unable to achieve what a quaternary 1:3 fan out from evaluation can (Figure 4.20), which is a better way to fill the gap.

Scenarios can be written to create a quaternary *fan in to purpose*. Unlike personas, scenarios are inherently comprehensively integrative. However, too many HCI scenarios pay inadequate attention to design purpose. Envisionment scenarios must express worth delivery as "happy endings" to anchor outcomes in purpose. For current usage scenarios, endings may be less happy.

My 12-year programme of research for design added a worth-focus to existing scenario approaches by stressing the importance of happy endings in Worth-Oriented Delivery Scenarios (WoDS; Cockton, 2009b). However, purpose was already understood as an important element in well-formed narratives as "a valued endpoint" (Gergen, 2005), along with causal linkages (as in MECs) and selecting events relevant to the endpoint. Other important features of good narratives are a matter of choice for design teams. Gergen (2005) also argues for the importance of demarcation signs, ordering of events, and stability of identity. Nielsen (2002) argues that good scenarios are character driven. A wide range of considerations thus apply to scenario authoring, but a focus on "valued endpoints" or "happy endings" does need to be prioritised, even though initial scenario versions may focus on beneficiaries (Muller, 2004). The MADS for WoDS is very similar to Figure 4.17, but purpose rather than the a_tefact is the focus for the fan in, and the graft to evaluation is ideative rather than argued, because creative writing puts evaluative words into the mouths of scenario characters.

A WoDS thus must cover all four arenas. Figure 4.18 presents a WoDS for the UXC in Table 4.2 (its numbers in brackets match paragraph numbers). Quaternary scenarios improve balance of interfaces (Cockton, 2020a, Section 5.4), so designers can not only write scenarios but also use them (Carroll, 2002). As scenario skeletons, UXCs offer a solution to Sutcliffe's (2003) two most critical problems: sampling and coverage. Where the expressivity of UXCs needs to be improved, e.g., for communication with key stakeholders or via video envisionment, scenarios can be written for a worth map's UXs. This is possible in concurrent methodologies but not RILED ones, as quaternary worth maps can be made early in design work and be refined and extended as arenas fill out. Worth map UXs provide a population for scenario authoring, supporting informed judgements on sampling and coverage. Sutcliffe (2003) wrote that there "are no easy answers to these problems," but concurrent design work, UXCs and worth maps provide structure for such answers.

A quaternary *fan out* from purpose borders on the magic of a self-implementing product strategy, where a value proposition generates a market segmentation, product design, and market testing plan. However, such a fan out can be used for critical reflection at the end of a design episode where purpose has been transformed, requiring review of other design arenas and connections. Such reflection could come close to a product repositioning. This aside, a single focus on purpose as an independent arena only makes sense for binary and ternary chain connections. Only a 3:1 fan in is realistic, whereas only 1:3 fans outs make sense for a_tefacts and anyficiaries.

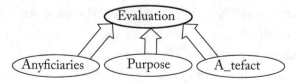

Figure 4.19: BIG planning testing with target users as a quaternary connection to evaluation.

A quaternary *fan in* to evaluation is possible (and desirable) by giving HCD test planning (Figure 4.14) an additional Wo-Fo, as in Figure 4.19. HCD has long-established connections both to and from evaluation, as in ISO 9241-210 (2019), although downstream utility remains a concern. Even so, evaluation is the only design arena with both a realistic quaternary fan in and fan out. A quaternary fan out occurs when evaluation results have good balance in BIG terms. Empirical

1. Sally saw a classified advert in the Carlisle paper and agreed to buy a *chaise longue* after visiting the owner to have a look and check its measurements (206 x 107 x 84cm,). She and her husband Harry now need to go and pay for and collect it, so they visit www.lovelyvan.com, the web site of a national van hire franchise. They have seen a press campaign for the company, and friends in London have used it and recommended it.

2. Sally lets Harry drive their PC. He finds a prices and availability link, but Sally asks him to check depot locations. There's no point in checking on prices and availability if the nearest depot isn't close enough. There's a clear area on the home page for finding your nearest depot. Harry types in their post code. A map appears in the large blank space below showing nearby depot locations with an information list below. Sally points to the nearest depot on the ring road. Harry clicks on it. The map changes to a local one for the depot, with address and phone details, and driving directions.

3. "Cool!" exclaims Harry (there's a cute animation as the map and info change). Another animated transition places a circle of vans in the blank area to the left. Next to each van there's an example load and below that, there's the van's load space dimensions. Sally immediately spots the van with a settee next to it. "That should do" she says. "Hang on," says Harry "Let's check the small print. OK, load space dimensions 240 long by 170 wide by 140cm high. Something 206 x 107 x 84cm will fit in easily, and there'll be enough room down one side to manoeuvre it from inside the van. So, we want a medium panel van".

4. Harry clicks on an obvious red "Book Me" button over the right edge of the van photo (no fancy animations this time). The other vans disappear, and a calendar appears in between the medium panel van and the depot details. It clearly indicates that there are medium panel vans available for the coming weekend. Below the calendar is a clear informative statement on hire periods, prices and depot opening times. Vans can be hired for up to 24 hours, or for short four-hour hires. The local depot is open from 8AM–8PM over the weekend. Harry notices a "hire planner" button below the information and moves the mouse to click it. "Hang on" says Sally, "let's see how much it is first." "I can see," says Harry "it will be £44 for four hours." "The chaise longue was only £100" said Sally "that hardly seems worth it." "A new one's over £500," said Harry "and you said it was as good as new. I can take some things to the recycling centre on my way back." "In four hours?" asked Sally. "Maybe not, let's see" said Harry and he clicks on a chunky "hire planner" button. A simple spin box appears with 2 in it, labelled "Number of drops/pick ups." Harry clicks this up to 3: "let's see, there, here, recycling, yes, that's 3." He clicks on OK and text boxes pop up one by one to the right of the spin box. At either end is the depot's post code in a non-editable text box, with the OK button moved to the right as well, but disabled. "That's smart" says Harry "I just need to fill in the seller and recycling centre post codes and ours." He sees a link to UK post code look up, clicks on it. A website opens in a new window and Harry gets the two post codes that he needs

5. Harry types in each post code into a blank text box, and presses the OK button once it is enabled. Three more spin boxes appear below the post code ones labelled "time needed at each drop off/pick up" with default editable times of 20 minutes in each. There's an OK button at the end again, and Harry presses it: "If we're quick, 20 at each will be enough." A summary of the route comes up "From the van depot to … From … to your location. From your location to … to the 12van depot." It's all clearly laid out, with a time estimate for each leg for the date and time, and a total time based on these legs and the time at each drop off/pick up. Below this is a very obvious clear statement that while lovelyvan have done their best they can to be accurate, they cannot guarantee time estimates. Sally is really impressed "that's so helpful" she cries out. The total estimated time is three hours. "That's enough leeway for us," says Harry, "especially if we have everything clear for getting the chaise longue in and the recycling stuff is stacked up ready to go." Harry selects a date and a time period, and navigates to the booking details and payment page, where Sally helps him with credit card and checking all details, which she does quickly *as the details are so complete and thorough, and laid out in a format that makes them easy to check*. Harry saves and prints the booking confirmation page.

6. Within minutes Harry has an email from lovelyvan. It's a well laid out html message with a link to an on-line pdf as an alternative layout. Harry follows the link to the pdf out of curiosity. "That looks very smart," says Sally. The document contains details of the hire, the depot and directions to it, the documents that drivers need to bring, instructions on what to do at the depot, time estimates for these activities, and a map with the route between drop offs. There's legal information at the end, but this is clear and well set out, and written in a reassuringly straightforward tone. Harry prints the pdf off, staples it, and pins it to the cork board near the PC. The printout even looks good when pinned up.

7. "I'm really looking forward to getting the chaise longue now," said Sally. "I'll be glad to get the stuff to the recycling too," said Harry "really easy."

Figure 4.18: **Worth delivery scenario (WoDS) for good plan UX** (Cockton, 2009b).

user-based evaluations can always be extended to become research methods for all other design are-nas. The approach works well with lean design-led work, integrating user research into evaluation as a verification for early vision (Löwgren, 1995). Such practices reduce tensions and frustration, ease integration, and reduce waste by only collecting relevant user data in the context of a_tefact usage, as came to happen when applying usability principles in more design-led circumstances at IBM, where 75% of the HCD effort shifted to post release user research and evaluation (Cockton, 2008b).

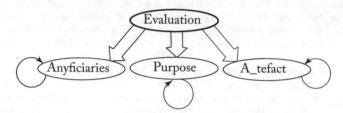

Figure 4.20: Downstream utility from BIG evaluation as a quaternary connection.

As with all evaluation, breadth must be planned for and delivered on in practice. In consul-tancy work carried out in 2005, my team at Sunderland carried out an evaluation that extended beyond the usability of an antefact to research on beneficiaries and purpose. As well as sending daily problem reports to the developer for overnight fixes to major usability problems, we collected insights into the target market (UK over 50s) and possible business models (especially pricing and one-off purchase vs. subscription). After two weeks of rapid iteration we saw no further usability problems of significance and switched to out of the box testing for a home internet device ("set top box") using a prototype user manual. This broad approach was planned and revised in close col-laboration with the product owner. Beneficiary and product strategy insights (i.e., design purpose) were fed back via a report, with a DVD of smooth use and positive feedback provided to support bids for further investment. The MADS for this evaluation were Figure 4.19 (planning) and Figure 4.20 (evaluation).

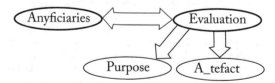

Figure 4.21: Cooperative and participative evaluation as a quaternary connection.

Not all quaternary connections with evaluation are fan ins or fan outs. Cooperative and par-ticipative evaluation (Monk et al., 1993) has a 2:3 fan in-out. In Figure 4.21, anyficiaries are equal partners in the conduct of an evaluation, which in turn can result in new insights about them, as well as feedback on purpose and the a_tefact.

75% of the basic quaternary connections can be covered by existing approaches or critical reflection. In contrast, only 50% of the basic ternary connections were covered by existing approaches, with an additional novel approach to inception brainstorming (from purpose to anyficiaries and antefacts). Gaps may be easier to fill during inception and reflection than elsewhere, but this needs to be followed through to make substantial design moves.

4.6   WHAT'S IN A CONNECTION?

Integration is not achieved through faith in arrows, but through careful consideration of the interfaces at both ends of them and when and how connections can actually be made. A ninth meta-principle of *integratability* applies to all arenas, requiring "hooks" for connecting. However, as with all functions of approaches and resources, there is only a potential here that has to be realised through critical creative practices. The presence of any arrow any MADS diagram only indicates a reasonable potential that lies in between possible and probable: there are no guarantees.

The connection approaches in this chapter make explicit what can only happen tacitly in RILED processes with diagram arrows that mislead. There is no complete analysis that finds all the parts prior to synthesising them (Gedenryd, 1998). Little is actually transported along the arrow from one phase to the next. Instead, work within design arenas (not phases) is coordinated concurrently with other arenas through co evolution. Agile practices have formalised this in their management of backlogs (Cockton, 2016a), but retain many linear process elements.

RILED language is hard to shake off. Having acknowledged the realities of creative practice, Löwgren (1995) still wrote of a "chain of transformations from the abstract (requirements) to the concrete (resulting artifact)." There are relatively few transformations, and these apply to unary loops (i.e., arenas are transformed, but not the whole design situation). The vast majority of connections take other forms. There is not one chain, but many. Chains are a relatively simple form of complex connection. More complex ones fall into place as design work develops. Sixteen years later, Löwgren (2013) wrote of "discursive knowledge production" in design work in a move away from a RILED "chain of transformations," implicitly acknowledging the role of argued and articulated connections.

For Wolf et al. (2006), design considerations are multifaceted and complex, happen simultaneously, and tend to affect each other. Regular critical reflection keeps design work aligned, supported by a lexicon that restricts rationalist and other often unsuitable vocabularies to specific aspects of design work where their use is apt. Also, as noted Cockton (2020a, Chapter 2), treating design work as *storytelling* (Erickson, 1996) is a key to telling the story of how the right idea was found, not just its *rationale*.

This chapter has presented many approaches to connecting. They are diverse and vary in form, development and outcome. The balance of connection types reflects the balance of disciplines in the example integration approaches above (*indicates Wo-Fo extensions and adaptations):

- *Software engineering*: Domain Analysis, Use Cases (*UXC), User Stories;

- *HCD*: Personas (WoP*), Scenarios (WoD*), Test Participant Screening, Design Rationale, Inherent Value Testing, Inspection Methods, BIG User Test* planning and implementation;

- *Marketing and advertising*: Hierarchical Value Maps (*Worth Maps and Sketches);

- *Creative design*: How Might We? Brainwriting, Inception Workshops;

- *Innovation and strategic design*: Business Model Canvas, Value Proposition Canvas, Lead users, Lean UX MVP experiments, Feature-Benefit/Artefact Connection* Tables; and

- *BIG Wo-Fo approaches*: Design Arena Canvas*, Element Measurement Strategies*, Direct Worth Instrumentation*, Worth Integration Tables*.

As well as differences in disciplinary values and origins, different structures combine different connection forms (unary, binary, ternary, quaternary, concourse, directed, grafted, chain). All structures support reflection (especially at episode ends), where increased scope and connections increase benefits. Approaches with greater scope integrate more, usually more quickly, and with a better affiliative function (involving all a design team expertise), and thus a better invigorative function through consensus, coherence and a sense of progress to(wards) the "right idea."

4.7   CHAPTER SUMMARY

BIG Design sees a worthwhile design progression as balanced, integrated, and generous. Chapter 2 covered Wo-Fo approaches to purpose that support generosity. Chapter 3 covered several forms of balance. Balance of connections is challenging, needing a mix of disciplinary inputs and values, and forms and reach of connections: far broader than RILED one-way links across adjacent phases.

MADS provide a useful structure for identifying the range of possible connections. This has in turn supported method innovation (Cockton, 2010) through identifying currently unexplored connection forms. Novel primary research approaches in Chapter 2 (adaptation of field research and sentence completion to direct and inform work on design purpose) are examples of extending existing single arena approaches to connections from beneficiaries to purpose. The reach of existing HCD approaches such as personas and scenarios has been extended by Wo-Fo versions above.

The Working to Choose (W2C) framework (Cockton, 2013b) of which ADS form an important part, extends the bases for method innovation. Connecting between design arenas, coupled with multiple resource functions, opens up an immense underexplored space for BIG Wo-Fo approaches. The value of resource functions is explored further in the next two chapters on case studies.

A worthwhile creative design progression must be open. It cannot be completely prefigured in advance. A worthwhile progression must fall into place to some extent, perhaps to a great extent for the most innovative design work. Innovative forms of connection with broad reach are key here.

Chapter 3's (Cockton, 2020a) manifesto has now been thoroughly addressed.

1. Balanced design work areas are a_tefacts, purpose, anyficiaries, and evaluation (Cockton, 2020a, Chapter 4).

2. Concurrent working is the norm, sequence is the exception (Cockton, 2020a, Chapter 5).

3. Connections between work areas are created, not preformed (this chapter).

4. Interfaces between work areas can be prepared to support connection work (Chapter 3).

5. MADS progressions are complete at every level of their abstractions (Cockton, 2020a, Chapter 5).

6. Design work can be tracked across work areas in ways that reveal progress (Cockton, 2020a, Chapter 5).

7. Most (but not all) RILED language can be retired. This chapter has shown that some types of connection can satisfy RILED values, so some RILED language can be retained.

Chapters 5 and 6 provide further support from a selection of case studies.

CHAPTER 5

Supported Case Studies: From Grounded to Worth-Centred Design

This and the next chapter survey over two decades of projects that have taken BIG and/or Wo-Fo approaches. All involve IxD, in keeping with the HCI focus of this book series. Detailed case study examples provide evidence that Wo-Fo and BIG approaches meet Gedenryd's test (1998) that proposed practice innovations "have been used with success," and not only "by their inventors."

There are five groups of case studies. The first two are in this chapter and the last three in the next. The first group introduces the antecedents of BIG. Literate Development's (LD) origins are first presented, then Clarke's (1997) pioneering LD tool, and lastly LD's extension into a full Grounded Design paradigm with HCD design arenas of evaluation, anyficiaries and a_tefacts, but more extensive connections than ISO 9241-210 (2019).

In the second case study group, I provided decreasing support and facilitation for worth mapping (Section 4.3.2). Within the Family Archive project at Microsoft Research Cambridge (MSRC, UK), I led on, facilitated, tracked, and advised all worth map work (Cockton et al., 2009a). In this group's second study, I provided support on MEC concepts to a research group whose lead had participated in the initial Family Archive worth mapping workshops at MSRC. This project drew on his first-hand experience in a situated shared display project (Otero and José, 2009). This first supported use of worth maps by independent researchers was followed by further supported independent use in the VALU project (Cockton et al., 2009b) and the first commercial applications of worth maps.

There was a decade between Clarke's embryonic research on integrating connections and the Family Archive project. During this decade, the role of values in design research became clear in my Sunderland research group's work on extreme accessibility (e.g., Doherty et al., 2000). Grounded Design was replaced by VCD when the need to foreground value as design purpose became clear (Cockton, 2004a). VCD began as a modified RILED framework (Cockton, 2005), with limited concurrency and a very basic design arena for purpose, but became worth-centred (WCD; Cockton, 2006). Alongside this, work on evaluation approaches and resources (e.g., Cockton et al., 2004) developed the foundations for resource function theory and MADS analysis of approaches (as in Chapter 4).

The second group of case studies indicated that being worth centred may risk swapping HCD's silos (anyficiaries and evaluation) for a purpose silo. To avoid this, work on purpose needed to be better integrated with other design arenas, where worth maps could not provide complete support. The required a shift from a worth *centre* to a worth *focus* in the context of BIG Design and the W2C framework (Cockton, 2013a, 2013b). The third group of case studies used a Wo-Fo independently. These are reviewed in Chapter 6, along with two other groups. The fourth group has only one case study, the first combination of Wo-Fo and BIG approaches (George, 2016). The fifth group is primarily based on postgraduate teaching at the Technical University of Eindhoven.

Although only the fourth and fifth groups involve explicit use of BIG design approaches, there are clear examples of some BIG practices in the first three. This and the next chapter close with a summary of insights and outcomes for BIG and Wo-Fo approaches for the case studies covered. In contrast to the high-level overviews in Book 1 (Cockton, 2020a) and Chapters 2 and 4, the case studies focus at the lower level of approaches, resources, and their functions, around which insights and outcomes from the case studies are organised.

Four of the case studies are research theses—one Master's (Vu, 2013) and three Ph.D.s (Clarke, 1997; Camara, 2012; George, 2016). All contain extensive examples that cannot be included in the space available for this book. All are available online, with URLs given in the appendices. Questions arising from these four case studies should be answered by consulting these theses. Similarly, there is further detail on the other case studies, with references to other sources of information, in the papers on the Family Archive (Cockton et el., 2009a), teachers' shared displays (Otero et al., 2009; Otero and José, 2009), and the VALU project (Cockton et al., 2009b). These too should provide answers to many questions arising from the short accounts below.

5.1   SOME ANTECEDENTS OF BIG DESIGN

The first case studies cover BIG antecedents: Literate Development (LD) and Grounded Design. LD's origins are presented first, then Clarke's (1997) LD tool, and lastly Grounded Design (Cockton, 1998).

5.1.1   LITERATE DEVELOPMENT

BIG originates in second wave HCI's gap between rhetoric and reality. Claims were made on the need to consider context in design, but there were few convincing examples of contextual research having clear concrete impacts on design decisions. While reviewing the literature on contextual design for his Ph.D., Steven Clarke observed that a focus on beneficiaries' activities could be mirrored by a requirement that UI dialogue orders should match users' established orders for work activities. Reframed in terms of design arenas, this connected from anyficiaries to an a_tefact subarena. The a_tefact subarena is (dialogue) *structure* (Garrett, 2002; Section 3.2.4). Section 3.2.3 did not mention an equivalent anyficiary subarena for activities, but locales in L-ERG-IKK+ (Section 2.3.2) could include them.

A specific example for this connection was writing disrupted by specifying footnote markers, which a change in dialogue order would avoid, but changing an artefact's object model (Garrett's *Scope*) could remove all need to repeat specification, and also avoid perverse notes in documents. This connects different subarenas to those in the activity-centred example: domain (anyficiaries) and object model (a_tefact, Garrett's scope). We wrote that "theories of context" influenced a_tefact design (Cockton et al., 1995), but looking back these were anyficiary subarenas and not theories.

Such explicit connections were similar to Literate Specification (Johnson, 1996), which linked formal specifications to Design Rationales, inspired by Literate Programming (Knuth, 1984). We thus called our approach to linking across design LD (Cockton et al., 1996), which could potentially cover all documents and data used in software development. This would enable rich and varied links between specific data analyses and design decisions. LD extended Literate Programming to the logical conclusion of linking all major work products in software development. Rather than merely link refinements of a program's design to its code implementation, anything can be linked to anything, where that makes sense. This generates many ideas for HCI research with regard to how work products relate to each other. LD focused on the integration and holistic assessment of IxD approaches at a time when there was little research on method integration in HCI, which was more focused on technologies and application areas then.

5.1.2   THE LD TOOL

Clarke (1997) developed an experimental tool to explore LD. It linked development documents, which are often referred to as artefacts in Agile software development, losing a vital distinction between what is being designed and the memoranda brought to bear on it. They have also been referred to in earlier chapters as *work products* (Parnas and Clements, 1986) and (the best term) *co-products* (Carroll, 1990).

The research was motivated by curiosity and uncertainty. Strong claims for second wave HCI had some substance, but first wave HCI had also seen strong IxD (e.g., development of Spreadsheets and Word Processors), so extensive attention to context was not absolutely essential for design success.

Clarke first prepared paper documentation for a system to manage the application, review, offer and acceptance process for an M.Sc. IT programme, which was implemented by a Master's student for her graduation project. The paper exercise revealed a need for tools to support multiple views of a design and its context of use (i.e., not just one document for context and one for design). It also indicated that connections should be separated from the documents that they link. With no representation of connections separate from the documents that contained endpoints, it was hard to see the big picture of how all connections combined. Clarke thus developed and iterated his LD tool to track how contextual data influences design decisions.

The LD tool maintained a database of connections between five co-product documents: two covered antefacts: a low-level *task model* (UAN) and an *object model*; and two covered anyficiaries: a *contextual focus* and *contextual scenarios*. The contextual focus was similar to value lists (Section 2.3.1), but was filled in with project specific detail rather than being reduced to a list. It became the main repository for what mattered about and to beneficiaries. Contextual scenarios envisaged an antefact in use, and thus were a concourse between antefact and anyficiaries, and potential aspects of evaluation and purpose. The initial paper exercise also included visual models from Contextual Design (Holtzblatt and Beyer, 2014), but diagram editors were beyond the scope of a minimalist experimental tool. This had no adverse impact because all model content transferred easily to the contextual focus as textual notes.

The fifth co-product used the *QOC format* (Questions, Options, and Criteria; Maclean et al., 1991) for argued connections between context and design: direct transfer connections link from contextual focus items to Questions and Criteria, and from a_tefacts to Questions; *realisation* connections link from Options to a_tefacts. This use of Design Rationales (Sections 4.1.3 and 4.4.1) connected antefact and anyficiaries arenas, complementing the concourse connections in the scenarios document with further concourses (QOC Questions blend anyficiaries' contexts and a_tefacts).

Connections in the LD tool had a name, source, destination, and some explanatory text that could hint at the connection's type, with varying clarity. The source and destination for a connection were initially single parts of documents, specified in their document editors, forcing explicit creation of interfaces for connections, as argued for in Cockton (2020a, Section 5.4). Parts were linked in the LD tool's *relationship editor*, which became the tool's main window. For examples of links and parts, see Clarke and Cockton (1998) and Cockton and Clarke (1999).

The LD tool was used in three studies, mostly by its developer (Clarke), since it was deliberately minimalist and continuously evolving. In the first, Clarke retrofitted the paper documents for the M.Sc. admissions system into the LD tool to assess how easily connections could be made. In a second study, Clarke retrospectively reconstructed his experiences in designing the LD tool and recorded these as documents and connections. In his third use of LD, Clarke reverse engineered the 1984 Olympic Games Message System from Gould et al. (1987). Following this, the LD tool was also assessed in a formative evaluation.

During LD's first use, there was no further research on the context for the M.Sc. admissions system. Any changes to the design could thus only be due to use of the LD tool. Contextual and design documents were entered in parallel, i.e., not in a linear sequence. A few additions were needed for the contextual focus to let all insights from contextual models be added. Errors in direct transfer connections between object and task models were discovered and corrected, since making connections forced examination of interfaces. New connections were added, because this was much easier with the tool than on paper. For example, use of a shared printer in a shared office had been overlooked, so batch printing was added to the design to avoid letters (reference requests, offers, and confirmations) being lost in the shared printing.

The second study was completely design-led, as there had been no separate formal contextual research for the LD tool, as there had been for the M.Sc. admissions system, and thus no documents to work from. Connections could thus be overtly provisional, with explanatory text stating "just an option however" and "to the best of my knowledge" (Clarke, 1997). Documents were created from scratch in a record-reflect-respond cycle, with clear evidence of problem-solution co-evolution as documentation of the LD tool prompted reflection on its usage contexts. This often led to changes to the LD tool. For example, a range of filters were added to only show some connections (see Section 5.3.3). Also, the parts"(end points) of connections became sets of anchors (Clarke and Cockton, 1998), in response to how design arena elements often cluster into a family of related considerations (e.g., safety or security features in automobiles). Typically, combinations of contextual factors exert influence over designs. These additions further improved on existing linking tools such as Vista (Brown et al., 1998) that supported connections between one contextual work product (hierarchical task model) and three a_tefacts ones: a task model (UAN notation as in LD tool), a design architecture, and high-level code.

The third study used the LD tool to reverse-engineer the Olympic Message System (OMS). A single source of information (Gould et al., 1987) contained several scenarios, which were copied into the LD tool. A mix of realisation and direct transfer connections were made from these envisionment scenarios to the object model. As an HCD project, many (mis)fit connections addressed Olympians' mother tongues, relevant technology experience and the practicality of training, passwords, choice of telephone, climate, and further contextual factors. Task models were implicit in the scenarios, so none were created. The contextual focus was filled in from (Gould et al., 1987) supplemented by Clarke's expertise, resulting in a completed checklist that could be filtered using the LD tool's new features to show aspects of context without any connections from them. One of these was *noise* in the public environments where the phone-based OMS would be used. This oversight was later confirmed by a retired IBM researcher with knowledge of OMS.

The three studies produced different webs of connections with different extents and structures. There were over twice as many connections for the M.Sc. admissions system as for OMS, and one quarter more than for the LD tool. Over half of the connections involved the object model for the MSc system, but just over one third for the LD tool and OMS. Scenarios and/or design rationales mediated all links from contextual data to design documents. There were no direct implications for design (Dourish, 2006). Instead, implications from context for design were mediated by documents that included options for a design, i.e., a specific a_tefact. There were mediated implications for *that* design, but not for *any* design.

For the M.Sc. admissions system, connections were either via scenarios or design rationales, but not both. Scenarios were the dominant mediating co-product for the OMS and MSc systems, but for the LD tool this was QOC, resulting from the reflection and response that followed recording of a design-led project, where the LD tool was used retrospectively for reverse-engineering, identifying inconsistencies and omissions. Overall, these different structures demonstrated the LD tool's flexibility.

Following the case studies, a formative evaluation trained five participants to use the LD tool for a simulated software maintenance task. It was hypothesised that if a maintenance team had access to contextual information that had influenced the design, and indications of how it had been used, then this would ease such a task. Each participant had at least one year's software design experience and exposure to HCD practices. Four were Computing Science Ph.D. students and one was a software engineer in industry. Each used the revised LD tool, preloaded with the design and context for a hypothetical system. A log of all actions was recorded. Clarke providing technical assistance if needed. After being shown how to use the LD tool, participants were told about a particular change to the context: users' experience and attitudes to technology had improved. Participants had to individually form a design response to accommodate this change, thinking out loud. Participants discussed what each element of context meant and thought about the potential relevance of different elements. Some found names in the contextual focus ambiguous, with idiosyncratic definitions, but in a group situation, discussion should develop consensus.

No participants assumed anything about how context had been used, instead most used connections to attempt to understand how context had influenced the design. Some made conjectures and tested them, guided by connection names and explanatory texts. Mostly, participants successfully identified paths of connections to relevant design elements. Difficulties only arose when participants struggled to understand the explanatory text for some links. However, all participants except one created new connections, rather than examining existing ones before changing them. "Parts" were better understood once they had made new connections.

Overall, participants could articulate benefits that made explicit links worthwhile as part of their feedback on the LD tool. There was a brief discussion with each participant after the exercise. Two participants said that connections could be useful in maintaining a system, although one felt that creating links would be annoying, adding to workload and perhaps demotivating. Others expected to be able to access connections from documents, not just from the relationship editor.

On the whole, the LD tool delivered a range of benefits and insights that vindicated the minimalist approach to prototyping. It has been worth revisiting Clarke's thesis as it remains the broadest substantial research on connections to date. As will be seen with Wo-Fo case studies, resources such as worth maps can simplify the creation and use of connections.

5.1.3   THE EXPANDED SCOPE OF GROUNDED DESIGN

The major problem addressed by LD is to *ground* an appropriate design in all relevant data. The challenge is to identify relevant data and to use it effectively (Cockton and Clarke 1999). This research supported co-development of a design philosophy, Grounded Design, and an engineering approach, LD, tying the design philosophy to realistic case studies and giving the engineering approach an underlying theoretical motivation. A mix of top-down and bottom-up approaches supported this co-development.

After Clarke's Ph.D., Grounded Design was extended to consider all development documents (Cockton, 1998), starting with evaluation co-products such as usability evaluation results (e.g., inspection, testing). A full co-product range was proposed (e.g., ethnographic and Interview transcripts, edited video and audio recordings, screen layouts, and dialogue models including scanned sketches). Data was also proposed as co-products to connect to (e.g., video and audio recordings, scanned field notes and diagrams, user test data, application domain data). Clarke (1997) advocated explicit connection types, in response to problems with explanatory text in the LD tool, but looking back, this would risk losing some connection types that the tool's open text comments had made possible.

At the time, we felt we were on the brink of a new paradigm in HCI that effectively integrates the activities of contextual research, grounded design, and usability evaluation. We had overlooked the need for a separate purpose arena, which would lead us away from HCD to a radically different design paradigm.

5.2   WO-FO PROJECTS FOR WHICH I PROVIDED SUPPORT

In this second group of case studies, I provided different extents of support and facilitation for worth mapping. The first was within the Family Archive project at Microsoft Research Cambridge (MSRC, UK). The second project developed situated shared displays in Portugal (Otero and José, 2009), using worth maps with some support from me. This was the first supported use of worth maps by independent researchers. Extensive design and implementation was carried out, and consideration was given to meta-principles for designing (Cockton, 2008a), so the mix here was broader than the early stages of the first case study in this group. The third case study is the VALU project (Cockton et al., 2009a). This was the second supported application of worth maps by independent researchers, and the first commercial applications. In all three projects, I supported understandings of MECs and their components.

5.2.1   THE FAMILY ARCHIVE PROJECT (CAMBRIDGE, UK)

The Family Archive project at Microsoft Research Cambridge (MSRC) was the first application of worth maps in a live research project, through seven workshops that I organised and facilitated, with tracking and planning in between. Worth sketching began as a review approach. Both worth sketches and maps were changing during use, making it infeasible for others to facilitate, construct or record them.

The Family Archive was conceived as an enhanced tabletop computer that could manage digital and physical media. Digital media could be stored in an archive alongside scans of physical objects, letting the latter be disposed of (e.g., transport tickets from holidays), stored safely (e.g., fragile items), or sold or passed on (e.g., heritage items). The archive could be used individually or by family groups. The project team spanned hardware and software engineers, interaction designers, and user researchers. Details of this worth mapping project are in Cockton et al. (2009a).

Worth maps evolved significantly during this project, alongside novel UXCs (Section 4.3.2) and worth sketches. Worth Map was a new name for Worth/Aversion Maps (W/AMs; Cockton, 2007), which were misnamed (worth includes aversions). "Worth maps" was simpler and more apt. Worth maps continued an evolution from HVMs, a marketing tool (Cockton et al., 2009a). Only terminal values (Section 2.3.1; following Rokeach, 1973) were preserved from HVMs (as outcomes). HVMs' abstract and concrete product attributes were renamed to be qualities and features, respectively, with materials separated from features during a VALU project workshop (Section 5.2.3). This resulted in three antefact subarenas.

HVM consequences (functional followed by psychosocial) had been replaced in W/AMs with physiological, psychosocial, financial, environmental, and low-level functional consequences, but these also changed following the VALU workshop to simpler consequence elements focused on the user interactions that realise MECs in use: actions, feelings, and experiences. Actions were design independent and based on field research.

To make use of these new MEC element types (i.e., materials, features, qualities, usage consequences, outcomes), DANs were needed to populate a worth map. Richard Banks had led on initial design work for the Family Archive and had recorded progress in a document, which I reduced to an antefact DAN with subarenas for materials, features, and qualities. Dave Kirk had led an initial field research into family archiving practices, investigating the sorts of objects that families retained and how and why they did so. This had been summarised as an early draft for (Kirk and Sellen, 2010). I reduced this to usage outcomes that became the items in a purpose DAN. There were also notes for the usage consequences (actions, feelings and experiences), informed by the field research, which could be thought of as an initial Connection Note (CoN) for a usage articulation. The DANs and CoN provided content for a PowerPoint stack with one element per slide. Background colour codes distinguished element types.

Two series of workshops were held: review and mapping. Three review workshops developed common ground and consensus through discussion of my preparatory DAN work. Four mapping workshops then developed specific worth maps. In the first review workshop, Richard Banks presented the design document. I next explained MEC element types, and how explicit consideration of, and connecting to, design purpose offered important benefits. I then presented the PowerPoint stack in MEC order, from materials, features, and qualities, via actions, feelings, and experiences, to outcomes. The validity or appropriateness of each element was discussed in relation to design and field work to date.

After the first review workshop, I began a living document that initially contained the DANs and CoN, with glossaries and tutorial material on MEC element types. This and the PowerPoint stack were updated before and after all subsequent workshops. For the second review workshop, blank cards were added for each element type to the stack. The handout was printed out two slides to a page and cut into cards.

At each workshop, cards were laid out on a table that was big enough for around 25 people. When cards were printed two per page, the resulting set was too large for the big table. For subsequent workshops, I printed slides four to a page. Cards were laid out in rows one MEC type at a time and reviewed and discussed before proceeding. Some were moved from one subarena to another following discussion (e.g., from a feeling to an outcome). Several team members had not been able to attend both the first two workshops, so the third review workshop reviewed and extended work to date with everyone in the meeting. This resulted in consensus on the cards, with additional ones added as a result of either brainstorming (e.g., networking capabilities as a "material") or referring to recent MSRC projects on family media use. As well as developing consensus on the elements, we discussed possible connections, but had no way to indicate these physically on the cards or table. This link-free representation was called a worth sketch. It was initially a way of laying out all worth map elements (or "worthies"; Cockton, 2007) for review and discussion, but it became the basis for a lean approach to worth mapping.

The review workshops were a success since we proceeded to the four main workshops. Worth sketching was received positively, as worthies spanned the expertise in the team, from hardware and software through interaction design and user research. Everyone in the team had rows of worthies that were "theirs" professionally. The materiality of cards on a table let specialists reach for, move to, and talk about their cards. The non-verbal cues helped to bring reticent individuals into discussions, resulting in a better balance of contributions from engineers, designers, and user researchers. Worth sketching thus had *affiliative* and *protective* functions by team building and inclusion. It also had *inquisitive*, *deliberative*, and *ideative* functions, prompting questions and discussion, and adding new elements that had not been proposed in work so far. There are many similarities with Dorst's (2015) account of problem framing (Cockton, 2020a, Section 2.1.3) here, which must inspire, provoke, captivate, inspire, unite, evoke, elicit, share, and more.

Halving card sizes had not been enough to make a worth sketch manageable. In a *protective* move, Abigail Sellen, the project lead, suggested preparing worth maps for each life cycle phase of archived objects: capture, organisation, editing, and consumption. Each became a focus for one main workshop. This life cycle contrasts with an engineering practice of basing work process structure on internal product structure (Gedenryd, 1998), resulting in linear refinement of work products (Parnas and Clements, 1985). Instead, worth mapping sessions followed the structure of an archived object's life cycle. For each phase, we selected relevant features from the antefact DAN (and added to it).

Another success from the initial workshops was the living document. It had an *informative* function, acting as a reference during and between meetings. It recorded the initial consensus on usage consequences (CoN), antefact, and purpose (DAN) as a prerequisite for worth mapping.

In the four mapping workshops (each two hours long), we focused on forming MECs. As in the review workshops, materials cards were placed in a row along the long edge of a large table by the facilitator, with outcomes along the opposite edge. Features, qualities, actions, feelings, and experiences were arranged in rows in between, in positions based on likely vertical MECs. We considered how elements could connect into MECs, starting with materials and working up. This resulted in extensive discussions. In a worth sketch, we could move cards around to form MECs, using proximity and overlapping clusters to indicate links in chains. At the end of each session, I drew lines to indicate adjacent cards (Figure 4.2). I used photographs of the marked card layouts to reassemble the worth sketch in my office, and then formed a worth map in the living document using a drawing editor.

During the workshop for the first *capture* phase, two features were split through refinement. Some qualities were sidelined as not relevant unless commercial branding was being considered. The remaining qualities were grouped by ease of learning, relaxed use, magical play, and versatility. This worth sketch prompted many questions and seeded much discussion.

During the workshop for the second *organisation* phase, features were added (e.g., links and tags within the archive for individual family members) as were materials (e.g., a microphone for voice identification and recording reminiscences; a removable drawer containing a hard disk). Later phases were anticipated, with remote situated displays being added as materials for consumption. There were no revisions to existing elements. This allowed swift updates to the living document, freeing up time to triangulate purpose elements against 118 photos from the field research. A Worth Board was made, using PowerPoint for speed. Photos that evidenced valuable outcomes were grouped together after a title slide with the name of a purpose element. Each group could have readily been formed into a large physical collage board with the purpose element named in a prominent position (e.g., centre, top-right), hence the parallel with mood boards. Photos were assigned to purpose elements collaboratively with the field researcher (Dave Kirk). As a result, 23 purpose elements were reduced to 17 and allocated to 3 groups (see Table 2.1).

During the workshop for the third editing phase, new features were added to support searching, safe editing of copies only, and other support for repurposing archived objects for subsequent consumption. However, there were some documented features that had not yet been associated with any archival phase yet, and would not be needed for the final consumption phase. They were not discarded because we had overlooked the background *enticing* phase for which they were intended, where an archive would attract attention and invite use. However, this third mapping workshop also faced some major problems.

Despite changes following the VALU project workshop, consequences were still unmanageable. Whereas qualities had been simplified for the first phase, and outcomes in the second, usage consequences had all multiplied to the point that overlapping cards had become small mounds. The viability of worth mapping was threatened. However, the table for consequences in the living document had a format that inspired replacing usage consequences in worth sketches with a single user experience, and then articulating each experience in a separate UXC table. These became UXCs (Section 4.3.1), where outcomes only come about as a result of user interactions. The resulting generic MEC—materials→features→qualities→experiences→outcomes—was simpler than all previous ones.

UXCs were quickly used to revise and greatly simplify the *organising* phase worth map in the living document. There had long been problems with consequences in HVMs, with research revealing complex loops developing through feedback that made HVMs unfit for purpose in complex consumption domains.

The workshop for the fourth *consumption* phase began with demonstrations of new materials from the software engineers, who had developed physics capabilities for objects in an archive, allowing objects to be dropped into boxes and tipped back out again. Boxes could organise the archive and be rolled or bounced around. These were more relevant to earlier phases, but we were able to reflect on how new features and qualities could be added to existing worth maps, and how usage experiences could change. UXCs made this much easier to consider.

After considering new possible physics features, the UXC format was presented, and was found to be very useful by the interaction designer, because it was more concrete than the worth map that had included the represented experience. Attention then returned the earlier consumption phase. Several additional "stuffcasting" features were proposed, along with any required hardware support. There was not time to complete the consumption phase worth sketch, so we used the remainder of the last workshop to review the worth of worth mapping.

The value of connecting was noted, referring back to positive experiences in earlier workshops, especially for innovation, since new forms of value could be identified and realised through proposed antefacts. Effective support for both creative and critical discursive practices was acknowledged, as was the value of the living document (and some of it lived on for years). The team appreciated having a shared big picture that placed their individual contributions in context. However, as no one had used worth mapping without my continuous support, no-one was confident that they could use it independently. However, the next case study showed that this had become possible.

5.2.2   WORTH MAPPING FOR SITUATED SHARED DISPLAYS (MINHO, PORTUGAL)

While I was at MSRC Rui José, a visiting researcher from the University of Minho, participated in initial worth mapping workshops. He was impressed with the potential of worth maps and applied his first-hand experience in a project to develop a situated shared display for an educational setting (Otero et al., 2009; Otero and José, 2009). A Master's student, also a teacher at a school, worked with Otero and José to develop and deploy a shared display in the teachers' common room. This team had a good understanding of a recent WCD publication (Cockton, 2008a; which I had discussed when Rui visited Newcastle) and were comfortable with WCD's flexible structure spanning a family of approaches, with the actual progression falling in place as design work advances. Evaluation would draw on EMS (Section 4.1.4) and Direct Worth Instrumentation (DWI; Section 4.1.3), which was not fully fledged but experiences with a prototype deployment were expected to develop confidence for them.

The project was driven by the researchers' technologically motivated design vision with no expectation of solving problems or satisfying requirements, but instead accepting the challenge of creating an appropriate mix of activities across design arenas, explicitly connecting between them, moving design work on with reflection and deliberation, and seeking to generalise findings to similar usage settings.

The project inception was similar to the initial meetings for the Family Archive and followed (Cockton, 2008a). There was a focus on understanding worth maps and other aspects of WCD. Rui José's first-hand experience of worth mapping helped, as did the associated living document. However, José left MSRC before worth mapping completed, so I provided support, updating his team on important changes during the main workshops. My support was limited to answering questions arising before and after their inception, largely related to worthies.

The inception was similar to examples in earlier chapters where design arena canvases or similar were formed (Cockton, 2020a, Section 3.1.6 and Figure 5.8). For example, the teachers, school directors, and the education ministry were identified as anyficiaries. As in Cockton (2008a) these were called "sensitivities," but they were effectively DANs, with a few misplaced items.

The next activity checked several key assumptions before moving to design and prototyping. Interviews collected information to fill gaps, check assumptions and complement what was already a rich landscape of inception knowledge. With this new information complementing existing understandings, four issues provided a focus for the next step (Otero and José, 2009). These spanned both positive outcomes to achieve (e.g., a less formal common room) and negative ones to avoid (e.g., missing information, perhaps through inappropriate "showreel" style timings). These informed four purpose items, and directed ideation on antefact subarenas, for which five quality items and six feature ones were identified. A wireframe for the display added a material subarena that realised four features.

The next activity was worth mapping (for a large format version, see Otero et al., 2009). The worth map only included outcomes, qualities, and features. There were no experience elements since the interaction with a physical display would be very limited. Outcomes would result from attending to the features and interpreting the qualities of the display. This informed development of the display, which was deployed in the teacher's common room. A small evaluation at the end of the deployment established that the approach to information provision was promising and other content added informality to the common room.

This first supported use of worth maps and related approaches by independent researchers resulted in valuable reflections. The team valued support for understanding the relationships between features and high-level interaction goals, critical thinking (reflection and deliberation), brainstorming, managing trade-offs, and in-built support for the WCD principles (Cockton, 2008a; Wo-Fo versions of Meta-Principles for Designing). They drew similar benefits from explicit connection to Clarke (1997), and also recognised the need for tools similar to Clarke's LD tool. Better approaches to populating the purpose arena were wanted on the assumption that the interviews had not been good enough.

5.2.3   THE VALU PROJECT (FINLAND)

The third case study in this group is the VALU project, which investigated how technology companies can identify user needs and values for product and service development purposes. The project team was multidisciplinary and included researchers with business backgrounds. This was the second supported application of worth maps by independent researchers, and the first WCD project to included existing commercial products. The support was similar to that for the previous study, but a workshop at Nokia's headquarters on Wo-Fo approaches was held 8 months into the project (several weeks before my work with MSRC). It was attended by the VALU team and their collaborators. A key aim was to recruit industrial collaborators for Wo-Fo case studies.

There were two workshop exercises and a third set of further work. The first exercise identified purpose and artefact elements from three HCI research papers and then formed worth sketches for them. This approach was similar to the inception of worth mapping within the Family Archive project. The second exercise asked participants to update three worth/aversion maps (W/AMs; Cockton, 2007), extend their antefacts, and connecting them to usage consequences and outcomes. The third set of exercises was largely "homework," including: stakeholder identification and consequent extensions to worth sketches and maps (W/AMs) from previous exercises; Worth Boards

(Section 5.2.1); WoDs (Section 4.5); EMS tables (Section 4.1.4); and association tables. The last resource is a form of CoN (Cockton, 2020a, Section 5.6), with columns for: endpoints of a binary connection; favourable and unfavourable factors; and how likely the connection would happen in practice, given the balance of factors.

As mentioned in Section 5.2.1, one workshop outcome was revisions to the generic MEC structure for worth mapping: Materials were separated from Features, and five types of usage consequence were replaced with Feelings, Actions, and Experiences, which later inspired the creation of UXCs as the most workable solution to explosions of usage consequences in worth maps.

The main workshop outcome was experience of worth mapping and related Wo-Fo approaches for the project team and representatives from several companies. I next worked remotely with the project team after the workshop, who were preparing tutorial material on worth mapping for the planned case studies. In this material, MEC elements were called "worth map elements" and grouped into human and technical sensitivities, as in Cockton (2008a). Positive outcomes were called "motives," and negative ones "aversions." The tutorial material contrasted top-down (HOW) use of MECs (reading down from purpose) with bottom-up (WHY) use (reading up from a_tefacts). These bidirectional readings are consistent with research on HVMs that show that consumers construct MECs in both directions (van Rekom and Wierenga, 2007). There was a HCD focus, with value coming "from users: what they wish/want to achieve."

Several companies began case studies. The most successful was with a money gambling operator owned by the regional government of the Åland Islands, operating via Baltic cruise ships, the internet, and in Finland, Estonia, Latvia, Norway, Spain, Sweden, and Switzerland. Its profits are distributed to a range of non-profit associations within health, culture, education, and sustainability. The use of worth mapping with this company is reported in Cockton et al. (2009b).

Sentence completion (Section 2.3.3) was used to gather primary data for the purpose arena (as a composite of overlapping values, needs, wants, motivations, emotions, etc.). It was important for credibility to ground purpose in anyficiary data. Closed question interviews were thought unsuitable, especially when making direct use of a single existing list of values, such as the Rokeach Value Survey, which had been unhelpful in a value-centred study (Voida and Mynatt, 2005). However, in the first months of the project, an extensive survey of lists of values had resulted in a reference table with 27 values in 7 groups (Cockton et al., 2009b, Table 1), with 4 additional groups related to consumer behaviours. This was used indirectly when designing studies and analysing results.

A pilot study assessed the viability of sentence completion questionnaires as a research method for design purpose. The reference table was used to design sentence completion questions and to code the results. As a projective research method, it proved to be more suitable for the project's needs than standard interviews: it replicated existing results that had showed that projective methods elicit values and judgements better than standard interviews.

An online sentence completion questionnaire was designed to explore the motives and experiences of two distinct groups of players, who were recruited from the player database. An online questionnaire was easy to set up and was efficient to administer relative to interviews. The quantitative results replicated the company's existing market segmentation, but also provided new more detailed information. For example, less active players were more likely to play alone and were more loss adverse. New information was also collected on players' aversions. The players' sentence completions were analysed to prepare histograms for each question, as in Figure 2.1.

The results were used by the researchers, and a UX and a Player Intelligence specialist from the company. Two workshops reviewed the results, collaboratively transformed values into worthies (worth map/MEC elements) and formed the first partial worth maps. The results for each question were stepped through in sequence, with formation of worthies guided by sentence completion frequencies and also from existing player intelligence. A_tefact and purpose elements co-evolved with connections between them. Worthies for relevant product features were also added, as were logically obvious or otherwise known connections "even without direct support from user data" (Cockton et al., 2009b), which, along with the use of player intelligence expertise, relaxed the tutorial material's HCD focus.

Two worth maps were created in the Visio drawing editor, one for each player group. Data from sentence completion was noted for relevant elements, e.g., for an excitement outcome, 22% of players had mentioned feeling excited and active after playing online. Layers in Visio were used to gather all connections in the MECs passing through a single UX element. This made a focus on a few sets of MECs at a time possible by hiding layers. There were also blank a_tefact elements in the worth maps to draw attention to user values that as yet had no features that could deliver on them. Figure 5.1 shows an example worth map prepared in Visio.

There were three lessons from the first two workshops. First, the materials elements added at the Nokia workshop were hardly used because the games were developed and delivered using a web infrastructure that was rarely worthy of note. Second, feature and quality elements were confused. Looking back, this might have been because some tutorial material had listed qualities as both human sensitivities and technical ones (as non-functional requirements).

There were new participants at the third workshop. Its objectives were to review, discuss, and extend the worth map. The workshop began with a 90-minute presentation of the results of sentence completion and the two worth maps. After lunch, two groups worked on the worth maps. Each was facilitated by a researcher, with two company participants in each. One was the Player Intelligence specialist from the first two workshops. The other three were product owners, who experienced a steep learning curve. One found MEC elements difficult and confusing (all three a_tefact subarenas were still in both worth maps). However, all understood connections from product to use values. They could reassess existing ideas for new features, reposition existing features against a wider range of values, and consider alternative value propositions to current ones. New a_tefact elements were added (e.g., control over some game attributes), and broader responses were considered, such as re-design of visual appearance and adding social computing features. Some of these had already been identified in previous product reviews and had been in the Scrum backlog, but connecting them to outcomes or aversions increased their credibility and the commitment from the product owner.

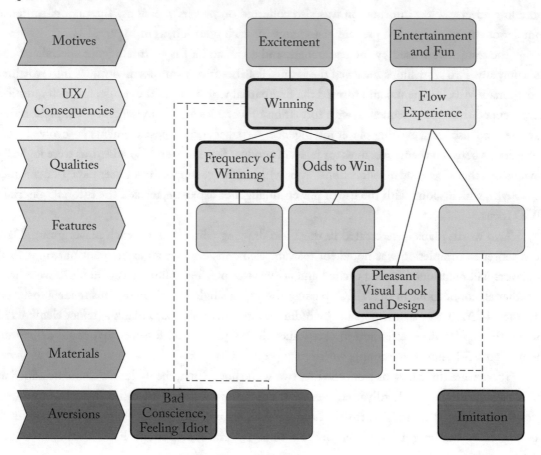

Figure 5.1: Worth map for a player group showing MECs for two UXs.

After the workshop, participants rated 15 questionnaire statements on a using a 4-point scale (4 was the best score). Two statements were deliberately out of scope, so unsurprisingly one of these received the lowest average score (1.75): "worth maps allow business value to be estimated and can be used strategically." With no business outcomes in either worth map, this indicated that participant responses were well judged. The average score for the other out of scope statement ("worth maps help to design more successful products") was 2.67, indicating that business value could well result from worth mapping. The other low average ratings for worth maps were for intention to use in future (2.33), ease of communication (2.5), and wanting to learn more (2.67). Setting a threshold of 3 for confident use in practice, the highest average rating (3.75) was for the importance of understanding user values, followed by worth maps developing a better conception of value for products (3.5), better marketing communications and customer relations (3.33), better connections of features to what matters to users (3.25), and being useful for design work tasks (3). The average rating for the other 4 statements was 2.75 (Cockton et al., 2009b).

Given the challenges faced by some participants, these were very encouraging ratings, but even more encouraging was how the case study closed in the two biggest office locations with onsite presentations (followed by workshops), and a video conference presentation to management in the overseas offices. The worth maps were carefully stepped through layer by layer. One workshop was product focused. The other focused on marketing and sales. Each focused on the top 4–6 issues for each player group. As in the first three workshops, existing product ideas and truly new ones were both better anchored in user values. Some ideas were high level, others very specific. Photos from the workshops and notes were sent back to attendees.

It was clear from this case study that worth maps and sentence completion combined well as bases for understanding user values and provided genuine business value to the company. The success of new and revised features cannot be disclosed due to commercial confidentiality.

5.3   WORKING WITH A WO-FO BEFORE BIG: INSIGHTS AND OUTCOMES

The case studies in this chapter span a dozen years. The first group predate Wo-Fo approaches by a decade and BIG approaches by even longer, but contain the seeds of both. The second groups all adopt Wo-Fo approaches, but predate explicit accounts of BIG design. Even so, some BIG practices were effectively followed in some. For example, the VALU project embraced the need to localise and adapt worth mapping before resource function analysis became part of the W2C framework. Similarly, for their staff room display project, Otero and José (2009) stressed the need for project teams to own their language for worth mapping. This willingness to learn and adapt is vital once teams accept that they cannot rely on predefined processes or pre-imposed methods to do the heavy lifting in design work. Only approaches and resources pre-exist design work (Woolrych et al., 2011), along with paradigm templates (Cockton, 2020a, Chapter 4).

All design approaches and resources have a *preparative* function, in that they prefigure design work. They do not fully resource it or fully direct it, but they do make their marks on what would otherwise be a blank canvas at the start of a design project. Despite the need to adapt, extend, complete, and augment preparative resources, there are important commonalities across the case studies above. These are summarised below and extended by the second set of case studies in Chapter 6.

The W2C framework provides a structure for presenting commonalities. Its resource functions operate at a more concrete level than the very abstract Meta-Principles for Designing and ADSs (Cockton, 2013b). All three are relevant, but resource functions are best suited to analysis at the level of specific practices within design work. Innovative worth mapping and related practices activate multiple functions, which is evidence of high worth design resources.

Approaches and resources have potential functions that are activated and realised by both intent and surprise (Section 2.1). Design work does not unfold, nor do designs emerge. Design work and the resulting designs have adventitious elements that are unplanned and unanticipated. These are part of a mix that involves intent, insight, judgement, reflection, and deliberation. Designs do not result from choices and like "creativity," "design choice" is a convenient shorthand for a complex assemblage of considerations, explorations, affirmations, and integrations. However, it is important to understand and acknowledge the complexities that underlie these potentially trite shorthands.

Four groups of resource functions underlie the commonalities in the first two groups of case studies. The first relate to *knowing* in a very wide sense, rather than a narrow one of objective knowledge that pre-exists design work and miraculously shows up on cue to save the day. The second relates to *collaborating*, which is essential for contemporary multidisciplinary design teams. The third relates to *caring* through explicit attention to psychological valences. The fourth relates to *steering* through strategic and tactical resources that scope and direct action.

5.3.1 KNOWING THROUGH CONNECTING

Design cognition has long been contrasted with other forms of thinking (Cross, 2001). Currently, Design Thinking (Brown, 2009) remains in vogue, albeit moderated by complaints about commoditised consultants' versions of it that are closer to engineering design than creative studio-based practices (Kolko, 2018).

Designerly ways of knowing (Cross, 2001) have become attractive beyond established creative craft disciplines because they are not bogged down in knowledge as "true justified belief," nothing more, nothing less. Knowledge practices in design are broad based, ranging from curiosity through common knowledge to critical reflection. Almost half of currently identified resource functions are associated with knowledge practices:

- *inquisitive* functions are activated when resources trigger questions from the design team;

- *ideative* functions are activated when resources spark ideas from the design team;

- *informative* functions are activated when resources provide timely and relevant knowledge;

- *reflective* functions are activated when designers appraise their work so far;

- *integrative* functions are activated when connections are made within or between co-products; and

- *expressive* functions are activated when resources are manifested materially or in utterances.

Worth maps and the LD tool have expressive and integrative functions by design, which are readily activated due to the extent of their preparative functions. Both also had ideative functions. Use of the LD tool led to ideation in response to the shared printer (Section 5.1.2). Making connections had an ideative function that added to documents and led to further connections. Once made, a connection could have an inquisitive function, indicating "the need for further investigation [that] may not have been obvious" without it (Clarke, 1997). Overall, making connections is worthwhile, even though one of Clarke's evaluation participants had concerns about the cost of the effort. All Clarke's evaluation participants could articulate the benefits of connecting development documents.

Ideative functions were also seen in the worth mapping projects. New worthies were added during Family Archive worth sketching that were not in the DANs formed from existing documents. For example, in the second organisation phase, features were added (e.g., links and tags within the archive for individual family members) as were materials (e.g., a microphone for voice identification and recording reminiscences;). While there was a feeling in discussions at the end of the fourth mapping workshop that we had stopped designing (separate design and field work was on hold), additions to the antefact arena were clear evidence that creative design work had continued. This microphone was proposed without initial field evidence for any "user need." The proposal was conceptual rather visually led. In later field trials of the implemented Family Archive (Kirk et al., 2010), a six-year-old "would regularly engage in long play sessions, moving around and resizing his [scanned toy] characters, and narrating a storyline." A microphone became essential in the related TellTable system for children's story animation (Cao et al., 2010).

Participants in the formal evaluation of worth mapping in the VALU project (Cockton et al., 2009b) noted that "new products are found with it" and found that it was a "tool to brainstorm and to try to innovate new features." The inclusion of blank feature elements in the worth maps "drew attention" inquisitively. Qualities such as *pleasant look and design* led to questions about the quality of current visuals and sound in the games.

As with other forms of sketching, worth sketching and mapping are thus not only expressive, but are also ideative and inquisitive. For example, the Interaction Designer for the Family Archive shared his interest in missing connections. The lack of a connection between elements that could be in a MEC led to questions on whether we had missed something. Overall, good questions make for good design work, so mobilisation of inquisitive functions is a valuable contribution to any project.

A wide range of informative functions were also activated in the case studies. DANs were formed through a range of primary and secondary research, as well as personal and creative resources. DANs for the Family Archive were formed from existing documentation and presented for review before further reflection and deliberation with worth sketches that prepared for the four mapping sessions. Changes to DANs, UXCs, and worth maps were recorded in the living document. Its final purpose DAN (list of relevant values, Table 2.1) continued to inform related projects for several years after.

For their staff room display, Otero et al. (2009) made good use of existing expertise and experiences on technological opportunities and design challenges. For example, previous use with shared displays had revealed the need to attract usage (as with *entice* phase of the Family Archive). Experience from the display's deployment informed the evaluation arena, with future possible measures added, along with considering Living Lab and Research in the Wild approaches for future evaluation.

Clarke's contextual focus for his LD tool can be thought of as a form of prestructured DAN for the anyficiaries arena, acting as an informative checklist. In the VALU project, a previously developed value table (similar to the value lists in Section 2.3.1) informed the design of their sentence completion questionnaire and the analysis of the results. This informed an implicit purpose DAN, not only adding elements, but also noting their frequency of mention and other information.

A lack of informative resources was felt in the staff room display project (Otero and José, 2009) where better approaches to populating the purpose arena were wanted. They did not find their semi-structured interviews adequate. The Family Archive and VALU projects has been able to draw on richer, broader, and more systematic resources for realising their purpose design arenas.

The VALU worth mapping team also added logically obvious or otherwise known connections to worth maps, which were appreciated for the improved conception of value in the website under consideration. As with the Family Archive, the implicit purpose DAN in the worth maps informed future product developments. Overall, primary and secondary research informed VALU's worth mapping, supplemented by essential personal and organisational information resources. As in the other two worth mapping projects, all three forms of research in Section 2.3 were used to fill out a purpose DAN.

"Creativity" methods aside, which are often kept separate from serious systematic design and evaluation work, inquisitiveness, and ideation are less associated with design and evaluation methods than information, direction, and expression. Worth sketches and maps, like all manifested design resources, automatically have an expressive function. Worth sketches and maps record and communicate for designers and others, especially when formed collaboratively (which is much easier for worth sketches than worth maps). When presented to anyone who was not involved in the mapping work, worth maps can look complicated. However, formative evaluation did not see this with the LD tool, where users browse their way around an unvisualised web of connections. The

LD tool only had single links between documents single links, but each MEC had several. Some literacy is required to read worth maps. The use of Visio layers in the VALU project reduced visual complexity, resulting in positive evaluation comments including worth maps being a "good tool to work with visually with information" and providing a "good overview." With appropriate handling, both readers and writers can realise worth maps' expressive function. Writers could move forward with pace and confidence.

In their staff room display project, the team valued support for facilitating "the process of making explicit the connections between high level concepts related to desired ends/worth/values and simple/basic/atomic features composing an (or to be) artifact" (Otero and José, 2009). This in turn supported a broad range of design practices: critical thinking (reflection and deliberation), brainstorming, managing trade-offs, and support for WCD principles (Cockton, 2008a; Wo-Fo versions of Meta-Principles for Designing). Multiple functions can be activated during worth mapping, with reflection and deliberation common to all case studies above.

Expressive functions provide good support for reflection. Initial Family Archive worth sketching workshops were primarily reflective and deliberative in function. Individual team members reflected on what was presented and the team deliberated on whether DANs contained appropriate elements. Explicit context in the LD tool activated participant reflection on the potential relevance of various elements. Link notes could contain reflection such as "just an option" and "to the best of my knowledge."

Worth maps were designed to be integrative, as was Clarke's LD tool, which anticipated the need for separate connection tracking (CoFs/CoNs; Cockton, 2020a, Chapter 5) by two decades (Cockton, 2016b). Link names were very short Connection Frames (CoF; Cockton, 2020a, Section 5.7). From a BIG perspective, the LD tool focused on integration via connections, both between and within arenas.

It is interesting to consider the LD tool case studies from the perspective of connection structures and modes.

- There were three QOC loops for the MSc system, and one each for LD tool and OMS (Section 5.1.2). These QOC loops created design rationale chains. Two connection modes can be seen. There were realisations, e.g., a task sequence elaborates an object model action. There were also direct transfers, e.g., a contextual focus entry transfers into a scenario, a scenario object or action transfers into an object model, revealing the antefact when scenarios contain application representations (Carroll, 1990).

- All OMS connections and all LD tool connections from QOC and scenarios to the design were one way, but binary connections were made in both directions between:

  ○ object model and scenarios (MSc—1 from/6 to);

- object and task models (M.Sc.—1 from/2 to);

- contextual focus and scenarios (M.Sc.—1 from/1 to);

- QOC and focus (M.Sc.—2 from/5 to; LD tool—5 from/3 to); and

- QOC and scenarios (LD tool—1 from/1 to).

- Chains extended binary connections to ternary and quaternary ones (based on documents on a link path). Clarke identified these and the need for grafts, for example to underpinning information for a connection that is not included in its endpoints.

- Clarke (1997) presciently saw types as a potential aid for understanding connections and unwittingly encountered all but two of the nine modes identified in Section 4.1.7:

  - *argued* from Design Rationale;

  - *realisations* from QOC options via the object model to low level task sequences;

  - *ideative* from scenarios to design documents;

  - *(mis)fit* involving the contextual focus via QOC; and

  - *direct transfers* from contextual focus to scenarios.

Connections were *latent* or *implied* when explanatory text could not indicate an explicit mode. These seven modes resulted from a creative bottom-up exploratory approach. All three CREAM types (Section 4.1.7) were present, and two each of hybrid and RILED ones: the missing ones being respectively *articulation* and *statistical*. The latter was not possible without quantitative data. Articulation is central to worth maps and their multi-step MECs. Articulated connections in worth maps make more focused concrete use of positive and negative connections than in QOC. MECs' quasi-causal nature makes articulation inspectable. Had modes been available and used, some LD tool connections may have been clearer, especially realisations that map from one design (sub)arena to another.

The LD tool makes single unidirectional binary connections between parts of documents with some loops and chains. It was thus less able to discover the range of connection structures that have been revealed in BIG analyses. Wo-Fo design's separate purpose arena has brought many complex connection structures into existence. Many of Clarke's (1997) links were wholly within arenas, and not between them, but even so, he was able to demonstrate that "contextual [focus] information was never used to immediately influence the design."

Experiences with the LD tool are also relevant to creating interfaces for connections in design arenas (Cockton, 2020a, Section 5.4). In the LD tool to make connections between documents, interfaces ("parts" or "bags") had to be created. Some evaluation participants saw this as extra work, but Clarke (1997) correctly argued that the quality of design work overall would be improved by thinking about interfaces before making connections. An exception applies to concourses, where latent and implicit connections precede explicit design arenas, preventing creation of interfaces. Again, Clarke's findings were prescient and anticipated the key BIG practice of explicitly identifying interfaces within design arenas.

A decade after Clarke's pioneering Ph.D. thesis, the value of connecting was again demonstrated through worth mapping. For the Family Archive, a removable drawer containing a hard disk had been proposed but had not been included in the design documentation. During worth mapping, it was restored as a material element once a purpose was identified for it (even today with cloud storage, such a component may remain attractive, if only to preserve links to cloud storage). Similarly, in the VALU project, evaluation feedback appreciated how a MEC "helps to connect abstract and concrete." The goals of worth mapping were understood and connections were formed readily. As a result, antefact capabilities in the backlog were given a higher priority once a worth map linked them to a credible purpose. In two projects, a single MEC was sufficient for "parked" features and materials to be given a pole position on the roadmap.

Overall, worth mapping, with connections in the LD tool, was associated with the mobilisation of a wide range of knowledge functions, beyond the informative and expressive functions that are typically expected from design and evaluation methods. Integrative functions were to be expected given the centrality of connections in worth maps and the LD tool, but ideative, inquisitive, and reflective functions were also activated during worth mapping and LD tool use.

5.3.2   COLLABORATING WITH WORTH SKETCHES AND MAPS

Interaction design work typically requires multidisciplinary teams, and thus individual knowing must be complemented by social knowing. This depends on strong social bonds and dynamics within a design team, which are strengthened whenever an affiliative function is activated through design work, which happened in all the worth mapping case studies above. Design teamwork requires presenting, explaining, and persuading. Performative functions support these social aspects of design work.

LD tool use was individual, but Clarke (1997) anticipated how group discussion could develop consensus on the meaning of contextual focus items, just as worth mapping teams spent time on understanding the meaning of different types of worthy. In these situations, deliberative functions were activated. While deliberation can be an individual knowing practice, unlike reflection it can be a social practice and is thus grouped here with other social functions. Forester (1999) surveys deliberative planning work and provides many insights into the effective facilitation of wide-ranging discussions between planning professionals, politicians, and communities.

Affiliative functions were realized in all worth sketching and mapping above. Teams worked effectively together, united by the big pictures that worth sketches and maps provided. Co-learning approaches were also affiliative, with teams willingly working to develop common understandings of worthy types, MECs, and sketching and mapping. For Otero and José (2009) a cross-disciplinary "lingua franca" facilitated a common ground for progressing the project. The materiality of paper on table Family Archive worth sketches physically brought the team together, looking both at their specialist rows and also the sketch as a whole. Practices here were inclusive, further activating an affiliative function, as well as a deliberative one.

Deliberation had a range of roles. It could trigger ideation, reflection, or integration. It could also activate directive functions through discussion and agreement of plans and tactics, and modest next steps. It realises Habermas' "friendly" (or communicative) epistemology, which combines "scientific inquiry with communication (about objects, values, and even aesthetic experiences)" (Dallmayr, 1998). Such a social epistemology is more relevant to multidisciplinary design teams than wholly cognitive ones focused on individual "true justified belief." It is not enough for one person to "know," they must bring the rest of the team with them.

There were extensive presentations on the VALU project. These compensated for expressive limitations of worth maps. In this project's formal evaluation, the average rating on whether the results of worth maps was easy to communicate was 2.5 out of 4, one of the three lowest of 15 ratings. Despite this, three presentations at two offices and by video conferencing followed this evaluation. It is important to look at the balance of activated and realised functions for an approach or resource, since limited performance on one function can be compensated for by others, in the case realisation of a performative function.

5.3.3   CARING WITH WORTH SKETCHES AND MAPS

Knowing and collaborating in design work are guided by feelings. Design teams *care* about their projects. Three relevant functions have currently been identified. The main axiological function is *ameliorative*, and when realised makes for better experiences and outcomes (to ameliorate is to make things better). These apply to both design products and also to how they are progressed. While good progressions do not guarantee good outcomes, design teams must believe that their purpose is appropriate and their work will progress to achieve it. Worth maps' built in support for WCD principles was appreciated on the VALU project, with the inherent *expressivity* of worth maps complemented by *committedness* to worth (as a balance of positive over negative outcomes). *Credibility* followed from grounding MECs in collaborative work to combine results of sentence completion with knowledge of the existing product and its agile backlog (receptiveness). The experience was similar for Otero and José (2009), letting them focus on progressing the product and not the process. In their experience, all six WCD principles (Cockton, 2008a, 2009a) were supported: "a virtuous cycle is in place: somehow the design principles seem to be encapsulated in the design cycle envisioned while adherence to the design principles makes the design process and corresponding methods meaningful." José's experiences with worth sketching within the Family Archive project were strengthened by independent worth mapping.

Each worth mapping project took different approaches to developing the purpose design arena, using approaches covered in Chapter 2. Observation, photography, and interviews were used for the Family Archive, interviews complemented existing understandings and the personal experience of the second author in Otero et al. (2009), and sentence completion in the VALU project all realised ameliorative functions. They all identified positive outcomes to design for and negative ones to design against ("possible to see strengths and weaknesses"; Cockton et al., 2009b). For the Family Archive, three purpose elements were genuinely new in the sense that no competitor technologies in 2007 could support such outcomes. This anticipated Generosity in BIG design, providing value that current families had not asked for or otherwise indicated a "need."

A purpose design arena can give teams a clear sense of direction, but they also need to feel that they are progressing toward delivery of intended worth. Well-expressed and inspiring purpose can make teams confident about what they are doing. Building on this is important. Effective use of approaches and resources results in continued and increase confidence, activating *invigorative* functions. Design work is affective as well as cognitive and social. In the VALU project, worth maps were evaluated as "good for boosting workshops." "Boost" is good evidence of realising an invigorative function. Positive emotions progress projects. However, not all design work proceeds positively.

Design teams can sense when a project is veering off track. A focus on balance is important to avoid an excessive focus on either benefits on the one hand, or costs and risks on the other. In the third worth mapping workshop on the VALU project, one product owner challenged basing worth maps on sentence completion, preferring questionnaires with closed questions as being less leading, and requiring less interpretation and time. However, the subsequent presentations and workshops confirmed the worth of realised purpose. Keeping projects on track requires appropriate responses to concerns raised, which in this case was to listen and reflect. *Protective* resource functions are involved here.

There are several examples where action was taken in the VALU project that realised protective functions: a pilot use of sentence completion before its use with the gambling company; the use of Visio layers to simplify presentations of worth maps by focusing on MECs through a UX; and presenting sentence completion results in batches. In the second worth mapping workshop, stepping through all the results in a single pass was too labour intensive, so in the third, the focus alternated between sentence completion results and the worth maps. Success cannot be simply attributed to worth mapping and sentence completion. Sensitive adaptive use of both approaches was essential to keeping a risky innovative project on the rails.

Some possible protective moves are only identified by later reflection. For example, some evaluation participants of the LD tool struggled to understand some explanatory text. Clarke

(1997) proposed connection types to improve comprehension. Explicit connection modes could do the same. Also, in the VALU project, worthies based on a_tefact subarenas were not affiliative, but isolated business roles, so a possible simpler MEC structure was proposed for project teams with a low proportion of design and engineering teams (Cockton et al., 2009b). This would only contain a_tefacts, UXs, and outcomes. However, MECs including a_tefact subarenas had worked well at MSRC and Minho, where teams had a majority of technical and creative roles. It would be equally protective to retain a_tefact subarena elements in such contexts.

Protective functions were activated on the Family Archive project. One was proactively realised by the materiality of paper worth sketches on a table, which as mentioned, was an inherent protection against exclusion, thus activating an affiliative function. As the first use of worth sketches and maps with an external team, this was also a risky innovative activity that could have gone off the rails without sensitive adaptive practices. Overly complex worth maps were a major threat. The first protective move came from the project lead, Abigail Sellen, who recommended modularising the worth maps by phases of the life cycle of an archived object. However, worth sketching was never constrained to only focus on the current phase. Much was identified in advance before worth sketching for the consumption phase, with remote situated displays being added as materials when sketching the organising phase. You can't stop people having ideas, and nor can you stop people remembering features and materials that had been briefly proposed during initial design work but not documented. Attention could thus shift forward and backward in time relative to an intended work order. The protective move was motivated by the need to manage complexity, which could be achieved without constraining ideation.

There was nowhere to include the background *enticing* phase in the life cycle of an archived object, since this phase wasn't part of that sequence. The phase was thus not initially scheduled for worth sketching, but it was once the features DAN was reviewed for elements that had not been allocated to a phase's worth sketch. This review had a protective function, as did creation of UXCs to replace complex consequence networks. Overall, future uses of worth maps benefitted from important adaptations to their creation and development during Family Archive work.

There were also examples of protective moves with the LD tool that arose from Clarke's record-reflect-respond practice when adding to documents and adding links. Inconsistencies between documents were picked up, along with oversights such as not initially desiging for use of shared printers in open plan offices (Section 5.1.2). Similarly, noise was seen to be an oversight for the Olympic Message System. Discovering oversights through a lack of connections (revealed by one of the filters added after the second LD case study) reduces waste in software design work. A similar manual practice revealed an overlooked phase for the Family Archive. The LD tool filters activated protective functions by:

- only showing connections in the link list to/from a single document;

- highlighting all elements of context that hadn't yet a role in any connection;

- presenting all paths that traverse from a document in a separate window to identify all dependencies; and

- only showing connections with identical end points (to check for duplicated connections to merge).

The extent of required creative work and sustained design management should not be underestimated (Cockton et al., 2009b). A shared understanding of ameliorating design purpose and invigorating progress support self-organising teams, who can also be trusted to make timely and appropriate protective moves. If not, subtle management control should be enough, as with the suggestion of modularising worth maps around archived objects' life cycles for the Family Archive.

5.3.4   STEERING WITH WORTH SKETCHES AND MAPS

The last group of resource functions steer various levels of design work. *Adumbrative* functions realise loose scopes. To adumbrate is to sketch an outline, by analogy with casting a shadow (*umbra* in Latin). A MADS can model design work at all levels from enduring paradigms to transient one-off moves. The move from LD to Grounded Design (Cockton, 1998) added an evaluation arena to anyficiaries (context) and a_tefacts (design). The move from Grounded Design to VCD (Cockton, 2004a) added a novel purpose arena, thus laying the foundations for Wo-Fo BIG design and the scope for Family Archive worth sketching. The shared staff room display project had a good balance as regards design arenas, aiming for a foundation based on "a thorough understanding of the social milieu that the system is meant to integrate and a clear view of the respective value position" (Otero et al., 2009), thus covering anyficiaries and purpose, but also building on existing expertise and experience with situated digital public displays. Their a_tefact arena had a solid foundation, protected by giving engineering and design ideation the same value as human-focused practices.

The mix for the shared staff room display was broader than for the Family Archive worth maps. There was extensive design, implementation, and deployment. There was also a commitment to use a broad range of Wo Fo approaches, in particular EMS (Section 4.1.4) and DWI (Section 4.1.3). The project anticipated some key future developments for BIG design, especially awareness of the design situation (before Cockton, 2010), avoiding big upfront problem research and analysis (as agile development does), seeing incomplete information as unavoidable (as Lean UX does), and embracing design judgement to decide on what data to value, and what to include in each arena. A report on VALU project experiences (Cockton et al., 2009b) contains a surprising slip, advocating equal attention to design arenas, framing balance in terms of weight rather than mix. The actual mix cannot be reported for commercial reasons, but the project's outcomes were fed through to product and territory teams. One interesting extension to scope was the inclusion of new marketing content for review in one workshop, as part of an activity to align online positioning of products with the worth maps. This work on online content could proceed more quickly than software development work on adding features and improving qualities.

The VALU project took a broad view of design purpose, developing a table resource that generalised over existing value lists and groupings. This scoped design purpose by framing value as a composite overlap of needs, motivations, values, emotions, and feelings. This contrasts with studies that used a single list of values, for example Rokeach Value Survey (Rokeach, 1973) in Voida and Mynatt, (2005). In all the worth mapping projects, the concept of worth had an adumbrative function, focusing attention on both aversions and motivators.

More detailed scopes are formed as projects progress. Otero and José (2009) acknowledged helpful aspects of VSD (Friedman et al., 2006), but found it too abstract and focused instead on specific individual or collective values in context as they arise at specific points in time and space. This more concrete focus would interface better with the evaluation arena, for which EMS and DWI approaches were under consideration. During the first Family Archive capture phase workshop, some antefact qualities from my review of initial design work were side lined as being commercially oriented branding concerns that were out of scope for initial exploratory work.

MADS are one resource for expressing scope. Design paradigms are another. Family Archive worth mapping was the first BIG project in spirit if not in name. A basis for identifying generosity was identified. Integration and generosity were well covered, but balance was only addressed in the early stages of worth mapping. In contrast, balance and integration were well covered for the shared staff room display. The LD tool and VALU project were largely focused on integration, but the focus on worth in the latter did improve balance relative to existing agile development practices at the online gaming company.

MECs also realised a scoping function, with each worth mapping project making use of different structures, but without any clear consequences from these differences. Indeed, without these differences the projects may not have gone as well. Adaptation of MECs could activate a protection function, with usage difficulties indicating a need for more adaptation.

Adumbrative functions can thus steer at multiple levels of abstractions: projects, episodes, approaches, resources and brief design moves. The resulting scopes have some persistence, and some will stabilise for the remainder of a project. In contrast, directive functions focus attention on what to do next.

The LD tool did not impose sequence on entry of documents, marking up parts, or creating links. The parallel entry of M.Sc. admission system's context and design documents anticipated HCI's slow embrace of creative design practices. The paper-based study on which it was based had followed an HCD paradigm, initially studying the context of use before design commenced. However, once the initial documents had been entered, antefact work next began to focus on user interface details. It was soon apparent that further contextual research was necessary to plug gaps (as with MVP experiments in Lean UX). This was just as well, since this research was in the month before a new cohort arrived, exposing an alternative "next fit" admissions procedure that filled remaining places rather than waiting for completion of better applications.

Clarke's experiences with his LD tool exposed flaws in RILED processes, since "context can be used in different ways and at different times throughout the lifecycle of a project" and documents "make a contribution not just at one stage of the cycle but whenever required" (Clarke, 1997). While the sequence in which design arenas are visited cannot be fixed, prioritisation can guide design work with "a careful definition of the ultimate purpose of the system" and subordinate the other arenas to that arena's needs: "even small variations in the purpose of a system may lead to different design approaches" (Otero et al., 2009).

This move away from sequence in design progressions can sometimes be compensated by resources with content ordering that can sequence subsequent approaches that make use of them. In the first review session for the Family Archive, worthies were presented for discussion in groups by element type, and then in order within groups (each element was given a number). Similarly, on the VALU project, sentence completion results were presented and discussed in their order on the questionnaire (but a single pass was too onerous, so consideration of results was batched for the third workshop). These sequences within resources thus realised directive functions. However, direction does not entail sequence. Clarke's contextual checklist directs designers to complete relevant entries, but not in any predetermined order.

At other times, information for one type of worthy would focus attention on another. In the VALU project, one sentence completion had indicated that some multimedia features in games were irritating. The defect was clear here, but not the features to which it applied, so a close review was needed of current games. Similarly, the use of filters in the LD tool was directive by drawing attention to unlinked parts in documents, to duplicated connections, and to a chain of connections originating from a part of a document.

Design and evaluation methods are often expected to be directive, with scopes restricted to a single design arena. However, Chapter 4 has presented many Wo-Fo examples that extend approaches beyond their initial scopes, e.g., personas, scenarios, mood boards, and user testing. Similarly, contextual design can be re-scoped to become an evaluation method (McDonald et al., 2006).

Projects do need to be steered by self-organising teams with subtle management control as needed. The scope of scoping and direction work is broader than often assumed. Scoping occurs at every level of design work from millennia old paradigms to minute long moves. Direction can occur at any level of this scope, and not just at the levels of process and method. Direction does not require a sequential procedure. An agenda is often enough (Keinonen, 2009), and it may take several episodes of design work to address one in full, since "designers often have to deal with uncertain or incomplete knowledge" (Clarke, 1997) and thus information that is logically required at some point may not be available. Lean UX is a recent approach that has embraced realities here and lets design work proceed in the absence of required memoranda, with the expectation that MVP experiments fill gaps as and when possible.

5.4   CHAPTER SUMMARY

Worth maps and the LD tool realised the functions expected from traditional design and evaluations. They were informative through the concepts of worth, worthies, and MECs, although more so after deliberation that improved affiliation. They were expressive, although with occasional and mostly manageable difficulties. They were directive, but not through a fixed prior procedure that authors had to follow. Direction was in the moment and more finely grained, although some work sequences could be planned in advance around modularisations of worth sketches and maps, or following content order within completed resources.

Worth maps realised their intended primary ameliorative and integrative functions, doing "what it says on their tin," but also ideative, inquisitive, reflective, invigorative, protective, deliberative, affiliative, adumbrative, and performative functions are activated in specific project circumstances. Resource functions are only potentials. Some are easier to activate than others, but all contribute to successful design work.

Chapter 6 considers further case studies as a basis for adding to the analysis.

Unsupported and Taught Case Studies: Adding BIG to Wo-Fo

This chapter surveys the second decade of projects that have taken BIG or Wo-Fo approaches, or both. It begins with a third group of case studies that used a Wo-Fo independently, without my knowledge or involvement. Reynaud and van Biljon (2010) used Wo-Fo user research to balance consideration of positives and negatives for UX and outcomes in mobile phone use by the elderly. Vu (2013) used worth maps and related approaches to develop an information system for the Finnish Golf Union (FGU). Camara (2012) sought to fully orperationalise the VCD framework (Cockton, 2005). With colleagues over four Wo-Fo projects, she developed support for several innovative uses of worth maps and synthesised this in the ARROWS framework (Camara and Calvary, 2017). Meta-principles from W2C supported some aspects of BIG design in both Vu's work and the ARROWS framework.

The fourth "group" has only one case study, the first and only current combination of Wo-Fo and BIG approaches (George, 2016). BIG Wo-Fo and George's Ph.D. research co-evolved, with the value of BIG and Wo-Fo resources demonstrated in episodic reflection and retrospection. George's research complemented worth maps with several important new Wo-Fo approaches (e.g., Figures 4.3 and 4.7), and made use of others such as EMS (Section 4.1.4).

The fifth group is primarily based on three one-week design courses that I taught at the Technical University of Eindhoven (TU/e) in 2015, 2016, and 2017. BIG Wo-Fo approaches have also been taught at seven conference courses and tutorials since 2013 at WUD, NordiCHI and CHI, and in undergraduate teaching at Northumbria and Reykjavik universities.

Three of the case studies in this chapter are research theses: one Master's (Vu, 2013) and two Ph.D.s (Camara, 2012; George, 2016). All are available online, with URLs given in the appendices. They contain extensive examples that cannot be included in the space available for this book. Questions arising from these three case studies should be answered by consulting these theses. Similarly, there is further detail on the other case studies, with references to other sources of information, in the papers on mobile phone design for older users (Renaud and van Biljon, 2010), and projects within the ARROWS framework (Camara et al., 2013a; Camara and Calvary, 2015, 2017). These too should provide answers to questions arising from the short accounts below.

This chapter ends with a cumulative summary of insights from the case studies in this and the previous chapter.

6.1   INDEPENDENT WO-FO PROJECTS

The Family Archive case study made it clear that moving the centre of design to worth just shifted a silo to purpose from HCD's anyficiaries and evaluation. To avoid this, work on purpose had to be better integrated with the other arenas, which worth maps did not achieve well enough. The result was a shift to a Wo-Fo in the context of BIG Design and the W2C framework (Cockton, 2013a, 2013b). The third group of case studies all made independent use of a Wo-Fo. All except one used worth mapping.

Reynaud and van Biljon (2010) adopted a Wo-Fo in user research to avoid trading off hygiene factors against motivators (Section 2.3.1). Vu (2013) assessed worth-centred approach in development of an information management system for the FGU. He was partially motivated by Camara et al. (2010), who were improving the operationalisation of the value-centred development framework (Cockton, 2005). Camara developed support for several innovative uses of worth maps. The BIG Wo-Fo paradigm had not fully developed when Camara completed her Ph.D. thesis. Work on worth mapping mostly suspended while BIG matured. Vu (2013), however, could consider aspects of BIG in his research. Camara and colleagues have continued to develop worth mapping and related approaches. Several projects can thus be reviewed in this third case study group.

6.1.1   AGE-APPROPRIATE MOBILE PHONES (SOUTH AFRICA)

This group's first case study (Renaud and van Biljon, 2010) is based solely on my advocacy of worth as a core design concept, with some support from the main account of VCD (Cockton, 2004b). It follows the logic of WCD (Cockton 2006) in balancing positive motivating value against negative hygiene factors of usability and contextual fit.

The authors criticise simplification as a response to accessibility issues for elderly users. Instead, they argue that worthwhile features (for effectiveness) must be accessible. The aim should be to maximise fit, not minimise features. Feature reduction must be properly informed by a suitable range of users' needs. Retained features must be accessible for a range of capabilities and usage.

For their usage context, they construct worth as a function of positive effectiveness and adequate accessibility (i.e., averted negatives). They thus avoid the single valence drawback (Section 2.1.1) by not only focusing on negatives, as is common in usability and accessibility work. Inclusive design too often fails to keep effectiveness and accessibility separate, focusing on the latter at the expense of the former.

Features can be aligned with needs through a *usage space* (Marcus and Chen, 2002), which has a similar function to Hillier et al's (1972) *codes*, associating feature groups with usages. van Biljon's (2007) Ph.D. had developed a usage model for mobile phones. As a *concourse* (Section 4.2), a usage space is a broad applications locale of general activities supported by broad classes of capabilities. A chain can be formed from abstract user needs via usage spaces to artefact features. The risks of a concourse's implied connections are low when single button presses make usage so simple that the articulated connections of UXCs and worth maps (Section 4.3) cannot improve connections.

A model can be formed from core and additional usage spaces, integrated through an individual's identity (Marcus and Chen, 2002). In Marcus and Chen's model, the five core usage spaces were information, self-enhancement, relationships, entertainment, and m-commerce. Each contains more specific application domains, e.g., health/safety, education, and active assistance. Van Biljon's (2007) core usage spaces were personal information, relationships, and safety and security. Her additional usage spaces were personal history, non-personal information, image, expansion, entertainment, and m-commerce. These were based on 20- to 30-year-old mobile phone users, and would not exactly match older users' (i.e., over 60) usage spaces.

Reynaud and van Biljon (2010) reviewed some secondary literature on value, values, motivation, needs, wants, and related concepts (Section 2.3.1) for ways to start their chain of connections from abstract user needs via usage spaces to features. They settled on Deci and Ryan's (2000) Competence, Autonomy, and Relatedness model of core needs, which is more appropriate for older people than Alderfer's (1972) Existence, Relatedness and Growth. For the "old old" (over 80) maintaining Autonomy and Competence can take precedence over Growth. Deci and Ryan's model thus drops Growth from Alderfer's and refines Existence to Autonomy and Competence. As well as these three core needs, Reynaud and van Biljon (2010) added open categories of wants based on Herzberg (1966) and Kano et al. (1984). Herzberg's hygiene factor is retained, but his motivators are replaced with Kano et al.'s "performance" factors. Unsurprisingly, Kano et al.'s generous "excitement" factors were out of scope for what was mostly a remedial exercise. Together, these basic needs and motivation categories could be used to establish a baseline that could then be mapped into usage spaces, which would be associated with phone features using a concourse structure similar to "codes" (Hillier et al. 1972). This would improve links between beneficiary contexts, a_tefact design, and evaluation.

Having established a theoretical framework for considering basic needs and (de)motivators, Van Biljon's (2007) core usage spaces and their twin components of worth (effectiveness, accessibility) structured a competitor analysis of mobile phones for seniors. A Japanese phone performed much better than the others, but it appeared that basic needs could be better met, especially for the specific context of elderly South African users: "it is impossible to assess worth without considering the context of the user" (Reynaud and van Biljon, 2010), a position similar to Winkler and Spiekerman's (2019) that values must be examined in the intended operational context of a planned system (Section 4.4.1). Hence, older South Africans's usage experiences were next studied.

Thirty-four South Africans from 60–92 years of age were interviewed. They were asked to comment on five very short scenarios that focused on one, two, or all basic needs. Competence and autonomy were of particular interest, since mobile phones clearly connect people (relatedness). Responses would reveal how well basic needs could be met with mobile phones or other means.

Participants were next asked to identify and demonstrate their four most-used phone functions. The seven identified functions were associated with a valence (performance or hygiene, i.e., satisfiers or dissatisfiers) and a basic need or a want, which in turn was associated with a usage space. The aim of demonstration was to count keystrokes, but with so many navigation errors that the counts were unreliable. Some participants asked a researcher for help to find functions. There were clear negative hygiene factors here as regards accessibility.

The last activity designed an ideal mobile phone by placing up to eight prepared buttons for functions on a cardboard mockup, with blank buttons used to add functions. This identified 15 desired features, which were only associated with basic needs, and no wants.

Results from this primary research were used to adapt van Biljon's (2007) usage space model for use with older users, resulting in three core usage spaces (Relationships, Organisation, and Safety and Security), which, respectively, correspond to Deci and Ryan's (2000) Relatedness, Competence, and Autonomy. Two additional usage spaces corresponded to the most used "want" features: image and personal history.

The revised model informed the design of a mobile phone prototype. Navigation problems with existing phones favoured simple button presses over menu navigation. Only six buttons were available, so only the top six desired features could be allocated to them (the police button could reasonable provide access for the seventh, ambulance). Three buttons were for features in the Relationships usage space, two for Organisation, and one for Safety and Security.

The value of a Wo-Fo in this study is that it avoids a single negative valence that can let accessibility direct feature retention. By considering positive basic needs and favoured usage spaces, these could support choice of features, which then had to be made accessible. Tables similar to feature-benefit ones, another form of concourse (Section 4.2), were used to associate features and purpose. One table related used (demonstrated) features to needs (basic needs, hygiene) or wants (usage spaces, performance). Another table-related desired features to needs alone. Interestingly, the two least used features satisfy wants (performance, usage space) and not basic needs.

This case study had a very simple concrete design situation. Its anyficiaries DAN is the most complex, with elements based on information from the primary research. There are three purpose DAN elements (Competence, Autonomy, Relatedness) and six initial features in the artefact DAN, with more in a backlog. The main interfaces for connections in the anyficiaries DAN were frequencies for use and desired features. Other elements in this DAN were not interfaced. The endpoints (interfaces) of direct transfer connections were anyficiaries (feature preference and use) and a_tefact (feature list). Two concourses connect a_tefacts to purpose: a usage space model, and used and desired feature frequency tables. The associated diagrams and tables are in Renaud and van Biljon (2010).

Reflection on this case study's concrete design situation quickly raises questions about the backlog of unaddressed features with no associated button: How these will be accessed? How accessible will this be if menu hierarchies must be used? Knowledge of existing mobile phone designs can guide exploration of options here, such as a roller button for scrolling through one flat menu containing all the features on the backlog in a suitable order (desirability or use frequency).

6.1.2   FINNISH GOLF UNION

This detailed case study was the focus of a Master's project at Aalto University (Vu, 2013). A new network information system (Verkkotietopavelu) was developed for use by Finnish Golf Union (FGU) headquarters staff and their member clubs. This was a much more extensive system than in the previous case study (Reynaud and van Biljon, 2010). Vu (2013) contains detailed examples of the approaches that were developed and used.

Vu's dissertation begins with an extensive review of 16 publications on the development of WCD (Cockton, 2006, 2008a, 2009b) from its VCD origins (Cockton, 2004a, 2004b, 2005), combined with the early stages of BIG Design (Cockton, 2008b, 2009a, 2010). A unified vocabulary is created across these sources. Specific Wo-Fo approaches are reviewed: W/AMs and worth maps (Cockton, 2007, 2008a, 2008d, 2008e; Cockton et al., 2009a, 2009b); UXCs (Cockton, 2009b); and EMS (Cockton, 2008c, 2008e, 2008f).

This was the latest of this chapter's case studies to start. The two that follow began a few years earlier while WCD was still developing, but extend beyond 2013. Vu had the advantage of beginning from a broader and better base for WCD than the other development projects below. He could present WCD as a coherent set of *principles* that guide design *processes* and *approaches* that are grounded in an understanding of the concept of worth. What follows has all been covered in Chapter 4 (Cockton, 2020a) and Chapter 2, but it is worth summarising Vu's independent synthesis of WCD practices.

As noted by Gilmore et al. (2008), value, values, and worth are a complex area with complex semantics. Vu (2013) works with worth as a balance of positives and negatives in experiences and outcomes that accumulate with usage. With Renaud and van Biljon (2010), he understands the limitations of usability, UX, and accessibility processes that focus overly on negatives and can waste time on addressing negatives that have no significant impact on the balance of actual worth. With Renaud and van Biljon (2010), Vu focused on wants and needs first and deals with usage problems as they become relevant. Artefacts have to be *useworthy* and not just usable, indeed quality in use is only a concern once intended worth is compromised as a result.

Vu understood the need for a separate design purpose arena to ensure that there is a focus on worth as well as on a_tefacts, anyficiaries, and evaluation, and that values for design purpose are not high status, abstract ethics, wisdom, etiquette, or otherwise dependent on the approval of others. Purpose (as intended worth) provides "happy endings" as a unifying target for design that will be achieved to some extent through interaction, and evaluated in the world, not in a design specification or usability lab.

In WCD, process is secondary to principles. Vu reviewed the WCD principles (Cockton, 2008a; later *Meta-Principles for Designing*; Cockton, 2009a) which the approaches that drive them forward should instantiate. Given an ADS for a design paradigm, the principle of committedness requires due commitment to all of its design arenas and forms of connection. For each design arena, receptiveness, expressivity, and credibility, respectively, require an openness to alternatives, appropriate recording and communicating, and arena specific criteria such as feasibility, generosity, validity, and relevance. Connections also need to be well expressed. Inclusivity requires sufficient stakeholders as net beneficiaries in terms of outcomes and experience. Sustainability and accessibility are covered by Inclusivity. Improvability requires evaluation to be focused on achieved worth, with approaches that can identify causes of inadequate worth and the capacity to respond creatively with effective design changes.

With these principles in focus Vu updated the VCD process (Cockton, 2005) to use WCD terms, resulting in four practices for design episodes (logical processes): worth identification, worth design, worth evaluation, and worth iteration. Episodes can involve one or more design arenas. Worth identification thus is not wholly focused on purpose via sketches of user and sponsor goals, wants, needs, dreams, and aversions, but can also involve anyficiaries and also antefacts through sketches and prototypes, with either "leading." Both worth design and worth evaluation connect to purpose (by interaction/UX and measures, respectively), and worth iteration often involves all four design arenas as worth issues are understood and addressed relative to purpose, anyficiaries, and a_tefacts (total iteration potential). Most of BIG Design is thus covered in Vu's WCD, despite it not being fully expressed until after his project was well underway (Cockton, 2013a, 2013b). Vu frames his project as Action Research, of which Research through Design can be thought of as a creative form.

In WCD only the approaches that direct activities within episodes can instantiate WCD principles, which are actually meta-principles that are too abstract to apply directly. Instead, design and evaluation approaches instantiate WCD principles in practice. For Vu, worth maps were WCD's core "anchor" approach, connecting human and design sensitivities that are essentially DANs for purpose and antefacts. Vu also used Worth Sketches, UXCs, and EMS (Section 4.1.4). L-ERG-IKK and worth boards were noted but not used, as the existing system to be redesigned had already advanced understandings beyond the point where these could add value.

Vu complemented WCD with two established HCD methods: SUS for evaluation (Brooke, 2013) and informal walkthroughs with users. He began his project with Bipolar Laddering (BLA; Pifarré and Tomico, 2007; Pifarré et al., 2009), which takes a structured approach to covering both positive and negative usage experiences and outcomes. BLA is not focused on usage. It investigates what is best, most important, and useful about a product. These factors are rated and ranked and form the input to a final laddering phase that asks why the factors are important, why these reasons are important and so on.

In his opening BLA activity, two staff from FGU headquarters and four managers from member clubs were interviewed. Most played golf. They used the current system freely and pointed out likes and dislikes and rated them on a five-point scale. Laddering then explored the reasons for their ratings. Ideas for improvement were asked for. Marketing and information documents were collected, along with other relevant artefacts. A system usability scale (SUS) questionnaire was completed, resulting in an average value of 32.1%, almost as low as "the worst imaginable" (25%) in SUS practice (Bangor et al., 2008). All four design arenas were covered by this opening activity.

Only one feature received a positive rating, the ability to export the data to a spreadsheet for external use with other tools, but the three separate exported files and their data quality were problems for HQ staff. All participants found the layout outdated and the navigation confusing. Club managers found checking their information for the annual printed handbook (Kenttäopas) very difficult and hard to verify. Club officials' details were hard to edit, golfers' handicaps were often out of date, and other information on golfers was hard to find. These stakeholders were clearly anyficiaries, and more maleficiary than beneficiary, especially the club managers.

With interviews with four senior FGU staff, this completed the worth identification episode, with far more negatives than positives encountered. The following worth design episode had three phases in response to these negatives. The first addressed layout and navigation. The second addressed flaws in existing functionality. These first two phases could only bring the system up to its threshold acceptability in Kano et al.'s (1984) model by addressing Herzberg's (1966) hygiene factors. The third design phase added new features with the aim of improving the system with performance or even excitement factors in Kano et al.'s (1984) model.

The first design phase used hi-fi prototyping, adding one feature at a time, presenting for comment, and making improvements as appropriate. The correct colour palette and logo were used for the FGU brand, and best practice was followed for primary and secondary navigation, with carefully spaced options and breadcrumbs for context and backtracking. A playback tool (Selenium IDE) was used so that previous users' interactions could be re-used with each new version.

The evaluation at the end of this phase used informal walkthrough and SUS. Users were asked to navigate through the website to different sections (e.g. officials, fees) as they would with the current system. Two participants felt unable to comment on a non-functional prototype, which reduced their SUS scores, but the average score was 70.1%, just edging into an acceptable score (Bangor et al., 2008). As well as evaluating the prototype and suggesting improvements, some further user needs emerged that had not been found by the BLA activity.

A realistic evaluation would need a functioning system, so in the next two worth design phases, Vu worked with the development team (project supervisor, project manager, back end developer, database designer) to create the Verkkotietopalvelu (network information service) system. The focus was on improving search, editing and validation functions.

Vu facilitated an introductory session on WCD for the development team. He then presented the human sensitivities (Purpose DAN, with some anyficiary elements). There were eight for the club managers and caddiemasters, and seven for the HQ staff. These were used in initial brainstorming by the development team when forming design elements (a_tefact DAN) for worth sketching and mapping, adding to those identified during the BLA activity, resulting in 11 elements. These were laid out as a worth sketch, with some worthies coalesced from two or three sensitivities, indicated by item numbers from anyficiary and a_tefact DANs. Most merges were of human sensitivities for the two anyficiary groups, but one defect worthy was marked with a design element and HQ staff sensitivity, and two features were marked with a design element and a club managers' sensitivity. Connection structures for realising worthies were mostly binary but with some ternary.

The worth sketch was laid out with element groups (e.g., defects, features) arranged horizontally to suggest likely MECs vertically. Two worth maps were then formed, one for HQ staff and one for club managers. Both had full positive and negative MECs, with features, qualities and positive experiences and outcomes above materials, and defects and negative experiences and outcomes below materials. These worth maps were used to prepare a full list of features for implementation, with a major focus on improving web form validation. Five validation rules were designed to support this.

Evaluation in the second design phase again used informal walkthrough and SUS. One problem in informal walkthroughs was that participants felt lost and confused when adding officials for a club. Vu followed the WCD tactic of only looking at an interaction in detail when it was causing loss of worth. A UXC was formed to locate problems in the asscociated interaction, and redesign resulted in confident assured interaction. The average SUS score was 83.6%, just on the edge of excellent (Bangor et al., 2008). The negative hygiene factors had been well addressed, but there were few of Kano et al.'s performance or excitement factors in evidence. To quote one evaluation participant:

> *The system is now working as it was supposed to be seven years ago, but we still see no value in this system.*

Usability and quality of implementation are threshold factors in the Kano model. They cannot add value. They are what is expected for a product to creep past the threshold of bare acceptability through a lack of dissatisfiers. Vu's experiences align with Renaud and Biljon's (2010) position that accessibility alone cannot deliver on satisfying performance or outstanding delight factors.

The third design phase aimed higher within the Kano model. New features for golf club managers included: handicap history reports; registration of green cards for golfers who had passed their test at a club; and automatic email reminders to update information for the next guidebook (Kenttäopas), with confirmation of this update to the sender. New features for HQ staff included: improved club memberships' address export and automatic email features. The green card registration could deliver positive benefits as well as removing the negative costs of the previous paper-based system, with details added at HQ. It became possible for club managers to identify golfers who had passed a green card test at their club, but, were not members of their club. Marketing material could then be sent to these golfers. This is an example of generosity, creating unexpected value through design.

Evaluation for the third design phase benefited from remote use and feedback, alongside formal user testing. The test scenarios were piloted in a lab setting at Aalto University with experts, before beginning the full evaluation. SUS was used to assess usability. There was a slight drop from the second phase (83.6% to 82.8%), which could be explained by a simple error margin, or perhaps due to having to learn new features (as opposed to using improved existing ones). Whatever the explanation, the drop is not significant, as SUS questions that focused on future intentions to use were associated with the highest scores (4 or 5).

A simple but very sensible approach to EMS was devised to focus measurement on users' perceived worth for the new features, rather than create a set of objective measures. Users tried out the new features and were asked to provide feedback. Both positive and negative outcomes were considered, e.g., loss of club revenue arising from incorrect contact details in the Kenttäopas guidebook, unfair golf tournaments due to inability to find golfers' information, and low quality of information causing tedious and redundant work. A follow-up email survey contacted ten club caddiemasters with a link to Verkkotietopalvelu and questions asking for their feedback. Of the seven who responded, four felt that the new features were valuable as they helped them to do their jobs faster, two found them worthwhile but asked for further functionality (specific search and reporting capabilities) and one felt that two competitor systems were still better.

Overall, many of the problems and missed opportunities identified during the BLA study had been resolved. Vu concluded that the "WCD framework was totally applicable for Verkkotietopalvelu information system design." As argued in the early years of VCD (Cockton, 2004a) and WCD (Cockton, 2006), valuable capabilities make more of a difference than quality in use, but this needs a multidisciplinary team whose respected backgrounds in design, implementation, and management create important synergies for working faster and better. For Vu, a WCD role is needed to keep "the team constantly updated and focused on the worthwhile outcomes and at the same time keep all the design elements technically feasible throughout the design and development stage of the information system." This is a clear example of Takeuchi and Nonaka's (1986) *multi-learning* factor that is absent from much documented advocated agile practice.

For Takeuchi and Nonaka's other factors, no *built-in instability* arose because the tutorial "waterfall" version of WCD (Cockton, 2008a) was followed. Its episodes of *overlapping development* phases caused no problems. A *self-organizing* team benefitted from *organizational transfer of learning* in both directions between Vu (WCD, HCD, Usability) and the FGU (business knowledge and strategy, operational knowledge and difficulties, aspirations). Communication between stakeholders appeared to be very direct and forthright, with no need for any *subtle management control*.

Most participants "unanimously agreed that the new features not only made their working life easier but also brought benefits to their organizations (e.g. golf club and golf union)," i.e., there were now more beneficiary than maleficiary, as at the start of this project. The system was now "easy to learn and usable on first try." There were still new features to implement after the third design phase, beyond the end of Vu's Master's project. The worth maps had supported a roadmap for future development (a backlog in agile terms) with features including "event calendar for creating golf events and making such events' information available to every other golf clubs in Finland, single sign-on for service/tee-time payment, tee-time booking" (Vu, 2013) with "many other features are also being planned and designed." WCD had provided a framework for identifying "the right amount of features and at the same time keeping them simple and usable" as "the right formula of creating a worthy product."

Vu felt slowed down as he and the project team were new to WCD and needed learning resources. His main difficulties were with EMS, for which limited support existed in the WCD and Lean UX literature at the time. However, he acknowledged a need to improve WCD by putting it into further realistic use by practitioners who need to "simplify the used terminology, the process, and the tools (i.e., worth map, UEF), making it more comprehensible to commoners or those whose domain is not in HCI or psychology, e.g., programmers, customers, product owners, or any stakeholders in general."

Vu's project with the FGU is very encouraging, since it demonstrated that a capable Master's student with appropriate collaboration and support could implement a WCD process from worth identification through worth design and worth evaluation to worth iteration, with each episode addressing a different framing of design arenas.

6.1.3   THE ARROWS FRAMEWORK

ARROWS (Camara and Calvary, 2017), the result of several projects (Camara, 2012; Camara et al., 2013a; Camara and Calvary, 2015, 2017), is a support programme for the core concepts in the ARROW framework (hence ARROW-S), which uses worth maps as snapshots: materials and features and related MECs are as currently implemented, i.e., for artefacts not antefacts. The framework began as PEW (Perceived and Expected Worth; Camara et al., 2013a) but became ARROW (Appreciations, Requirements, and Rationale of Worth; Camara and Calvary, 2015). Hardware and software components (materials) are located along the middle of a worth sketch or map. Actual appreciated positive associations between design and human elements are in the upper half, and negative MECs that expose unmet requirements in the lower one.

The ARROWS programme originates in Camara's (2012) Ph.D., where she aimed to completely operationalise WCD (Cockton, 2008a), developing Cocoon, an adaptive mobile information system. Cocoon was a context-sensitive recommender system that exploited a social network to present relevant personal and public information (and not solely the latter, as in most prior recommender systems). A broad view of context was envisaged, augmenting locations with current physical and social contexts, as well as knowledge of individuals' family and social life (Camara et al., 2010).

Cocoon's design was guided by the same WCD framework, principles, and process as Vu's FGU system (Cockton, 2008a). The VCD process (Cockton, 2005) was followed, beginning with opportunity identification via secondary literature on mobile services and quality of life, combined with a competitor analysis of existing services. This was a sensible addition to the VCD framework's opportunity identification through "personas within usage contexts" (Cockton, 2005), which was narrowly focused on users. A further sensible addition, more in keeping with the concurrent development of 'worthies' (human and design sensitivities) in (Cockton, 2008a), was carrying the competitor analysis and secondary research through to "the vision of Cocoon, a mobile application that automatically provides the user with different types of information in context" (Camara and Calvary, 2015). Personal information would be related to contacts. Capabilities were envisaged via 16 scenarios of use with a Cocoon antefact, illustrated as storyboards, with similar content to WoDS (Section 4.5). These storyboards laddered from "what" (envisaged features for Cocoon), via "how" (interaction with it) to "why" (motivations for using it). MEC elements in the storyboard (Camara et al., 2013a) included contextual information push (features), discovery of new places and stories (consequences), and maintaining ties with family and friends (outcomes). The storyboards were concourses that connected human and design sensitivities (Cockton, 2008a)

Semi-structured interviews were used to better ground six of the storyboards' human and design elements. There were 10 participants each from 2 cities in different French regions, with ages ranging from 21–84. Nine were students and 8 were managers (Camara et al., 2010). All interview participants were experienced mobile phone users and mostly regular users of social media.

Each interview began with a welcome. The study and its objectives were then explained. The interviewer then asked each participant about their mobile phone usage. There was a specific focus on use of social networks and tools on mobile devices, as well as memories and their management, especially the role of digital tools in communications with close friends and family.

The six storyboards and their backstories were then shared one by one with participants, who were asked to give their initial impressions, and then their motivations to use, buy or recommend an app like Cocoon. Once they were prompted to consider reasons to buy, learn, use, or recommend, participants could share both positive examples of perceived worth (motivators) and negative ones (demotivators). Such specific prompts elicited more than an open question on worth (Camara and Calvary, 2015). They are "the simplest 'hook' for designers" provided in Cockton (2006), again showing the value of being specific about worth and purpose.

Participants grounded their perceived outcomes in likely use of Cocoon, and directly valued its features (such as a pico-projector) as much as the illustrated consequences and outcomes that they made possible. This multi-dimensional nature of worth (Camara et al., 2013a) justifies calling all MEC elements "worthies." Enablers of worth can be valued as much as worthwhile outcomes that are witnessed in people, places, and things. This is consistent with doubts about the hierarchy of HVMs and unidirectionality in MECs (e.g., van Rekom and Wierenga, 2007).

The interview ended with a collection of demographic information. Two approaches were used to map interview data to sensitivities for worth mapping (Camara et al., 2010). A card sort was used to manually group identified MEC elements in the storyboads. Text analysis software was also used, with results very similar to those from the card sort. PEW's distinctions between *perceived* and *expected* value were apparent at this point, with respondents raising concerns as well as appreciating Cocoon in use. Expected worth included avoidance of adverse usage through detailed user controls for protection of privacy. Potential features and qualities were proposed to address defects and negative experiences and outcomes, as well as other features and qualities that were not (clearly) present in the storyboards.

The text analysis software created a hierarchy of groups, with a very abstract highest level. As argued (Section 2.1.2), abstract values are unsuitable for connecting between purpose and other design arenas. For example, the text analysis generalised from valuable (personal and family) memories to neutral "cognition," losing all useful connotations. Values were thus framed at an appropriate lower level of abstraction and grouped into four "universes of worth" (Camara and Calvary, 2015). These became a basis for both later evaluations of prototypes and a design strategy.

While 12 participants gave positive reviews to the Cocoon storyboards, 5 gave mixed reviews, 2 would not give one, and another didn't know if he was ready to use such a system. Quantitative data was used to scope the artefact and beneficiaries: identifying the most "voted" features; limiting hardware to mobile devices with small displays, and interaction to touch; and reducing target beneficiaries to adults and young users (Camara and Calvary, 2015). In publications after 2010, data for only 19 participants was presented as an elderly user was scoped out.

Creative vision and storyboarding had created an initial set of human and design sensitivities. Some were removed and others were added following the interview responses. These worthies needed to be connected into a worth map, but a choice had to be made from the spread of published MEC structures (Cockton, 2007, 2008a; Cockton et al., 2009a). Decisions on an appropriate set of elements were made in collaboration with design and development experts from the R&D lab of a large telecommunications company: a project manager, an IxD/UI specialist, a psychologist, a graphic designer, and a software engineer. All had worked together in agile development teams.

Before discussing possible content and structure for MECs, each expert was asked about their role in development work, the resources that were used to communicate design work, and goals set for evaluation work. Expert feedback was then sought on the PEW MEC template, which was called a "canevas" in French (Camara, 2012), translated to "canvas" in Camera et al.'s papers in English. The template showed a generic MEC structure as a chain of single elements for each type (e.g., features, qualities). The template had a simple linear positive MEC running up from hardware and software components, and a negative one running down from them. This provided a basis for understanding an example worth map, which was revised collaboratively with each expert (Camara et al., 2013a).

These activities made it possible to assess the experts' comprehension of worth maps and the initial PEW framework The applicability of the framework was discussed, along with the experts' interest in worth maps. Expert feedback led to minor changes to the framework, focused on form rather than MEC content. All the experts could see value in worth maps. The software engineer, graphic designer, and IxD/UI specialist were attracted by the qualities and defects in the worth map, which could provide useful direction for non-functional requirements and IxD work. All felt that worth maps gave an overview of a system that was suitable for multidisciplinary teams. In particular, the software engineer appreciated how worth maps convey what matters to users, giving "meaning to his work" (Camara et al., 2013a). Interactive (deliberative) use of worth maps was suggested. Re-use of existing human sensitivities in worth maps for future projects was also proposed. Worth maps thus support designs in several ways (Camara and Calvary, 2015), as would be expected from the multiple potential functions associated with most design and evaluation resources (Cockton, 2013b).

One difficulty that arose was that, to understand some connections, user interview data had to be revisited to see how users had made connections when responding to the storyboards. This led to a suggestion that users participate in worth mapping (Camara and Calvary, 2015). An alternative approach would have been to create UXCs when writing each scenario and revising these to align with participants' responses during interviews about the storyboards of the scenarios.

Identification of design purpose elements thus need not be labour intensive, but construction and revision of the worth maps using Microsoft PowerPoint was tedious and time consuming (Camara and Calvary, 2015), just as it had been for the Family Archive (Cockton et al., 2009a). WCD would benefit from an integrated set of tools.

The worth maps supported creation of wireframes and workflows using the Axure tool, which were evaluated in one-hour testing sessions with 11 participants. This Cocoon antefact was easy to learn and use, and thus a Cocoon artefact was implemented as an instrumented Android widget (Camara and Calvary, 2015). Instrumentation recorded low-level usage rather than the outcomes favoured for DWI (Sections 4.1.3 and 4.4.3; Figure 4.10). Cocoon's instrumentation was part of an evaluation strategy that included a field study, SUS questionnaires, and group feedback interviews.

For the field trial, five groups of three people who knew each other were recruited (they were mostly friends). After one week of use, participants were asked to complete a SUS questionnaire.

At the end of the field trial, the groups were interviewed. The data collected was used to build a new worth map based on actual usage. This new worth map, showing appreciated (achieved) and requested (missing) worth was compared to the initial worth map that had guided design of Cocoon. Forming this second worth map created an implicit EMS through judgements about the achievement of worthies.

Comparing two worth maps without support from a software tools was difficult, but nevertheless supported evaluation based on the judgements in Cockton (2005) as to whether a design *donates* unexpected positive value, *delivers* on intended value, or *degrades* or even *destroys* it. The judgement was that Cocoon almost delivered on its intended (appreciated) value, with no requested value in the evaluation worth map, but with some unexpected positive outcomes. For example, Cocoon spurred users into photosharing in ways that had not been anticipated. Any donation of expected value here is from the users, not the design team, and could be thought of as a simple form of appropriation.

All possible aversions identified in the storyboard discussions were avoided, even though requested control capabilities were not used. Three of four universes of value were delivered on, but the fourth (strong emotions and feelings) was not in evidence, probably because the groups lacked deep social ties or the relatively short usage period, which may also explain the lack of use of control capabilities.

In group interviews, participants appreciated learning about their contacts and places where they used their phones. They liked the clear split between personal and public information, the information push feature, adaptation to context, and enjoyable threads of shared images and texts. As in the storyboard interviews, both features and outcomes were appreciated, as would be expected given the true bidirectional nature of MECs (van Rekom and Wierenga, 2007). As with Vu (2013) evaluation was based on perceived worth, but with doubts expressed as to whether an EMS (Section 4.1.4) can cover all worthies. Some may not be possible to measure (Camara and Calvary, 2015).

Both Cocoon's design and evaluation had made good use of the worth concept's twin focus on positives and negatives (appreciated and requested worth in the ARROW framework). WCD principles supported a "mind-state" (Camara and Calvary, 2015) that was supported by resources' functions that focused design work on the standards set by WCD principles (Cockton, 2008a). WCD had been completely operationalised from inception, unlike Vu's FGU case study, which began with an existing system. An abstract MEC template (canevas) had been developed for tutorial purposes, with actual MECs in worth maps having the same structure as in (Vu, 2013) and (Cockton, 2008a). A novel approach to worth evaluation had been developed, based on comparing worth maps. All MEC elements could be valued by users, and not just experiences and outcomes.

Cocoon's two final worth maps were followed by four more for other systems. Camara worked with different teams of colleagues and developed two worth maps for worth identification for Colibri, an Advanced Planning System (Camara et al., 2013b), and one for worth evaluation of the FutureID system. A sixth worth map was reverse engineered for the Lyric central heating controller (Camara and Calvary, 2017), which could be compared with a worth map for an older controller in Cockton (2008a). The main use for the Lyric worth map was to disseminate and promote worth mapping. Worth maps had proven to be effective across three projects and Camara and Calvary wanted to encourage their use as an interesting tool for both product roadmaps and customer communications (as in VALU project). Explicit connections had proven their value, with further benefits from worth map's support for heterogeneous design teams.

Experiences with Colibri and FutureID led to an important development for worth mapping, with a new type of MEC element. A system "as a whole" is added as a feature, with a nested UI element which is also regarded "as a sub-feature of each feature" (Camara and Calvary, 2017). Making the whole a part is less illicit than may initially appear. In Assemblage Theory (de Landa, 2006), "the whole itself is a product, produced as nothing more than a part alongside other parts." Thinking of wholes as parts, even though very counterintuitive, brings several advantages in Assemblage Theory that can overcome longstanding systems theory problems associated with ambiguous boundaries around and between systems and their environments. The addition of the whole system as a part makes important connections possible while avoiding a proliferation of connections from individual features and qualities.

The Lyric worth map made good use of this new capability via three example MECs. This was one form of additional support for ARROWS, following its development from the PEW framework. ARROW Support provides a systematic approach to worth mapping. ARROWS provides definitions and additional knowledge on the elements in standard ARROW template that combines positive and negative MECs for appreciated and requested worth respectively. The additional knowledge includes guidance on four overlapping types of qualities and how to distinguish between them, and how much direct practical evaluation of qualities is realistically possible. There is guidance on practical approaches to evaluation, with example valuable outcomes expressed at a level that allows measurement. Anticipated and past value should be considered.

Given the multi-dimensional nature of worth (Camara and Calvary, 2015), any MEC element may be valued or disappoint. Thus, complete MECs from materials to outcomes need not be considered, but can be. The two complete forms of MECs create two chains, one resulting in appreciated worth and one giving rise to requested worth. The other four MECS considered in ARROWS are shorter, omitting either outcomes or qualities. The former supports a focus on UX where this is key to product quality. The latter supports a focus on instrumental use where outstanding UX is not critical to product success, or when a quality is a threshold factor in the Kano model and it must be assumed that materials and features combine to achieve it (e.g., accuracy in a thermostat). Together, these can simplify worth maps when it is judged to be appropriate. ARROWS also recommends a range of modularization approaches as another approach to making worth maps manageable.

The ARROWS framework was assessed in a workshop. The participants were a diverse ensemble of research project manager, innovative service designer, two human factors specialists, communications services architect, and psychologist. The first three were in one group and the rest in another. The workshop began with creative tasks using Lego building blocks, ending with making an ideal thermostat. Each group discussed what they had made. Two videos on the Lyric controller were shown, followed by an introduction to ARROWS and then the worth map. Questions were encouraged. Posters of other worth maps were then viewed. The workshop ended with a questionnaire that requested individual information, assessed the understandability and benefits of ARROWS and worth maps, and explored the Lego exercises.

The participants were "multilearners" in Takeuchi and Nonaka's (1986) terms, with expertise on design elements and a good understanding of human-oriented elements or vice versa. All five who defined worth maps did so accurately. While the communications services architect did not provide a definition, his perceived benefits indicated an accurate understanding. All but one participant saw worth maps as providing good support for opportunity identification, studies of needs and evaluation. The project manager saw them as a suitable tracking tool in agile development, replicating results in Camara et al. (2013a).

6.2   BIG WO-FO FOR MY CARE CIRCLE

This group is a single case study, the first combination of Wo-Fo and BIG approaches (George, 2016) in a research through design Ph.D. on supporting care circles of children with major communication difficulties. Much of the tracking framework in Chapter 5 (Cockton, 2020a) was developed here. George began using the VCD framework (Cockton, 2005), supported by me as her primary Ph.D. supervisor, but moved steadily from a worth-centred to a Wo-Fo approach, guided by BIG principles and W2C concepts. BIG Wo-Fo and George's research co-evolved, with the value of the former's resources demonstrated by the ability to apply evolving versions of them in an iterative approach to reflection and retrospective. George's research complemented worth maps with several important new Wo-Fo approaches, as well as using some proposed ones in practice for the first time. Resources used in the research can be found at resourcesbyjennifergeorge.wordpress.com/.

George's research through design coalesced into seven episodes of research, design, development, and evaluation. She did not name these episodes, but they can be framed as: (1) secondary contextual research; (2) first conjecture and exploration; (3) second conjecture and exploration; (4) uncertainty reduction; (5) design and implementation; (6) formative evaluation; and (7) summative evaluation. Superficially, this may look like a RILED process, but her tracking using MADS, PADS, DAFs, and DANs clearly demonstrates that each episode never just focused on a single design arena.

In her first research episode, George studied secondary sources on disability, assistive technologies, and disability assessment. This gathered information on accessibility, disabled anyficiaries, available assistive artefacts, World Health Organisation policy on disability as a guide for design purpose, and frameworks for evaluating the suitability of assistive technologies. As with all unconstrained project inceptions, all four design arenas came immediately into play, with three DANS having two entries (George used the first name for DANs, which was Design Arena Progress Lists).

This wide-ranging contextual research informed her first conjecture, that a decision support system (DSS) could be designed to support care circles in the choice and use of assistive technologies. George's teaching at the time included DSS, so her conjecture is consistent with how personal knowledge and experience is brought to bear in creative design practice. Her second episode of primary research focused on the assessment that supports the choice of assistive technologies for children with extensive communication impairment. The aim was to inform the design of a DSS. Through observation, formal and opportunistic interviews, and autobiographical reflection on a care circle known to her, George added 14 relevant insights about beneficiaries, 4 on purpose, 22 on artefacts, and 1 on evaluation (respective cumulative totals at end of second episode: 15, 6, 24, 3). The episode name (first conjecture and exploration) reflects the mix of findings with the majority (22 out of 41) related to the antefact.

At the end of this second episode, George explored connections between design arenas using a Worth Integration Table (WIT; Section 4.3.1), rather than a worth sketch or worth map. There were columns for artefact capability, beneficiary group, positive benefits, negative risks, and the source activity for the row entries (using numbers as in Cockton, 2020a, Figure 5.4). A MADS was formed for the episode, in addition to the WIT, DANs, and DAFs. There were also PADS for the anticipated and actual "findings" of each activity. The MADS (Cockton, 2020a, Figure 5.1, left, using artefact where antefact would now be used) was very revealing, with the generator for this episode focused on the artefact (first WIT column), with connections from beneficiaries and purpose (other WIT columns). Having an antefact in focus resulted in immediate implications for design (as possible capabilities and their worth) and downstream utility (through reframing the artefact).

The WIT-directed reframing of all four design arenas for the next episode. George used Iteration Shift Tables to contrast DAFs at the start of a design research episode with the DAFs at the end. Each table thus contained eight DAFs, two for each design arena, one for the start, and one for the end of the episode. The DAF for the artefact changed from a DSS to a social network with information resources. The DAF for beneficiaries was reframed from a child's family to a broader care circle. The evaluation DAF shifted from having no specific framing (but with two options from the first episode) to an explicit rejection of a DSS. The purpose DAF changed from supporting selection and use of assistive technologies to a much broader Wo-Fo, with both positive and adverse outcomes in focus (as in the WIT).

The WIT allowed rapid exploration of possible positive and negative MECs, with the table's rows providing a focus on potential MECs originating from an artefact capability. A WIT is a good precursor to a worth sketch or map. A WIT can focus on a set of MECs, whereas a worth sketch is a resource for broad consideration of possible MECs. The effectiveness of this WIT here was seen in the extensive reframings for the next episode. Doubts on the viability of a DSS had grown during the four research activities, but the WIT made it clear that a new conjecture was needed, and the Iteration Shift Tables framed the necessary shift here.

The third episode combined secondary and primary research with evaluation. The first activity extended the contextual review from the first episode to review communication and information sharing in sociotechnical systems. This added one insight to the beneficiaries DAN, two to purpose, and seven to the artefact. Two primary research activities added two further beneficiary insights, three additions to design purpose, and three more options for the artefact. As in the previous episode, a BIG process was in evidence through a mix of design arenas, reflecting on possible connections, and being open to a wide range of potential design purpose. There was no exclusive RILED focus on "understanding the problem." The episode ended by applying the CAT model (an evaluation option from the first episode) to two existing open social networking platforms, but neither could be materials for an envisaged artefact due to shortcomings on accessibility (George et al., 2010). Three further artefact options were added by this activity, and two notes to the evaluation DAN.

The fourth episode focused on uncertainty reduction across all four design arenas. In a first worth sketch, only some DAN items for artefact and purpose had corresponding elements. This used to initiate a second WIT to include all the additions to DANs from the third episode. This WIT was then re-expressed as twinned Artefact-Connection Tables. Purpose elements were in the left column and artefact options in the right. The first table was similar to a feature-benefit one (Section 4.2), but the second was a *feature-aversion* one. Artefact-Connection Tables thus pair to cover worth. Also, three Worth Shift Tables were drawn up for high, medium, and low levels of implementation priority. The left column expressed a current circumstance and the right an ideal one to indicate how "existing circumstances" would change "into preferred ones" (Simon, 1969).

The six tables exposed gaps and shortfalls in knowledge (missing or inadequate items in DANs). The Worth Shift Tables provided the best focus for identifying gaps and shortcomings in information and ideas. They were concourses due to their open textual nature, letting this episode's novel questionnaire investigate all the design arenas but focusing especially on worth. The worth sketch was returned to after completing the six tables. A second version was more comprehensive, but still with fewer detailed design (artefact) elements than the tables. It served as a single visual overview of the six tables. Proceeding to a worth map would have been wasteful, as the worth sketch was based on incomplete or poorly supported information.

This fourth episode had similar objectives to an MVP experiment (Section 4.5; Figure 4.17), but with no prototype. Instead, the first activity designed a questionnaire to address gaps and shortfalls in DANs. A second activity piloted the questionnaire and led to some revisions. The third activity analysed the results of the questionnaire, with a generator focused on evaluation. This episode could not be modelled by a single MADS. The MADS for the questionnaire design activity was identical to the one for the first episode (centred on artefact, connections from beneficiaries and purpose). The second had a complex MADS with grafts and a loop (Cockton, 2020a, Figure 5.1, centre), with both beneficiaries and evaluation as the generators for this activity. The third was similar to the second, but with evaluation as the sole generator and an additional connection from beneficiaries to evaluation. The MADS for the Assumption Checking Questionnaire in Figure 4.7 merged these three MADS into a ternary connection that omitted some detail. George's (2016) original MADS are of interest because they were the first to combined grafts, loops and multiple activity generators, exposing complexity beyond that in the initial analysis of ADS structures (Cockton, 2010).

As well as improving the evidence for several items in DANs, the questionnaire filled gaps, adding four notes on beneficiaries, three on purpose, eight on the artefact, and one on evaluation. Given the six prior primary and reflective research activities, this was a high yield that proved the value of critical integrative reflection. The questionnaire had not just focused on beneficiaries. It also had questions that collected information on acceptable artefact features and usage, and the attractiveness of the proposed design purpose.

Each item in the questionnaire aimed to collect information that would fill gaps or improve evidence. Implications for the envisaged artefact were expressed as traffic lights against the results for each question. Most were green, but a few ambers indicated a need for caution. On balance, there was evidence that the development of the envisaged artefact could proceed, and a fifth design and implementation episode began. The system was named *My Care Circle*.

The envisaged artefact was to be implemented as a website by a developer on a part-time basis, so further supporting documentation was prepared (a third version of the worth sketch had been prepared at the end of the fourth episode). The first activity in the fifth episode developed three worth-oriented personas (Section 4.5). There were a few "creative narrative additions" to improve the scenario elements in the personas, but otherwise these were explicitly grounded in contextual research from the previous four design research episodes. The second activity prepared task specifications were for walkthroughs in development, along with a requirements specification. As with the personas, these were explicitly grounded in previous research. A third activity creatively explored visual attributes for the user interface, with the results passed onto the developer. A social media questionnaire explored colour, shape, and image associations for care, and also asked for "creative or crazy ideas that you would use to describe care."

The final fourth activity implemented My Care Circle. There were no changes to DANs or connections during this episode. Its MADS did not explicitly involve the evaluation arena, but feedback to the developer was provided twice. The artefact was the episode generator, with connections from beneficiaries and purpose expressed through personas, task specifications and requirements. A loop on the artefact indicated the transformation from a specification to a working artefact. A graft from evaluation to this loop could be added to include the feedback to the developer.

The sixth episode was focused on formative evaluation in preparation for a field trial of My Care Circle. The first activity was a Cognitive Walkthrough using the three personas, with its results added to the evaluation DAN, which also happened with the next activity, Heuristic Evaluation. Change requests were forwarded to the developer. This was followed by a third activity with the revised website, user testing with think aloud, which as well as providing further feedback on My Care Circle (as three change requests), also gathered a further insight on a beneficiary group, and another element for design purpose.

A fourth final activity demonstrated My Care Circle in a different setting to the ones used for primary research in previous episodes. The setting was a school for children with behavioural rather than physical challenges. There was a positive response to the demonstration and there were suggestions for another feature, as well as a further insight each on beneficiaries and purpose. In the MADS for this episode, the generator is evaluation. Nine additions were made overall to the other three design arenas, demonstrating that the fan out from evaluation in ISO-9241 is not a choice of what to do next, but a concurrent set of connections from evaluation to other design arenas, as in Figure 4.20.

Further changes were made as a result of the four formative evaluation activities in the sixth episode, resulting in My Care Circle version 2, which was completed for the start of the seventh formal evaluation episode. After this, the information resources for My Care Circle 2 were added in collaboration with a health professional. There were no changes to DANs as a result of this activity, but connections were improved by drawing up a Worth Element Measurement table, which provided the EMS (Section 4.1.4) for the next activity. This is the most complete example of an EMS, and access to it may have helped with Vu's (2013) FGU and Camara et al.'s (2013a) Cocoon systems.

The second activity was independent use by one disabled participant, whose use added five new insights to the beneficiaries design arena. The third activity was another demonstration, to the special school that had supported primary research in the second and third episodes. Staff at the school were very supportive. They added a further insight to the beneficiaries design arena and suggested some online channels for recruiting independent users.

For the fourth activity in the seventh episode, independent use by care circles, the amber warnings from the questionnaire unfortunately manifested themselves as limited motivation to engage with a system that would probably not endure beyond the Ph.D. research. Most prospective independent users would not invest time in My Care Circle 2 due to concerns about wasting effort setting up an online care circle with no guarantee that support would continue. Partnerships in social innovation have rightly become more challenging over the last decade, so future work in this area needs to pay attention to "channels," a long-standing practice in commercial innovation approaches such as the Business Model Canvas (Osterwalder and Pigneur, 2010).

Six individuals for two care circles agreed to participate, but use quickly tailed off, with carers other than the legal guardian not making time to engage. Even so, one care circle did ask each other a question related to assistive technology, which did shows support can be obtained from a broader care circle. This added two further insights to the artefact design arena. Overall, the six and seventh evaluation episodes added eight insights to the beneficiaries arena and three to purpose, with six options added to the artefact arena, as well as three sets of evaluation results. The MADS for the final episode had evaluation as its generator with all three other arenas progressed. This further demonstrates the balanced nature of the My Care Circle episodes, which never once focused on a single design arena across the whole of this research through design project.

Even with the limited evaluation data, including feedback from two demonstrations, it was possible to make use of the EMS planned at the start of the episode. Adverse outcomes have been reduced from 10 to 6, which includes addition of a new risk arising from potential problems with peer support. One could not be assessed as there was insufficient usage, and no evidence was available for another. This reduction increased worthwhile outcomes from 11 to 14. The net increase was 3, with 4 added and 2 merged. There was (partial) evidence for half of the positive outcomes. Four could not be assessed as there was insufficient usage. One intended positive outcome was "requested worth" in ARROWS (Camara and Calvary, 2017), i.e., it was intended but had not been delivered. A final fourth worth sketch showed the outcome of EMS, as in ARROWS, a snapshot of the worth of My Care Circle 2 as it has been used, rather than how it had been intended to deliver worth.

In addition, new features for My Care Circle 3 were identified, including the following: legal primary carer control of access and privilege features for individuals and groups in their care circle; alert feature for emergencies to inform a care circle that someone looking for advice or support; support for recruiting care circle members; and a sponsor to reassure care circles about the system's longevity.

6.3   BIG WO-FO IN EDUCATION AND PROFESSIONAL DEVELOPMENT

The fifth group of case studies is a set of anecdotes from postgraduate teaching and continuous professional development. The postgraduate teaching is primarily three one-week design courses that I taught at the Technical University of Eindhoven (TU/e) in 2015 (Master's students), 2016 and 2017 (both Professional Doctorate students). The 2016 cohort were at the start of live collaborative projects on operational systems and early stage products. The 2015 and 2017 cohorts worked on a one-week sprint on an open brief to design a support system for TU/e students.

The course title was Balanced Interaction Design and Evaluation. In the 2017 version, the course began on a Monday with introductions and an inception exercise as in Section 3.1.6 brief (Cockton, 2020a), followed by brainwriting followed by sorting into a Design Arena Canvas. The afternoon began with a formal teaching session on MADS modelling of design paradigms and re-search into creative design (covering Sections 4.2, 2.1, 2.2, Book 1 (Cockton, 2020a)). The students then worked in groups on the brief. On Tuesday, teaching began with a lecture on worth (Chapter 2 apart from Sections 2.1 and 4.3), followed by a brief presentation on Lean UX (Section 4.5), connections (Chapter 4), and then coverage of approaches, resources, and functions (Section 2.1). There were practical exercises in between the lectures. By the end of Tuesday, the students had covered Design Arenas, creative inception, DANs, MADS, PADS, Lean UX, UXCs, worth maps, and other Wo-Fo approaches. These were sequenced in a forced inception process, after which groups progressed their work independently (Cockton, 2020a, Figure 5.7). The remainder of the week was taken up with studio-based work, field research and prototyping, presentations and critiques, and some further teaching on Wednesday on W2C (Section 3.3), agile, tracking, and reflection (Cockton, 2020a, Chapter 5). There were daily presentations and critiques on the Wednesday, Thursday, and Friday (final). Each student wrote a reflective document. Groups shared and tracked their work using blogs and/or shared file storage.

Previous versions of the course in 2016 and 2015 covered similar ground, but with less formal tracking. In 2015, only an early version of PADS was used. In 2016, PADS and DANs were used. The Wo-Fo material was largely unchanged across the three years and was similar to a three-week final year course at Reykjavik University in 2014. This course was taught for a half day each day, and so had 50% more contact time than the TU/e course. A similar design brief to the TU/e 2015 and 2017 courses was used. Presentations, critiques, studio work, and preparation for assessment took up much of the last week, so the formal lecture content only just exceeded that at TU/e. There was more formal teaching on evaluation at Reykjavik and in 2015 at TU/e than in 2016 and 2017.

In all four university courses, students worked effectively on design arenas concurrently as self-organising teams. All were surprised by the effectiveness of brainwriting as an approach to idea and information gathering. In 2016 and 2017, design arena canvases were also used, establishing a baseline for a response to the brief by Monday (2017) or Tuesday (2016) lunchtime (in 2016 much of the Monday was taken up with presentations by project sponsors). Groups that developed early prototypes found these to be more effective for user research than mainstream approaches such as interviews. PADS proved to be effective for end of day reflection and planning the next day's work. Most presentations in 2016 and 2017 grounded their planning in PADS.

Students' practical work shows the adaptability of BIG Wo-Fo approaches and the speed at which they can be learned and applied with tutor support. BIG Wo-Fo approaches have also been taught at conference courses and tutorials since 2013 at WUD, NordiCHI, and CHI. Courses were a half, three-quarter, or whole day. With between one fifth and one tenth of the course time as TU/e students, and no independent work between sessions, attendees could not reach the same level of competence across several approaches and practices. Even so, there were several examples of strong ideation arising from worth mapping and inception exercises based on design arena canvases. Interestingly, course participants worked more effectively in the half-day courses, with better ideation during inception and worth mapping. Participants on longer courses may have become progressively fatigued over the afternoon.

There are examples of effective use of PADS by the 2016 and 2017 TU/e cohorts in Section 5.5 (Cockton, 2020a). One innovative use of worth maps in evaluation was developed by a group of students in the 2016 cohort. They were starting a collaborative project with the local council, focused on their document management system. With increasing freedom of information requests, efficient and effective use of this system was now very important. The group created two versions of a worth map for the current system. For a third version, they used data from initial user testing to form MECs from artefact elements to negative outcomes through the use of defect and adverse UX elements (Section 4.3.2). This let them identify and explain the features responsible for negative outcomes. They also formed MECs to positive outcomes to show the likely impact of improvements to current problem features. Multiple MECs implicated some features in current negative outcomes and possible future positive ones. This approach was similar to identifying requested worth in ARROWS.

In the 2017 cohort, one group found a quick way to build MECs using post its. Features were stacked in use case order from bottom to top, with qualities interleaved to the right of this stack, and positive outcomes were spread above this stack. This was effectively a sketch of a UXC, with use of the features and experience of qualities in the stack order leading to positive experiences and outcomes. This practice would also support transitions from worth sketches to UXCs and worth maps. It had similarities to the agile story mapping approach (Patten with Economy, 2014), which had already been pointed out in a CHI course by an attendee.

A large gap on a flat work surface could be left between the rows of design elements and outcomes, to leave space for trying out MEC stacks, which would them form the basis for initial MECs and UXCs. This would help to identify and name relevant experiences for the worth map.

Both George (2016) and Camara and colleagues made limited use of experience elements in their worth sketches or maps, and Otero and José (2009) missed them out completely. Experiences and outcomes are fairly similar in George (2016), and Camara and Calvary (2015) have a loose collapsible structure for human-oriented elements in their ARROW framework. Naming UX elements can be difficult. When teaching I encourage the use of a "The one where …" format, as in many episode titles for *Friends* TV programmes.

One student from the 2015 cohort later extended worth maps from single projects to identify new business opportunities for a digital artist whom she has been mentoring. These worth maps go beyond project outcomes to link to new opportunities for sharing project experiences in workshop and course settings.

The first conference course where I taught worth mapping was WUD 2013 in Tallinn. During this course and another half day course at NordiCHI 2014, groups quickly generated a stream of innovative ideas for a van hire service with a web-based touchpoint (as in Figure 4.1). In the longer courses from 2016, a few participants had difficulties understanding the different types of worthies, whereas the pace in the shorter courses may have led participants to try first and ask later. An exception to this was a half day course at the University of Jyväskylä, taught in a tiered lecture theatre with limited flat working space and some external changes to the schedule. Despite this, some MECs were formed in less than ideal circumstances.

The longer courses most probably gave a better indication of actual initial understanding and is consistent with Vu's and the ARROWS experience, as well as the Chapter 5 case studies where considerable time was spent on developing understanding of MEC elements in practical contexts.

The conference courses had similar content to the TU/e course, but with less detail and some omission. Positive feedback from participants the four CHI courses included:

- direct applicability to their work, "new approach for old problems," connecting to own work practices, such as Story Mapping (Patton with Economy, 2014);

- the opportunity to reflect on design paradigms and methodologies, history and past practices, "historic and synthesizing aspects";

- high level of abstraction, "the theory parts," depth of research and ideas covered, "introduction to variety of vocabulary and theories," "inspirational word list";

- the value of co-evolution and balance;

- the ideas of worth and generosity, and other "cool design principles";

- creative inception (brainwriting, design arena canvas);

- the family ("playbook") of Wo-Fo approaches, especially worth sketching and mapping and Wo-Fo design research as practiced in exercises ("exercises were helpful to understand the theories");

- Wo-Fo and BIG in agile settings, need for integration ("design in a bubble doesn't work in an agile world."), "new connections"; and

- sharing relevant experiences in their groups.

The connection to story mapping is interesting, since the 2017 TU/e students found a way to use a story mapping structure for UXCs. There was some negative feedback on content, feeling that "lots of terms and jargons were not explained." This contrasts with two comments above that valued the new vocabulary, but it again reinforces the need for the whole team to understand BIG and Wo-Fo concepts. While many can pick up these quickly and work with them immediately, others need more time and support. The case studies do allow for optimism here, as the projects involving multidisciplinary teams developed a demonstrably effective command of BIG and Wo-Fo practices.

In total, at TU/e, Reykjavik, and Jyväskylä universities, and in 7 conference courses over 7 years, I have taught worth-focused approaches to around 280 students and professionals. I have taught BIG tracking approaches for the last five years, and these are also being used in teaching elsewhere by colleagues. Successful teaching in fast past settings of a half day to a week complements the evidence from project-based case studies that BIG Wo-Fo approaches can be worthwhile.

6.4   WORKING WITH WO-FO AND BIG: INSIGHTS AND OUTCOMES

The case studies in this chapter span a decade. The first groups adopted Wo-Fo approaches, but predated explicit accounts of BIG design. Even so, some BIG practices were effectively followed in some of these case studies (e.g., Vu, 2013). The second and third groups made explicit use of BIG and Wo-Fo approaches, resulting in improved synergies between work on design purpose and work on the other three design arenas. Further important commonalities across case studies are summarised below. We close this chapter with a second survey of insights and outcomes (grouped by realised resource functions).

6.4.1   KNOWING THROUGH CONNECTING

The six cognitively oriented resource functions are in evidence in this chapter's case studies. There is less evidence of ideative functions, but this may be due to gaps in reporting the worth-mapping process for Cocoon (Camara, 2012). However, creation of Cocoon's storyboards involved more ideation than information. For Vu's (2013) FGU system, worth mapping included brainstorming with the development team on the design elements for the worth mapping. For My Care Circle (George, 2016), creative work was associated with user interface design, and with worth sketches used as synthesis tools for reflection following ideative use of Worth Integration and Artefact Connection tables. Ideation also filled gaps in persona narratives for My Care Circle. The TU/e graduate's extension of worth maps to business development is an excellent example of an ideation function in extending the scope of a design approach to mentoring.

Inquisitive functions are rarely in evidence for this chapter, which again may be due to reporting rather than reality, with no details of the dynamics of design workshops. However, for My Care Circle there was a systematic approach to reflective questioning shaping questionnaire items in the third research episode.

The HCD focus for both the age appropriate mobile phone (Renaud and Biljon, 2010) and Cocoon realised many informative functions from user research approaches, sourcing user preferences for features, and (for the phone) usage frequency. For the FGU project, prototype evaluations in the first and second worth design phases added to purpose beyond what had been discovered from bilateral laddering interviews, as well as providing feedback on the prototypes, demonstrating non-binary connections from evaluation to other design arenas.

For integrative functions, the use of table resources such as WITs with concourse structures is interesting. Both the age-appropriate mobile phone and My Care Circle extended error prone feature-benefit tables (Section 4.2) from business practices into effective tools. Tables similar to feature-benefit ones were used to associate features and purpose. For the phone design, one table related used features to fixed sets of needs and wants, and another table related desired features to fixed needs, rather than the random quasi-benefits that are too common in feature-benefit tables. Given the accessible but worthwhile simplicity of the phone design, there was no need for articulated connections as in UXCs or worth maps. Specific purposes could reasonably be connected in a chain to specific features. Selection of purpose elements for consideration was statistical, selected elements directly transfer from anyficiaries to the antefact, where they were realised as buttons.

As with the VALU project in Chapter 5, Renaud and van Biljon spent no time elaborating on logically obvious or otherwise known connections. Connections from anyficiaries to purpose were provided by associating a usage space model with an interface of three basic needs and two broad motivation factors. As usage spaces can be thought of as concourses, the connections here are at best implied. Take such associations for granted allows agile work, although they may be risks with being tacit and uncritical when the reverse is possible without undue effort.

Similarly, George (2016) used a range of novel tables with better structure and content than typical feature-benefit tables. Her WITs related antefact features to both benefits and aversions, and also to the research activity to provide a context for the relation (connecting to an activity rather than a design arena reinforces the concourse structure). WITs are similar in structure to the PEW framework (Camara et al., 2013a). They consider antefacts rather than artefacts, but consider both positives and benefits as required by the concept of worth.

As concourses, George's table formats proved to be more flexible and agile than resources and approaches that require separation of discoveries and options into design arenas. Concourses were implicit in modelling of the Applied Arts design paradigm (Cockton, 2013b), but were only given extensive consideration and formalised during the writing of this book. Looking back, it is clear that WITs, Artefact Connection Tables, and Worth Shift Tables benefitted from their ability to accommodate design insights and options that spanned more than one design arena without explicitly associating insights and options with specific arenas.

George's Artefact Connection tables allowed a single focus on positive or negative outcomes, and her worth shift tables refine these by considering both the present (neutral or negative) and future (positive) to form design goals for an innovative product. With a worth sketch, these three forms of table gave George a range of broad and focused perspectives to guide the design of her novel multi-arena questionnaire. While worth maps may have allowed a more critical approach to connections than worth sketches, George's consideration of an EMS was compensating critical approach that focused on how to evaluate success rather than how to articulate the usage that would lead to it. The role of worth sketches for My Care Circle was to check for gaps in information in conjunction with the tables when designing the questionnaire, rather than as preparatory steps to worth maps. Similarly, the fourth worth sketch guided George's application of EMS. Worth sketches were thus focused on supporting evaluation rather than exposing MECs.

George also showed how co-products of design work, and not just the artefact (as in Gaver, 2011 and Gaver and Bowers, 2012) can be annotated to link between and within arenas. Two resources in her fifth research episode, Personas and the Requirements Specification, were annotated, as were her worth sketches and questionnaire design (fourth episode), and Element Measurement Tables (seventh episode). In each case, annotations make connections explicit and extend resources to span extra design arenas.

Another integrative alternative to worth sketches and maps was the use of storyboards for Cocoon, which like Clarke's (1997) scenarios, were concourse structures. Where worth maps were used, as for the FGU project, worthies could be integrative in addition to the MECs. Seven of Vu's worthies merged two or three positive or negative outcomes from each beneficiary group, and two features and defects were also directly associated with one or both groups. The latter is another example of bidirectionality in HVMs (van Rekom and Wierenga, 2007), where design elements may have immediate valences for beneficiaries, without no articulation in a MEC.

Only Vu's (2013) project and the Family Archive used UXCs. Vu only used one to model a single disappointing MEC with usability problems in his second worth design phase. A worth map was already in place, so the MEC could form the initial spine of the UXC. If no worth map is in place before evaluation, one can be formed, as TU/e students did in 2016 to model defects in the local council's document retrieval system. Articulated connections were made between an artefact and its evaluation, and implicit ones to purpose. Worth maps proved to be a good compact format for recording and expressing initial evaluation results.

Overall, this chapter's case studies add to integrative practices in Chapter 5, where Otero and José (2009) appreciated the benefits of explicit connections. Integration is not only achieved via worth sketches or maps, but also via scenarios, storyboards, EMS, UXCs, and a range of novel tables. The value of connections was first shown in Clarke's LD tool with its very simple connections. The other case studies have shown the value of having a rich range of connections.

BIG practices are most in evidence in George (2016) where a range of *reflective* resources were activated, initially by reflecting on the achievement of meta-principles (Cockton, 2009a) for specific design arenas, then reframing design arenas in between design research episodes, and later developing MADS and PADS as retrospective resources for research reporting. The co-evolution of progression resources for tracking, reflection and planning use reflects creative design practice. Retrospective use is a useful first test of new resources, but use in teaching has confirmed their effectiveness with scores of postgraduate students working on a mix of educational and professional briefs (Cockton, 2020a, Section 5.5).

George's multi-arena questionnaire design required extensive reflection on her first three research episodes. Her use of novel tables and worth maps combined integrative, expressive, and reflective functions to great effect. Expressive functions are in evidence in other case studies above, as would be expected for any resource use. What is more important is the quality of expression. For Vu (2013) worth maps and other WCD approaches proved themselves as a good tool for communicating between the triangle of stakeholders, HCI practitioners and the development team members. Vu "had no issue during the process of worth identification and worth design." This is as much due to Vu's hard work and diligence as it to WCD. He also benefitted from papers by Camara and colleagues, including an important one in French that others may not have been able to read (Camara et al., 2010).

6.4.2   COLLABORATING WITH WORTH SKETCHES AND MAPS

As with projects in Chapter 5, worth maps realised affiliative functions with heterogeneous multidisciplinary teams in VU's FGU project and ARROW case studies. There is no evidence of deliberative functions being activated by worth maps, but as with ideative functions, this may simply be due to gaps reporting. The development of the PEW/ARROW framework however did involve deliberation when developing the MEC template. There is also no evidence in this chapter's case studies of performative functions, as presentations of worth maps, as in the VALU project, are not reported.

6.4.3   CARING WITH WORTH SKETCHES AND MAPS

The concept of worth alone can activate ameliorative functions. For Renaud and van Biljon (2010), it prompted a critique of universal usability, accessibility research, and products for older users that focused on removing negatives with no regard to preserving positives. The other case studies in this chapter also made very effective use of the concept of worth, finding compatible user research methods such as bilateral laddering (Vu, 2013) and developing appropriate resources such as tables and the ARROW framework. Judgements were formed as to whether the priority was to address negatives or positives. Where new forms of artefact were being developed (Cocoon, Colibri, My Care Circle), the balance was toward positives. Where existing systems or products were in focus (FGU, mobile phone for elderly, council document management system), negatives were addressed first.

For Cocoon, the multidisciplinary team found worth maps invigorative, with each member finding support for their work in different elements of MECs. Protective functions are more in evidence in this chapter's case studies. This includes long established practices such a piloting study designs, as in Vu's (2013) pilot of user testing scenarios. Vu also proactively recommended having a WCD role on project teams, but this role could be shared by more than one existing team member, complementing their existing expertise from multilearning (Takeuchi and Nonaka, 1986).

George's (2016) multi-arena questionnaire realised protective functions, but not enough to ensure evaluation by fully engaged care circles. The questionnaire elicited more commitment from professionals (whose work should improve) than from families (whose work would increase). The reasons for this difference were not systematically investigated. It was only during the summative evaluation episode that family members shared their reluctance to a research system that may not remain available.

In relation to ARROWS, a psychologist expressed concern about the time needed to create a worth map manually from scratch, but no design-led project in either this or the previous chapter experienced no such problems. As with many questions of worth, knowing how long is too long depends on a cost-benefit ratio. Also, benefits may extend beyond the project (where project management will invest in the longer term), as with the purpose DAN from the Family Archive, which informed future projects involving family communication. Re-use of worth resources was suggested on the Cocoon project. A roadmap was created for the FGU system beyond Vu's Master's project.

6.4.4   STEERING WITH WORTH SKETCHES AND MAPS

The concept of worth activates both ameliorative and adumbrative functions. It scopes design purpose to include both positives and negatives. It can expand a project's focus beyond negatives that can predominate in accessibility, usability and UX work, as with the accessible mobile phone case study (Renaud and van Biljon, 2010). Worth initially focused Vu (2013) on negatives, but once these were addressed, he and the FGU development team moved onto positives. One of these, the incorporation of green test records into the online system, generated unexpected additional benefits, identifying potential new club members. A similar benefit happened with Cocoon, where users shared photos in ways that had not been anticipated. Any donation of expected value (Cockton, 2005) here is from the users, not the design team, and could be thought of as a simple form of appropriation. However, as with a child's use of the Family Archive (Section 5.2.1) to scan their toys, this incitement to share photos was not part of the initial intended worth, but after evaluation could be given further support for Cocoon or another system (e.g., TellTable was implemented separately from the Family Archive; Cao et al., 2010). Gaver and Bowers' (2012) Annotated Portfolios also include examples of user appropriations for separate spreads on users' experiences with their designs.

The scopes of approaches and resources can also be adapted or extended. The use of worth maps for mentoring (Section 6.4.1) is one striking example. George's uses of worth sketches for planning research and evaluation studies is a further example, as is the ARROW framework's transfer of worth mapping from the scoping of antefacts to the evaluation of artefacts. A group of TU/e students independently also used worth maps in evaluation work. Approaches from outside of WCD, such as feature-benefit tables were improved and repurposed (probably unknowingly) by Renaud and Biljon and by George. Far from following cookbooks, all teams in the case studies adapted, extended and completed Wo-Fo and other approaches and resources. Figure 5.7 (Cockton, 2020a) shows adapted approaches using blue post-its.

No project wholly used HCD. A mix of methods (ethnography, interviews, competitor analysis) is acknowledged in Camara et al. (2010), going beyond the VCD framework's opportunity identification solely through "personas within usage contexts" (Cockton, 2005). However, for WCD (Cockton, 2006) "Business strategy is … the primary discourse for the commercially worthwhile." WCD was never wholly user-centred and thus a broad multidisciplinary understanding of design purpose is needed, but this may not have been stressed well enough. Some projects were more commercially directed than others, and where not, showed examples of generosity that went beyond the results of user research.

Two projects built on the VCD development framework (Cockton, 2005) and three took direction from the simple tutorial "concurrent waterfall" process in Cockton (2008a). Work leading up to the ARROW framework was motivated by the need to fully operationalise a WCD version of the VCD development framework, but Vu (2013) could largely follow the VCD process structure without being constrained by it, blending in concurrent work practices from Cockton (2008a), renaming VCD phases to WCD ones, and adding approaches for worth identification (bilateral laddering) and evaluation (walkthroughs, SUS, user testing).

Scoping functions operate at high levels across several episodes of design work. Directive functions operate at activity level, within episodes. ARROWS (Camara and Calvary, 2017) provides systematic support for worth mapping. At a much finer grain, open questions on worth (Camara and Calvary, 2015) in interviews were not as effective as my "simplest 'hook' for designers" (Cockton, 2006) on collecting insights about design purpose for Cocoon (What would motivate you to buy, learn, use, or recommend Cocoon?).

Quantitative data could direct design work, based on frequencies of reporting (VALU project), use (mobile phone for elderly), preference (Cocoon, mobile phone for elderly, FGU), or dislike (FGU, Cocoon).

6.5 CHAPTER SUMMARY

Wo-Fo approaches, with varying adherence to BIG practices, have been used independently in three projects and in courses taught by me and a Ph.D. supervised by me (George, 2016). Experiences have been positive. Resource function analysis points to explanations for this in terms of the multiple functions that are activated and realised when using Wo-Fo approaches and resources.

CHAPTER 7

The Past, Present, and Future of BIG Wo-Fo

The case studies in Chapters 5 and 6 indicated the potential of BIG and Wo-Fo approaches in IxD. What matters most now is the future. However, it is first worth briefly retracing the history of Wo-Fo, and also the BIG practices that provided a better creative critical context than VCD (Cockton, 2005). A critical stance is exercised one last time on RILED practices before moving onto an assessment of current Wo-Fo in a BIG context, which in turn provides a baseline for discussing future work.

7.1 THE PROGRESSION OF WO-FO AND BIG

The progression from WCD to Wo-Fo is one from uncritical use of a RILED framework to its erosion by key realities of creative design that were only partially understood at the time. RILED process structures were abandoned to developed BIG as a replacement. A better conceptual habitat was needed for Wo-Fo practices. The account of the progression below draws on the first and third steps in Dewey's (1938) *Pattern of Inquiry*.

Unfortunately, long-standing RILED habits warped the first step, *The Antecedent Conditions of Inquiry: The Indeterminate Situation* into a *determinate* situation. Fortunately, key realities of creative design practice, while not in explicit focus, surreptitiously weakened RILED's hold and moved WCD to the second step, *Institution of a Problem*, a "precognitive ... situation ... adjudged to be problematic" (Dewey, 1938).

In the third step, *The Determination of a Problem-Solution*, the key creative reality of co-evolution was both problematic (having sneaked into a RILED process) and the solution, dismembering the RILED process. This new framing took care of itself without following the remainder of Dewey's *Pattern of Inquiry*.

7.1.1 THREE WAVES OF DETERMINATE SITUATIONS

> ...*it is of the very nature of the indeterminate situation which evokes inquiry to be questionable; or, in terms of actuality instead of potentiality, to be uncertain, unsettled, disturbed*
> (Dewey 1938).

The antecedents of the work in this book are a series of not indeterminate but determinate situations. They unfortunately lacked Dewey's perspective above. Each of HCI's three waves was determinately above question. It was clear that cognitive psychology held all answers to usability. It was clear that work ethnography held all answers to computer-supported collaborative work. It was clear that a phenomenological smorgasbord of emotions, values, cultures, meanings, interpretations, embodiments and the rest of Humanity 101 held at least some of the answers to networked multimedia on diverse digital devices and an accompanying shift from work to leisure and home use!

Such overconfidence hamstrung first wave quality in use and second wave fit to context (Cockton 2004a). Both could be described but not meaningfully evaluated. Each wave

> *set up a problem that does not grow out of an actual situation … to start on a course of dead wood, nonetheless dead because the work is "busy work"* (Dewey 1938).

Similarly, Carroll (1990) pointed out that psychology must efficiently add value to design work, i.e., it must make a worthwhile contribution. "Busy work" is wasteful. Value is added through understanding actual uage situations that reveal how slow is too slow, how many errors are too many, how much misfit is too much misfit, and so on. Actual situations calibrate targets. Desiderata are inherently axiological, requiring IxD to centre not on the user or users, but on value as the basis for e-valu-ation to be fit for purpose. First value (Cockton, 2005) then worth (Cockton, 2006) displaced quality in use and fit to context as the centres for design. Rather than study users, tasks or contexts of use prior to any design work, VCD would study *value opportunities*. A year later, WCD expanded this to *worth identification* based on both future positives and current and future negatives.

Worth as the new centre would not be subordinated to any existing software development focus. Worth opportunities were not to be found solely in current users' needs, wants, or pain points, nor were they to be found solely in a digital artefact's innovative materials, inspired features, or experienced qualities. Neither were they to be found solely in business perspectives on product strategy, perspectives that were much better understood within the Information Systems discipline than in HCI. Worth opportunities could be any mix of these, and thus design purpose added a first development phase to understand them (Harper et al., 2008). In such a phase, a synthesis of "economics and business understandings" and the "hard and soft nature" of value and values becomes possible to provide "missing links" (Poggenpohl, 2017).

The missing links of design purpose would fill gaps between existing software design phases. They would provide propositions for beneficiaries, goals for designed interactions, and targets for evaluation. They would thereby become the true centre of design. A range of WCD approaches and resources were developed to support this new true centre and to connect to its peripheries (Chapters 2–4).

There was only one problem. No actual situation for design had been taken into account. Yet another normative design process had been proposed without considering how design work actually worked.

7.1.2   DETERMINATION OF THE PROBLEM-SOLUTION

> *Statement of a problematic situation in terms of a problem has no meaning save as the problem instituted has, in the very terms of its statement, reference to a possible solution*
>
> (Dewey 1938).

The three waves of HCI proposed centres for an imagined design and development process. WCD followed suit. It was not just lack of a separate focus for design purpose that was a "problem" with HCD. Its very structure was too, and remains unchanged in the 2019 version of ISO 9241-210 (2019).

To be *worth-centred* was to have a fixed place in a fixed structure. To be *worth-focused* is to have a roving spotlight that pans across a field. This reframed the problem to the nature of the whole field rather than a single zone in it. The first explicit attempt to consider the whole field resulted in *Meta-Principles for Designing* (Cockton, 2009a) that could span the whole field, favouring no specific areas. The whole field was conceived as a set of design arenas. This reframing moved the problem from fitting worth into a RILED process to fitting a Wo-Fo progression to actual design practices.

Extensive studies of creative design practice regularly reveal two regularities: co-evolution and backtalk. Neither had been explicitly considered when creating the VCD framework (Cockton 2005, Figure 5.11). Both revealed themselves in VCD departures from RILED practices. Firstly, co-evolution between design and evaluation overlapped both phases. Evaluation started first and then waited for an a_tefact to evaluate. Secondly, iteration changed from being a property of the whole process to a phase at the end of each cycle. Within it, design and evaluation were considered in parallel with backtalk from each. Thirdly, while most connections were binary between adjacent phases, some were ternary between non-adjacent ones.

Conceptually, it was a simple step to consider all phases except iteration as design arenas. These would progress concurrently. Iteration becomes end of episode planning. The literature was clear on co-evolution and its dependence on backtalk, so it made sense to make concurrent connections between concurrent design arenas. This in turn reframed the problem as one of balance and integration, instead of phase order, arrows, and interfaces that depended on ordered phases. Flexible connections need to support concurrent work, because any arena can be connected to any others at any time when progressing design work. Given that the balance (mix) of design arenas and connections is not fixed in advance, continuous tracking is needed. Project management can no longer track progression through a pre-imposed fixed sequence.

The first two key realities of creative design practice are consistently named as *co-evolution* and *backtalk* (or in full "conversations with the materials of a design situation"). They are synergistic. Each enables the other in *conversational co-evolution*. The third key reality has no consistent name. It was called *generosity* in Section 2.2.2 (Cockton, 2020a), but it is rarely worthy of comment in much design research, beyond celebrating designers' vision in romantic accounts. Generosity also arises from "challenging the brief," e.g., Ken Grange's redesign of the Frister and Rossmann 804 sewing machine (Cross, 2011).

Although again unplanned and not based on knowledge of generous creative practice, VCD also anticipated generosity in its evaluation scale, where intended purpose is denied, destroyed, degraded, delivered, or donated (Cockton, 2005). Camara and colleagues used this scale when comparing planned and actual worth maps (Chapter 6). "Delivered" is like an agile definition of done, but requires a product to really work in the world rather than just pass software quality tests. Denial terminates a project as infeasible. Degraded and destroyed are worsening forms of failure. "Donate" generously exceeds intended worth.

Reframing WCD as creative design practice required rejecting imposed linearity and accepting a fully concurrent process. A fixed order with simple connecting arrows segued to a more challenging but much less distorting space: infinite possible integrating connections and a multitude of design arena mixes. This enabled generosity though multiple sources for design purpose: users' needs, wants, and pain points; creative and technological opportunities; and visionary product strategies for commercial, public, and third-sector organisations.

Sorting out RILED involves more than sorting out arrows. Boxes matter too. Each design arena has its own craft expertise, knowledge, and communities of practice. Productive capacities here create the a_tefacts and memoranda that connect to progress axiofacts. However, progression of design arenas must be mindful of integration with some focus on interfaces. It is one thing to fake a rational progression with fixed interfaces (work products) within an a_tefact arena (Parnas and Clements, 1986). Few would contemplate faking progression across for design arenas and integrating connections. Fortunately, there is nothing to fake. With nine connection modes (Section 4.1.7) honest connections can always be made. Some will be too creative for some, but adventitious aspects of design mean that all axiofacts will involve some latent, implicit, and ideative connections.

Sorting out RILED involves jettisoning its process structure, not its values. If it is possible to strengthen creative connection modes to RILED standards, this can happen if the effort is worth it, adding value to the product and its producing organisation. Scientific values can be ameliorative, but only when they are delivered on. Merely espousing them is not enough. Worse still is insisting that others deliver them irrespective of what is known to be possible. Possibility trumps desirability. We can live with enigmatic connections for an axiofact that has demonstrably progressed to generosity. Successful evaluation absolves all process sins.

BIG and Wo-Fo combine into a coherent and productive set of concepts. There is a theory here, but we must answer Latour's question: a theory of what? (Gaver and Bowers, 2012):

> *As soon as a divide is made between theories and what they are theories of, the tip of techno-science is immediately shrouded in fog. Theories, now made abstract and autonomous objects, float like flying saucers above the rest of science, which by contrast becomes "experimental" or "empirical."*

BIG Wo-Fo is a theory in Löwgren's (1995) sense of a "design methodology which can be seen as descriptive and normative … based on a creative design perspective." BIG is compatible with consistent results of research into creative design, and this thus a theory to the extent that it fits the facts. Being Wo-Fo is a normative directive and adumbrative resource that is an axiological theory. In axiology, there are no "facts" to "fit," only amelioratives to embrace. As with all axiological practices, design can be judged in terms of intentions, consequences, or the virtues of design team.

Generosity is a powerful intention. Perceived worth is a rewarding consequence. While an axiological "theory" fits no facts, it can predict futures: generosity should increase perceived worth. Generosity needs to be driven by vision and passion.

> *Reason is, and ought only to be, the slave of the passions and can never pretend to any other office than to serve and obey them* (Hume, 1896 [1738]).

Meta-principles for Designing (Cockton, 2009a) identify some virtues (receptiveness, committedness, inclusiveness). Additional ones associated with resource functions have been identified since, e.g., inquisitiveness.

7.1.3   THE ART OF THE EMPIRICALLY POSSIBLE, HISTORICALLY EVIDENCED, AND LOGICALLY SOUND

Dorst's (2015) Open Complex Dynamic Networked world makes wicked "problems" the norm. Yet many are drawn to process models with no basis in fact beyond tame problems. RILED's shortcomings may not be offset by expert judgement in areas in the absence of competent middle management. That situation is very common in software development where generalist project managers are given responsibilities for design and technical areas in which they have nothing educationally or professionally in common with team members. Rational project management may be their one available resource, creating false expectations for scientific management.

Agile and Design Thinking have not significantly reduced such false expectations. Neither has departed enough from RILED practices. Both abandon upfront requirements, but Jones' (1970) analysis-synthesis-evaluation model still sequences each iteration. Many design thinking models are still depicted with boxes and arrows (Waloszek, 2012). If there's no sequence, arrows should not be used. Their fixed iteration sequences evidence continuing strong pressures to approximate scientific method, with agile's "definitions of done" replacing a hypothesis to be proven. Continued hopes for a design science fuel continuing preferences for box and arrow diagrams. We need to critique unrealistic positions.

In philosophy, logical positivism has provided the clearest exposition of objective scientific bases of verifiable truths, but one of its key champions, A.J. Ayer later declared that "I suppose the most important [defect] ... was that nearly all of it was false" (Hanfling, 2003). Decades before postmodernism's Science Wars, formal logic had failed to provide a language for objective science. Instead, formal logic's universal quantifier (for all— $\forall$) exposed a flaw. $\forall$ introduces a predicate that is true for everything in some set. Popper (1959/1934) argued that we generally cannot know when all of a set has been observed, so universal quantification cannot be verified for an arbitrary set of phenomena, events or entities.

There is no systematic basis for knowing if enough observations have been made to induce an eternal universal law. Instead, Popper argued that potential for scientific truth lies in falsifiability, not verifiability. To scientifically investigate a hypothesis, it must be possible to falsify it. Failed attempts to falsify increase confidence in a hypothesis' truth, but it will always remain provisional and open to subsequent falsification. This first critical flaw undermines logical positivism's empirical basis for verifiability.

Quine (1951) questioned logic's contribution to verifiability. Logical positivism restricted rational deduction to analytical statements, which are true independent of observation. Quine demonstrated that definitions of analytical statements were circular, largely trivial tautologies (e.g., "all bachelors are men"). This second critical flaw weakens logical reasoning as a systematic basis for absolute scientific truths. As a result, Quine argued for "a blurring of the supposed boundary between speculative metaphysics and natural science" and "a shift toward pragmatism," supporting Fallman's (2003) pragmatic account of design.

There is thus currently no unproblematic basis for scientific truth. Any unease with creative connection modes must be assessed in relation to similar problems with scientific practices, which are more subtle than over enthusiastic high school teachers and dogmatic academics want us to believe. There are no formulae. Judgments of sound reason and adequate evidence are made within scientific communities where relevant arguments are made and supporting evidence is gathered. Disciplinary communities are good judges socially of sound arguments and adequate evidence, albeit with room for fair disagreement. Good science can and does happen (there is ubiquitous evidence of successful applications), but this is not due to adherence to universal principles of evidence or rationality. Scientism makes false claims here.

Scientism is a doctrine based on an extreme oversimplified ungrounded position on the nature and veracity of scientific method and the inferiority of unscientific knowledge practices. However, disproof of this extreme position is found in solid ethnographic studies of science work, detailed historical analyses, and philosophical enquiry, which continues to build on the positions of the later Ayer, Quine, Popper, and others. Much history and philosophy of science has been written by experienced scientists such as Polanyi (Chemistry), Lakatos (Maths and Physics), and Kuhn and Feyrabend (Physics).

RILED practices have remained in the cross hairs for much of this book in ways that may feel obsessive, but they are no more so than in the manifestos of Scientism. What is different is a willingness to engage with evidence on how design work progresses. A failure to engage fairly with the well-established results of a half-century of research into design is a local symptom of a much broader refusal to engage with evidence-based critiques of naïve accounts of scientific work. For example, in *Enlightenment Now: The Case for Reason, Science, Humanism, and Progress*, Pinker (2018) does not engage knowledgeably with Popper's specific writings on falsification (each of his mentions treats it as common sense), nor does he engage with Quine or Ayer when making a case for reason. Instead he writes of "Humanities" positions on Scientism as if these were Socrates corrupting the youth of Athens, irrespective of their origins or accuracy.

I make no apologies for uncompromising defence of and advocacy for critical creative practices. The evidence from studies of design and science, past and present, is unerringly on the side of pragmatic accounts of how both design and science progress. Those who promote RILED practices, even to the point of faking them (Parnas and Clements, 1986) should provide evidence that they work beyond tame problems. Until then, uninformed criticism of critical creative practices must be robustly corrected.

7.2   THE CURRENT STATUS OF BIG WO-FO

Hopefully the previous section has given a reasonable account of the intertwining of the ambitious, adventitious, and sometimes accomplished progressions of Wo-Fo and BIG, followed by identification of the two major intellectual flaws in the reasoning that stubbornly underlies RILED practices. Currently, the following claims can be made for intertwined Wo-Fo and BIG approaches.

1. BIG is creatively compatible.

2. BIG Wo-Fo is progressible and accountable.

3. BIG is reasonable.

4. BIG Wo-Fo is worthwhile.

7.2.1   BIG IS CREATIVELY COMPATIBLE

Wo-Fo is the current end point of a progression from VCD via WCD. Despite VCD's RILED framework of boxes and arrows creative practices crept in. BIG resulted from engagement with the literature on research into creative design practices. VCD's relaxed RILED process was dropped in favour of conversational concurrent progression that needs systematic monitoring of balance, integration, and generosity.

Letting go of pretences of control is not letting go of responsibility. On the contrary, it enables true responsibility. Instability can be unsettling, but in structural engineering Lev Zetlin accepted it robustly (as cited in Petroski, 1994):

> *Engineers should be slightly paranoiac during the design stage. They should consider and imagine that the impossible could happen. They should not be complacent and secure in the mere realisation if all the requirements of design handbooks and manuals have been satisfied, the structure is safe and sound.*

Informative and directive resources are not enough. They must be balanced by protective resources. At the same time, a design must be progressed by ideative resources, supported by integrative connection modes that admit imaginative conjecture. These modes are at the creative extreme of a continuum via reasonable design practices to ones that can meet scientific standards (as socially defined within a discipline—there are no absolutes).

In their detailed study of UK RDIs, Davies and Talbot (1987) looked for similar phenomena to the advent and experience of an imago and found intriguing matches in eastern mysticism. Similarities between imago experiences and spiritual ones such as "being the knowing" mean that we should be open to a broad range of understanding and explanation in design research. Such spiritual experiences could be a better model for the creative aspects of design practice than rationality. For example, the value of mindfulness has been explored in design education (Rojas et al., 2017).

7.2.2   BIG WO-FO IS PROGRESSIBLE AND ACCOUNTABLE

In "big upfront" RILED approaches, a whole process is planned. Agile methodologies have rejected big upfront approaches, with some coming close to eliminating any post-inception work prior to a first iteration of design and development. However, each agile iteration is planned with reference to a backlog of requirements. Concurrent work is possible within or across iterations, especially when combining UCD practices with agile development (Cockton et al., 2016). Processes and iterations enforce progression by forming plans in advance, moving through stages and gates (Christensen and Kaufman, 2008) or ticking off definitions of done in the "burn downs" of agile iterations. If Takeuchi and Nonaka (1986) had not replaced the sashimi of their Japanese writing with scrum in English, perhaps two decades of misunderstandings could have been avoided.

Long-established rational value systems have created expectations that progress must be against a plan. However, plans are not possible for truly creative work. BIG uses design arenas and connections to indicate progress. DANs fuse burn downs and backlogs. Backlog items require future work, whereas burnt down items currently require no further work. Rather than meet "definitions of done," these latter items need a short rationale on why they are currently "good enough."

A backlog item may be waiting to start, waiting for memoranda to connect, or in progress. Similar practices apply to CoNs, where a connection mode may be good enough to proceed for a few episodes, but need to be progressed to a more reasoned mode as and when possible. DAFs and CoFs for the start and end of an episode indicate progress at a higher level of abstraction than DANs and CoNs. They do so textually, whereas PADS do so graphically. George's (2016) Iteration Shift Tables showed an episode's progress using DAF pairs for each design arena. She used PADS to compare anticipated progress with actual outcomes of an episode.

BIG's tracking resources thus express progress. They can be used directively to indicate what progress should be made, with reviews to assess whether it has. They can also be used deliberatively, accepting co-evolution to revisit goals for current and previous episodes and revise these as necessary, rather than ticking off progress for episodes.

Adding Wo-Fo practices results in more meaningful expressions of progress. The risk of wasteful "busy work" is reduced by a Purpose DAN, which should give design teams a broad rich set of reasons for what they do (Gedenryd, 1998). Progress can be assessed against the achievement of design purpose.

As expressive resources, PADS, DAFs, CoFs, DANs, and CoNs make BIG practices accountable. Actual progress is expressed in several ways rather than having single acceptance criteria for each item of design and development work. The design purpose arena provides substance for accountability. Both BIG and Wo-Fo encourage explicit design practices that make accountability to the team and stakeholders possible.

7.2.3 BIG IS REASONABLE

Stebbing's *A Modern Introduction to Logic* (1930) addresses reasonable arguments. She does not turn human practices into abstract monolithic things such as Science or Rationality. Such a practice is called *reification*, and the nouns created become the subjects of sentences, with Science *this* …, Rationality *that* …, and for that matter Creativity *this* … and Design *that* … too. A single word stands in for a diverse range of human practices and experience. Were they explicitly the subject of a sentence, suspicions would be immediately raised. This is why Creativity has only appeared in quotes (Chapter 2) and Design has never been the subject of a sentence in this book. Instead, explicit references are made to designed artefacts or creative design practices, with plurals signalling a range of referents, over which generalisation is likely to be fraught. Fallman (2003) thus cautions against external rationalisation of design work as guidelines, which are best used ideatively or informatively and not directively, since the contexts where guidelines' antecedents were effective get lost in abstraction, stripping them out of a world that is "crammed with people, artifacts, and practices, each with their own histories, identities, goals, and plans." Slavish following of guidelines takes designers into the sort of intramental space that we need to avoid (Gedenryd, 1998).

Reification is a gateway category to overabstraction. We need to be reasonable about rationalisation. Beaney's (2017) attempt to rationalise Stebbing's opening example of a non-swimmer stranded by the tide (Cockton, 2020a, Section 5.9) provides a good example of Quine's (1951) concerns about the credibility of formal rules of argument. Each step of Beaney's syllogistic reasoning is open to question, but that does make it unreasonable. Instead, it is simply not the last word on the mechanics of how the non-swimmer's behaviour was reasonable in the context of the cliff and the callers on it. Most connection modes in Section 4.1.7 look reasonable alongside Beaney's reasoning. We have to judge reasonableness in design against reasonable standards. Connection modes can meet these standards except for latent, implicit, and ideative. Again, those modes of connections can be progressed to a more reasoned mode as and when possible. Premature and political progression should be avoided. The effort of progressing the mode of a connection must be worth it. It should not be rushed, or even happen at all, just to make someone feel better. Issues can often be resolved by evaluation.

BIG is reasonable because most current connection modes are reasonable. However, the "R" in RILED stands for Rational. Stebbing examined what was reasonable, without recourse to any additional "Rationality." In contrast, Parnas and Clements' (1986) have recourse to both the reasonable and the rational in their claim that it is reasonable that a standard process should be rational. Quine's (1951) circularity is as clear there as it is in all single males (aka bachelors) being men. Who would have thought?

As with a mathematical proof, BIG's connections are checked reflectively and deliberatively as part of the progression of design work. However, there is only one connection mode in a maths proof. It is objectively verifiable, but mathematical competence is required to both check replacement of equals with equals and to see the accuracy of checking here. There are at least nine connection modes in BIG. Latent, implicit and ideative modes require connoisseurship to appreciate them aesthetically (Cockton, 2020a, Section 5.9). The other connection modes are more inspectable and make fewer demands on those who appraise them or judge their appraisals. Stebbing's wise non-swimmer's moves are no less dependent on expertise to judge their reasonableness. Someone ignorant of tides and their wrack marks could not see how deciding that the ledge was safe was reasonable. A lack of knowledge and experience can lead to an onlooker missing "the most interesting points" (Darke, 1979).

A reasonable test of reasonableness needs a reasonable tester. Connection modes support reasonable criticism by suggesting criteria for a reasonable connection. Direct transfer requires an unchanged construct to be in the connected arenas. Realisation requires the same construct to be expressed differently in the connected arenas, with a reasonable rationale for how one construct realises another. Articulation requires a valid usage case that draws content from connected arenas. Argument requires reasonable derivation, but per Quine (1951), no clear correct criteria are available for checking over an argument. We remain dependent on specific disciplinary practices. BIG's connection modes make space for a range of disciplinary practices.

7.2.4 BIG WO-FO IS WORTHWHILE

Any true Wo-Fo approach to design work should progress to an axiofact, and thus result in a product that is valuable to those who funded development, purchase it, or make use of it. Wo-Fo is worthwhile by intent. The purpose design arena supports explicit shared understandings of design and evaluation goals.

During the development of BIG and Wo-Fo approaches, agile development has become the dominant approach for software (Cockton, 2016a). Interestingly, Clarke (1997) drew attention to waste long before the term became established within agile software development. One LD tool filter directed attention to contextual elements that have not yet influenced design, which reduced waste on several occasions. As noted in Section 4.3.2, Wo-Fo approaches can deliver on a key agile principle (Beck et al., 2001):

> *Our highest priority is to satisfy the customer through early and continuous delivery of valuable software.*

While there is much talk of value in agile methodologies, there is limited evidence of systematic support being developed. This cannot only cause difficulties with what should go on onto an agile backlog of features waiting to be implemented, but also difficulties with what should next come off. On the VALU project (Cockton et al., 2009b), the online gambling company found that worth maps could prioritise new or revised features that could deliver high priority outcomes for users.

As well as value for the customer, agile seeks value through "better ways of developing software" when "helping others do it" through which the Agile Manifesto (Beck et al., 2001) came "to value:

1. individuals and interactions over processes and tools;

2. working software over comprehensive documentation;

3. customer collaboration over contract negotiation; and

4. responding to change over following a plan.

That is, while there is value in the items on the right, we value the items on the left more." The third and fourth preferences have long been established in creative design practice, e.g., in advertising. The first and second preferences can undervalue memoranda as key to developing an axiofact rather than an artefact. "Working" software in a wholly technical sense, and associated agile "definitions of done" that reinforce this, is not the same as "valuable" software. Agile approaches that have no systematic explicit way of working with value have no systematic approaches to delivering valuable software to satisfied customers. Wo-Fo thus offers agile practices a co-ordinated set of approaches for focusing on making software worthwhile.

Wo-Fo applies to the progression of design as much as its outcomes. If we are generous to beneficiaries, then we must also be generous to design teams. We need to understand what is worthwhile about a range of disciplinary and professional practices. We then need to take the best of each and reduce their drawbacks to enable a better use of design and better appreciation of how its worth is understood by senior management (Stevens and Moultrie, 2011)

Heskett (2017) sees the value of design as being mostly extrinsic, but it has intrinsic value when design strategies for products are supported by strategic design within organisations. Stevens and Moultrie (2011) have identified a range of design practices that add value beyond that realised through the achieved worth of a product. Design agencies that can demonstrate competence in multidisciplinary work gain competitive advantage and attract complex design challenges. Process, as how design organisations progress work with their innovative approaches and resources, cannot be easily imitated by competitors. Such progress can be evidenced for prospective customers in models and sketchbooks (as in Gaver, 2011). Further value is evidenced in design cultures that take a holistic approach to design strategy, considering not only the product, but strategic innovation programmes, intellectual property, revenue streams, and the backstory that can transform an antefact into an embryonic axiofact.

Weber (2017) summarises Heskett's theorisation of design's value in economics terms as "user design-oriented business development." This foregrounds the multidisciplinarity of worthwhile design work. The risk of waste with multidisciplinary working is reduced by a range of connections that turn multiple disciplinary inputs into memoranda for axiofacts. Heskett's Design Value theory combines (Weber, 2017):

- the market focus of neoclassical economic theory and social demand from institutional economics;

- the end-user-oriented product innovation and imperfect competition from Austrian economics; and

- foci on transaction costs, tacit knowledge, and technological and institutional factors from new institutional economics and growth theory.

With its broad view of design arenas and their connections, BIG let us consider Heskett's ambitious agenda for design value. BIG is an adumbrative resource that can span a wide range of competitive advantage.

7.3   ONGOING AND FUTURE WORK

The potential of BIG and Wo-Fo is still under exploited. There are some clear barriers to more widespread uptake and use, including:

1. the need for tool support;

2. sharing resource examples in a community of practice; and

3. organisational learning and BIG Wo-Fo.

In addition, further work is needed on research issues for BIG and Wo-Fo.

7.3.1   THE NEED FOR TOOL SUPPORT

An agile approach has been taken to the development of BIG and Wo-Fo approaches. George (2016) introduced several new BIG and Wo-Fo resources "just in time" to support her research. Worth maps have continuously evolved from W/AMs, via the VALU and Family Archive worth maps to ARROWS. Agility is required for research *for* design *through* design *into* design, where use of novel approaches (for) on realistic projects (through) is studied (into). Worthwhile approaches and resources can only be developed through use, so Beck et al.'s (2001) "early and continuous de-livery" is essential to assess how valuable they are and what needs to be improved. The tendency to date has been to not develop specialised software tool support, but for WCD and BIG to become more widespread, better tools are needed.

Wo-Fo work on the Family Archive project used Microsoft office tools: Word for the liv-ing document and worth maps; Powerpoint for the Worth Board; and Excel for UXCs. Cocoon's Worth Maps were drawn in Powerpoint and the VALU project's in Visio. This was appropriate when Wo-Fo approaches were developing rapidly and had not been proven. It would have been premature to develop software tools a decade ago, but the time spent on diagramming and main-taining consistency between documents means that widespread use of Wo-Fo approaches needs tool support. Automation of repetitive low-level tasks would be beneficial, as would automatic (partial) generation of alternative tables from the same underlying information, as in (Renaud and van Biljon, 2010; George, 2016).

The VALU project made effective use of online questionnaire tools, and Vu (2013) used Selenium IDE to record test user interactions that could be played back with a new version of his prototype. However, both recognise the need for better tool support, and work ARROWS (Camara and Calvary, 2017) reached the same conclusion, as did Otero and José (2009).

Clarke's (1997) LD tool showed the benefits of software support. His evaluation participants could all examine existing connections and create new ones. "Parts," which were needed to provide interfaces for connections, were better understood once new connections had been made. Experiences with the LD tool show that a current snapshot needs to be navigable via both design arenas (Clarke's bottom-up) and connections (top-down, ideally from a visualisation). Clarke (1997) also developed another tool, Geneva, while on an internship at Intel. This linked contextual reports to underlying data, giving access to deep connections within the anyficiary arena. Similar deep linking is possible for the evaluation arena. The Vista tool (Brown et al., 1998) had similar deep linking within the artefact arena to pseudo-code.

The VALU project's use of Visio layers shows the value of being able to avoid overwhelming design teams with a big picture that cannot be easily comprehended. Modularisation and information hiding capabilities will also beneficial. However, deliberation by the whole team or subgroups needs to be supported, so tools should not be designed for individual use only.

A further source of complexity is the dynamics of BIG Wo-Fo work. The cost of drawing a worth map is compounded by their rapid evolution. Comparing worth maps in ARROWS is also difficult without tool support (Camara and Calvary, 2017). The paper and diagram editing based resources used to date have proved to be viable for research project use, but wider uptake would be better supported by software tools for BIG Wo-Fo.

7.3.2   SHARING RESOURCE EXAMPLES IN A COMMUNITY OF PRACTICE

The Internet has transformed research for design. Professional innovators can share new approaches and provide examples from themselves and others. A large set of examples can be crowdsourced. Much of the research elements here are informal, without systematic evaluation of use. However, since approaches and resources are always completed and adapted in use, controlled studies are not possible. We should not expect to see simple method effects. Instead, when novel approaches and resources are used in specific ways, their users will associate them with specific outcomes. The evidence here will be largely anecdotal, but communities of practice will be able to detect trends and develop playbooks (Gajander, 2019) from palettes (Friedland, 2019).

The Persona Lifecycle: Keeping People in Mind Throughout Product Design (Pruitt and Adlin, 2006) contains early examples of crowdsourced resources. The example personas in this book were sourced from the authors' contacts in their community of practice. More recently, resource examples were collected for *Value Proposition Design: How to Create Products and Services Customers Want* (Osterwalder et al., 2014).

Detailed examples for Chapter 6 can be found in Camara (2012), Vu (2013), and George (2016). For Chapter 5, Clarke's (1997) thesis is also online. However, dedicated online resource collections and support are a better format for dissemination than academic theses, such as the interactive online companion for the Value Proposition Canvas at strategyzer.com. George's resource collection for BIG Wo-Fo is at resourcesbyjennifergeorge.wordpress.com, and Camara's for ARROWS at phdgirl911.wixsite.com/arrows-and-wms. Jones has an online resource for his storienteering resources (storienteer.info). One advantage of online resources is that they are accessible beyond the IxD, UX, and HCI communities. Jones' resources are in extensive use in home schooling.

Crowdsourcing has been extended to evaluation examples. For example, resources for learning space redesign have been shared online (classroomrecipe.blogspot.com/2013/11/classroom-design-recipe.html), with examples of their use shared on Instagram (Qaed et al., 2016). This greatly extended the reach of the evaluation study, reducing the need for site visits. As with Jones, Qaed's resources have been used beyond interior design for education, including home use and use by Human Resource teams.

Work on the online ARROWS and BIG resources is continuing. A larger community of practice needs to build around them. It is important for academic research to have a role in the development of approaches and resources for IxD work. It is important for researchers to adopt crowdsourcing and online community approaches from current professional practice. As well as hopefully demonstrating the value of systematic research approaches, feedback and examples are essential to improving resources from research for design. As with annotated portfolios (Gaver and Bowers, 2012), family resemblances between resource examples can be reasoned about and discussed. Deliberation is a vital research resource for understanding different usage patterns for IxD approaches and resources.

7.3.3   ORGANISATIONAL LEARNING AND BIG WO-FO

Design Thinking has brought simplified creative studio practices to a wide range of organisations at all levels of society. Junginger (2017) has stressed the need to involve government organisations in change process for service design, so that they understand how HCD approaches can help.

Dilnot (2017) noted Heskett's desire to influence business at C-Level to appreciate the relationship between design and value. BIG Wo-Fo approaches can make this more concrete, both for a product's design strategy and for the supplier's strategic design (Stevens and Moultrie, 2011).

Takeuchi and Nonara (1986) provided a well-researched model of successful commercial innovation. BIG Wo-Fo builds on this with approaches and resources that encourage *multi-learning* and support *organisational learning*. Progressions of BIG design have *built-in instability* through their *overlapping development phases*. Tracking resources support reflection and planning that empower *self-organising teams* and creates a window for *subtle management control*. Organisational learning may be the most challenging of these six factors.

Online examples and discussions allow independent learning by professionals, but this needs to be shared with teams. Formal training and facilitation were used in most Chapters 5 and 6 case studies. Design teams need to develop common understandings of BIG Wo-Fo resources and approaches that they use. Most will develop in use on projects, but some training is needed to support first use of innovative approaches. In these contexts, the provision of examples may not be a helpful tactic.

UX practices were introduced to agile development in a medical equipment developer (Øvad and Larsen, 2016). Templates for three approaches (Focused Workshops, AB-Testing, and Contextual Interviews) were refined over six iterations. Requests for examples were made on several occasions during training courses, but Øvad and Larsen did not provide any. Examples introduce a risk of surface learning. In formal training contexts with homework, it is better for attendees to develop their own examples. Examples can be presented in discussion sessions after exercises, but it is important to grasp the underlying principles for approaches and resources, and not just what a complete example looks like. A focus on expressive and directive functions will not develop broad understandings or robust competences.

In my courses, I show examples after attendees have completed an exercise independently. Questions arise and discussions follow, enabling individuals to grasp underlying principles that would lack salience in an uninformed glance at examples. Again, onlookers who lack relevant knowledge and experience can miss "the most interesting points" (Darke, 1979) in design work. Approaches and resources can rarely be developed for effective immediate use by anyone, regardless of their expertise. Design teams need to work to get them to work: "text book knowledge is not sufficient" (Jeffries et al., 1981). Examples work best when they become part of "a conversation among old friends [that] may be hard for an outside to comprehend" (Gaver, 2011). With the best organisational learning, everyone will become a friend of BIG Wo-Fo design.

The shift of focus in design from the artefact to value is relatively recent. In 1988, Thakara edited *Design After Modernism: Beyond the Object*. This focused on understandings of design work that were not wholly focused on artefacts. Jones' (1988) critique of design methods was one chapter in this book. In the decades before, design writing had been more focused on artefacts and making (e.g., Pye, 1968, 1978). In the decade after, design was increasingly reframed as the creation of value (Marzano, 1998). This move from artefact to axiofact makes single arena exemplars in design problematic, whether they are iconic artefacts, visionary purpose, inspiring personas, or innovative evaluation approaches. None of these can be appreciated in isolation.

Examples have short half-lives. Apple's iTunes did not last two decades. When launched, it was an early example of a product-service system, providing usable infrastructure for an iPod to improve the UX for iPod owners. At the same time, it created retail opportunities for Apple and expanded its services over the years to provide more value for Apple and its users, until for many it became a bloated and confusing bit of legacy software. It was withdrawn from Apple devices after less than 16 years of operation. It remained available on other platforms at the time of writing this book.

The story of Apple's iTunes is not a story of an iconic exemplary design. It is a story of worth. Initially it reduced negative experiences associated with getting music onto an iPod at the same time as adding positive value through music sales and additional functionality for backing up devices, storing photos and other capabilities. Eventually, the cost of using iTunes outweighed its benefits for many users and for Apple. How it looked, what it felt like to use, and what it could do are not central to its story. Instead, this is a story of worth, a story of an axiofact, not an artefact.

Moving from artefacts to axiofacts has expanded what organisations must learn about design. It is no longer enough to be inspired by artefacts alone. Inspiration must be balanced across design arenas and connections. Sio et al. (2015) add to the evidence that making connections is of primary importance in design work:

> *A distant example may be beneficial for experts who have a large amount of domain-specific knowledge. However, presenting the same example to novices may not yield positive effects because novices may not have the knowledge to see the connection between the example and the problem.*

Design exemplars for the 21st centuries are proven axiofacts, artefacts that have been shown to provide worth. In Chapter 5 this included the Family Archive, the staff room display and the online gambling system. In Chapter 6 it was a mobile phone prototype, the information system for the FGU, the Cocoon mobile app, the Colibri planning system (now a commercial product), and MyCareCircle. The achieved worth of these digital artefacts varies, and few stand out as outstanding exemplars of worth. However, they are examples of what design exemplars should now be. Looking at artefacts tells us little about their worth. We need to look at evaluations and what is evaluated, and how beneficiaries connect to an artefact's purpose.

We are still at a relatively early stage of understanding axiofacts. Further design research needs to improve our ability to recognise and communicate exemplary worth, and to communicate this to key stakeholders.

7.3.4   BIG AND DESIGN RESEARCH

Over the last few decades, creative design practices have been steadily embraced as the backbone of research methodologies in IxD and HCI. Frayling (1993) referred to this as *research through design*, drawing on art education practices *through* art rather than *about* art. The equivalent of the latter is research *into* design. These research modes can combine, with research into design reflecting on the progression and outcomes of research through design. Frayling's third mode of design research, research *for* design, adds further complexity. Developing support for design practice is research for design. This support must be assessed in practice, which must also involve both research into and through design.

Research through design is not only for research for design. Its wider attraction lies in how creative practices "build bridges between larger research issues and the approaches to these issues embodied by" (Gaver and Bowers, 2012) the axiofacts of research through design. Research through design for the world can have much greater reach than research through design for design.

Methodological reporting is key to research through design. As a creative practice, a research methodology cannot be wholly planned in advance, nor will a few pilots to shake down studies be enough to proceed with a final study plan, as for a questionnaire (George, 2016) and user testing scenarios (Vu, 2013) in Chapter 6 case studies. Creative progressions are unpredictable. Tight management is pointless.

Disciplines that examine yesterday's world seek generality through methodological practices that reduce bias, increase ecological validity, support replication, and allow confidence in results. While research through design does not necessarily "have to make enemies of generality. ... [its] characteristic contribution ... may be watered down if excessively 'scientistic' criteria for the validity of its research are laid at its door" (Gaver and Bowers, 2012).

Creative progressions must trade upfront planning and control for retrospective reflection and deliberation. No process is fully known upfront (as with significant mathematics proofs), so reasonableness of progression needs to be demonstrable. BIG's tracking representations can support reconstructions (George, 2016). They can also be used to report research, but previous representations such as Wolf et al.'s (2006) progress visualisations, and Gaver's Design Workbooks (2011) and Annotated Portfoilos (Gaver and Bowers, 2012) may be more suitable, especially for interim presentations to multidisciplinary research projects.

Retrospective representation, reflection, and deliberation are research practices for discursive knowledge production where knowledge value is added to practice value (Löwgren, 2013). BIG's tracking representations are suitable for high-level tracking and reconstruction of design research progressions, but the details will be found in co-products, as overlaid on Wolf et al.'s (2006) progress timelines. Research through design for the world will benefit from the use of Wo-Fo approaches, as they explicitly record and make use of new worth for the world that is best innovated through creative practice.

BIG Wo-Fo can thus resource creative research practice as well as professional practice. These are all forms of intermediate-level design knowledge (Löwgren, 2013), but research will benefit from deeper theory. One possibility here is *Assemblage Theory* (de Landa, 2006). With its origins in addressing limitations of systems theory, it is well suited to adventitious progressions in complex dynamic system. Its use of counterintuitive positions, such as "the whole itself is a product, produced as nothing more than a part alongside other parts" has already been used to good effect in the ARROWS framework (Camara and Calvary, 2017). It has been in the background for my thinking on design progression. The benefits of bringing Assemblage Theory to the surface and assessing its worth would be useful for future research. For example, it may provide a suitable context for understanding how "designs resource social interactions" (Gaver and Bowers, 2012).

7.4   ABOUT THAT MANIFESTO

In Chapter 3 of Cockton (2020a) a cast of fictional voices progressed toward a Balanced Design Manifesto. This design practice research fiction was deliberately polyvocal. The characters were based on colleagues, research acquaintances, graduates, a product team, hostile reviewers, and voices online and in social media. When Claudia proposed the Balanced Design Manifesto, it was based on what she had heard in the discussions, which was all based on positions that are readily encountered within relevant communities of practice. Chapters 4 of Cockton (2020a) and this book onwards have gone beyond these existing positions. Each manifesto position is considered in turn and the book's closing position on each statement is given.

7.4.1   WORK AREAS FOR BALANCED DESIGN: MEANS, ENDS, BENEFICIARIES, AND EVALUATION

Work areas are design arenas with names that reflect balanced positions: a_tefacts, purpose, anyficiaries, and evaluation. This answers the first question for this book: what are the main areas of design work? Sections 4.2 and 4.3 (Cockton, 2020a) introduced the design arenas. Chapters 2 and 3 reviewed approaches and resources for supporting work in the arenas.

7.4.2   CONCURRENT WORK IS THE NORM. SEQUENCE IS THE EXCEPTION

Sequence is an illusion, with the exception of routine work on tame problems. Attempts to impose sequence fail, but design teams may be forced to hide it rather than expose the true concurrent nature of their work. There is no correct structure for sequential or concurrent work. A template can guide specific BIG design paradigms to suit the need of specific projects, programmes, and organisations (Cockton, 2020a, Section 4.3). Iteration does not make sense in a concurrent progression model. Concurrency is limited by the number of design arenas (currently four). The case studies all show that is manageable. All organisations that work across the four design arenas would have to work concurrently after a first sequential iteration. They actually start working concurrently from inception onwards. This answers the second question group for this book: are there standard correct progression structures that can organise design work without regimenting it into a sequence of phases? With how much iteration or concurrency?

7.4.3   CONNECTIONS BETWEEN AREAS ARE CREATED, NOT PREFORMED

Connections are design resources with different structures, modes and framings. They can be partially preformed, as templates that are filled in by project specific work. Sections 5.6 and 5.7 of

Cockton (2020a) and Chapter 4 review connection structures, framings, and modes. This answers the first part of the fourth question for this book: What sort of connections would be in a comprehensive model of design work?

7.4.4 INTERFACES BETWEEN AREAS CAN BE PREPARED FOR CONNECTING

Interface items can be marked as such in DANs (Cockton, 2020a, Section 5.4). Several items may be grouped into a single interface (Section 5.1.2). Chapter 4 reviews a broad range of connection structures. Concourses can support connection work without a requirement for interfaces or explicit design arena items. Unary, binary, ternary, and quaternary connection structures can be extended with grafts of combined into chains or rings. This answers the second part of the fourth question for this book: What sort of connections and interfaces would be in a comprehensive model of design work?

7.4.5 PROGRESSION MODELS TO BE COMPLETE AT ALL ABSTRACTION LEVELS

ADS can model design work at all levels of abstraction, from paradigms through progressions, episodes, activities, and moves. Chapter 4 (Cockton, 2020a) develops the ADS concept as connecting between design arenas.

7.4.6 DESIGN WORK TO BE TRACKED ACROSS AREAS TO REVEAL PROGRESS

SoMADS and PADS can track progression, along with DAFs, CoFs, DAFs, and DANs (Cockton, 2020a, Chapter 5). Additional agile structures such as Kanbans can be associated with each item in a DAN or CoN. SoMADS and PADS are ADS based concepts. DAFs and CoFs draw on design research on framing. DANs and CoNs have a similar structure to agile backlogs, but there is no burn down. Items can be progressed, accepted as complete, reopened, stalled, or retired. Progress is indicated by improvements to DANs and CoNs. These leave trails of tacit design commitments. Explicit design decisions will not always be in evidence, but tacit ones are made whenever DAN items are progressed, and well-formed connections are added. This answers the fifth and sixth questions for this book: What forms of tracking would a new model support? What would progress look like when design work is tracked with support from a new model?

7.4.7   MISLEADING RILED LANGUAGE NEEDS TO BE RETIRED

We have replaced the RILED lexicon. Problems and solutions have been replaced with memoranda and a_tefacts. Processes have been replaced with progressions. Designs do not unfold or emerge, but fall into place in progressions of directed pushes and adventitious slides. Phases have been replaced with episodes. Methods have been replaced with approaches formed from resources. Satisfied requirements have been replaced with satisfying axiofacts. Nine connection modes have currently replaced a mechanical vocabulary of generation, derivation and translation.

7.5   MISSION ACCOMPLISHED?

Divisions of labour can acquire unhelpful hierarchies. The King of the Hill holds the centre of design. Different professional and disciplinary groupings vie for the centre stage: software engineers; HCD experts; business strategists; and creative designers. It would be much better if they could all get along and network more.

The foci in design work shift as design arenas are progressed and connections firm up. By replacing the RILED lexicon with a vocabulary that is compatible with the key realities of design work, by developing tracking constructs for reflection and replanning, by developing approaches and resources for progressing design arenas and connections between them, and by providing examples of these innovations in use, this book has developed an integrated framework that supports a Wo-Fo within a template for flexible connecting design work.

Conceptually, the mission appears to have been accomplished. Practically, there have been some demanding expeditions with new equipment, with teams ranging from Master's and Ph.D. students and their support, via commercial organisations, to a research group in a leading international IT company. Hopefully, others will be motivated to follow in their footsteps.

Glossary and Abbreviations

A posteriori: (Latin) a philosophical term for an inductive approach that proceeds from facts to generalisations. The development of most guidance and principles for IxD is a posteriori and limited to one or two design arenas.

A priori: (Latin) a philosophical term for a deductive approach that proceeds from generalisations to generalisations. The derivation of Meta-Principles for Designing was a priori and considered all design arenas (Cockton, 2009a).

A_tefact: an antefact or artefact; one of four design arenas (Cockton, 2017). Created and persistent.

Abstract Design Situation: a set of connected design arenas (Cockton, 2010).

Activation of resource function: a design move that mobilizes a potential function of a resource.

Adroitness: a meta-principle for design focused on the demonstration of craft excellence in the a_tefact arena, overlooked in Cockton (2009a). A virtue with a golden mean between the vices of clumsiness and obsessiveness.

ADS: Abstract Design Situation.

ADS template: a template that can be modified to create MADS for different design paradigms, especially BIG paradigms. Modifcation is mostly focused on connections and progressions (represented as SoMADS).

Adumbrative: a resource becomes adumbrative when it activates a function that roughly scopes design work (at any extent from millennia old paradigms to brief design moves). To adumbrate is to overshadow (*umbra* is Latin for shadow). Playbooks, palettes, processes, phases, episodes, approaches, and resources can all be scoped (Cockton, 2013a).

Adventitious: resulting from external factors or chance. Creative studio-based practices are very open to adventitious direction from insights, discoveries, accidents, fresh perspectives, etc.

Affiliative: a resource becomes affiliative when it improves the bonds within design teams. Activation of affiliative functions is often triggered by other functions (e.g., deliberative, integrative, invigorative). Affiliative functions were identified after Cockton (2013a).

Agile: a family of software design methodologies, represented in the Agile Manifesto (Beck et al., 2001), which rejects "big up front" analysis and fixed requirements to varying degrees, but always working in shorter iterative RILED cycles. There is some concurrency in agile development, but its extent beyond the artefact arena (e.g., concurrent development and testing) is contested. Concurrency in BIG applies to all design arenas, not just one.

Ameliorative: a resource becomes ameliorative when it activates a function that identifies positives and negatives that can contribute to an appropriate balance of worth for both the progression of design and its outcomes (axiofacts) Amelioration improves something. *Melior* is Latin for better (Cockton, 2013a).

Antefact: a mediating representation of a final artefact. A sketch or prototype of any form: Wizard of Oz, Paper, Lo-Fi, Hi-Fi, video, enacted (Cockton, 2017).

Anyficiaries: one of four design arenas. An anyficiary is a beneficiary or maleficiary. One person can be both due to a mix of benefits and sacrifices for an artefact (Cockton, 2017). A curated persistent arena.

Approach: coherent support for a practice, based on a set of resources. Use of an approach in design work results in a complete method once all missing resources have been added, incomplete resources completed, and other resources adapted as necessary. Approaches are rarely complete, and require additional resources to be sourced or created during design work (Woolrych et al., 2011).

Arena: an enclosed physical space, originally for competitive sport, combat, attention, argument, or discussion. It takes its name from its covering of *harena* (Latin, fine sand) that was laid down to absorb blood!

Argued: a hybrid connection mode where items in one design arena are argued to have consequences for items in another.

Arity: a mathematical concept that counts parameters for functions. Parameter values for a function comprise its domain. The results of applying a function to its parameters are its range. Arity is extended in this book to count all arenas in a connection, both those in the domain (origins of the connection) and its range (destinations of its connection). Most connecting transitions between RILED process phases are binary. Connections with the same arity can have different structures.

ARROW: Appreciations, Requirements, and Rationale of Worth (Camara and Calvary, 2015), previously PEW. An approach that compares intended and worth maps based on evaluation data. Simplified MECs are used.

ARROWS: ARROW Support (Camara and Calvary, 2017), a set of public resources and training for worth mapping.

Artefact: the final product of design and development work, which is functional and complete. It is not a prototype (that is an antefact).

Artefact Connection Tables: a Wo-Fo variant of a Feature-Benefit table paired with a Feature-Aversion table to create separate resources for considering connections between a_tefacts and purpose (George, 2016).

Articulated: a hybrid connection mode where items in some design arenas are combined into a usage sequence that progresses through and towards items in another arena (usually purpose).

Axiofact: an a_tefact that demonstrably delivers worth. In research through design, this could be an antefact. In most other design situations, it must be an artefact. BIG Design creates axiofacts, not just artefacts.

Balance: an appropriate mix, not an equal share, of effort and outcomes across design arenas and connections. In BIG Design as a result of rejecting the big upfront planning of RILED processes.

Beneficiary: someone who benefits from an artefact (Cockton, 2017).

BIG Design: design work that is Balanced, Integrated, and Generous (Cockton, 2013b), resulting in an axiofact.

Binary connection: a connection of any structure between two design arenas.

Chain of connections: a composite connection where one connection ends at a design arena from which another connection originates. Connections within chains tend to be binary. The chain of connections is ternary or quaternary.

Code: an early concourse structure across beneficiaries and a_tefacts, a designer's personal informative resource "expressed in terms of the users rather than in terms of buildings, … the designer operates a kind of informal code for linking one to the other" (Hillier et al., 1972). An implicit pattern.

Complex connection: a composite connection formed from other connections, via a graft, chain or ring.

Co-product: a resource produced during design work, in contrast to an a_tefact produced by design work (Carroll, 2000). Example co-products include personas and scenarios.

CoF: Connection Frame.

Committedness Meta-Principle: a design team commits to a scope of work within and across arenas and connections. A virtue with a golden mean between miserliness and excess. Related resource functions include adumbrative and ameliorative.

CoN: Connection Notes.

Concourse: an open space between design arenas, a connection structure where both connections and design arenas can be implicit or latent. No DANs or DAFs need to exist. Concourses are common in the initial progression of creative design work as codes, partis, patterns, and primary generators. Design Workbooks (Gaver, 2011) and Annotated Portfolios (Gaver and Bowers, 2012) are also concourse structures.

Concrete Design Situation: a detailed snapshot of design work. All current work activities for a project, resources in use, and progressed resources for a design project (Dorst, 2017).

Connection Direction: a connection's direction is from its origins to its endpoints, like the mapping from the domain to the range of a mathematical function.

Connection Frame: a pragmatic framing of a connection as a textual summary, which can be part of a CoN.

Connection Mode: the intellectual activity underlying a simple connection (or part of a complex connection). There is no automatic hierarchy. A RILED connection mode is not inherently superior to a hybrid or CREAM one. All connections remain conjectural until there is support from evaluation. CREAM connection modes can fare just as well as RILED ones, and may do better: "in most cases the [primary generator] design concept was arrived at before the requirements had been worked out in detail, and necessarily so, because these requirements could only become operational in the context of a particular solution" (Darke, 1979).

CREAM Connection Modes: tacit modes of connection, currently latent, implicit, and ideative.

Connection Notes: a collection of notes on connections between design arena. Each note can be a phrase, sentence or short paragraph. A connection's arity, direction, structure, and mode can be noted, as can its frame. Once a connection is progressed, there will be a corresponding resource that details the work on it.

Connection Structure: the arity and form of a connection, which can be simple or complex. Complex structures include grafts, chains, and rings.

CREAM: the Creative Reflective Exploratory Aesthetic Moves (Cockton, 2017) of studio-based practices. Creative exploratory work cannot be fully planned, so reflection and deliberation are important sources of rigour. Aesthesis is an important reflective practice, understood as Heidegger's "circumspective looking" (McNeill, 1999). CREAM mixes the adventitious and the deliberate, progressing designs through work within arenas and on connections (Goldschmidt, 2014).

Credibility Meta-Principle: requires a design team to consider how others will judge the validity of their work within and across arenas. A potential with eventual diminishing returns. The credibility of a connection is related to its mode and available relevant evaluation data. Multiple disciplinary standards can apply within a design arenas. CREAM disciplines subject ideas to extensive analysis and critique, with a "conjecture tested to see how far [requirements] can be met" (Darke, 1979) and "fine tuning … to make it a runner" (Davies and Talbot, 1987). Related resource functions include directive and informative.

DAF: Design Arena Frame.

DAN: Design Arena Notes.

Deliberative: a resource becomes deliberate when it spawns discussions during design work. Activation of deliberative functions is often triggered by other functions (e.g., affiliative, directive, integrative, protective) in specific social contexts such as design reviews, planning the next design episode, or coaching and mentoring. Deliberative functions were identified after Cockton (2013a).

Design Arena: a sociomaterial arena (ATELIER, 2011), adding material a_tefacts and co-products to a social arena in a design setting.

Design Arena Frame: a pragmatic frame for a design arena, written as an organising principle, perhaps using metaphor or analogy, to capture an arena's coherence, which an ADS cannot express. Originally called Design Arena Overviews (George, 2016) but renamed to align with Dorst (2015).

Design Arena Item (DAI): an item in a DAN.

Design Arena Notes: a collection of notes on items in a design arena. Each note can be a word, phrase, sentence, or short paragraph. Once an item is progressed, there will be a corresponding resource that details the work on it. Originally called a Design Arena Progress List (George, 2016) but renamed to loosen up on the list metaphor.

Design Paradigm: short for Design Work Paradigm, unless otherwise stated. Paradigm is derived from "showing side by side," so that patterns may be seen. Patterns can exist at any level of abstraction in design work, from the highest-level value systems (Dorst and Dijkhuis, 1995) to specific patterns of structural design failures (Petroski, 1994).

Design Rationale: a set of argued connections between artefacts (features and qualities) and other design arenas (memoranda), often represented using the QOC notation.

Design Work Paradigm: a distinct generic pattern of working in design, expressed as a MADS. The three major design paradigms are the Applied Arts, Engineering Design, and Human-Centred Design (Cockton, 2013b).

Direct Transfer: a RILED connection mode where items from one design arena are transferred with minimal changes into another arena.

Direct Worth Instrumentation: instrumenting an a_tefact to support evaluation of achieved worth, a ternary connection between purpose, evaluation and a_tefact. A possible resource for EMS.

Directive: a resource becomes directive when it guides design work (Cockton 2013a). Activation of directive functions is typically triggered when using an approach or planning a design episode, but informative resources can also be directive, including concepts such as anyficiaries, generosity, and worth.

Domain: in mathematics, a function's parameters. For a connection, its originating design arenas or start point(s).

DWI: Direct Worth Instrumentation.

Element Measurement Strategy: an approach that connects from purpose to evaluation by associating measures and required targets with purpose items, and selects or designs evaluation instruments for these measures. DWI is a possible resource.

EMS: Element Measurement Strategy.

Ephemeral design arenas: purpose and evaluations, arenas that have no existence after a project ends. Intended purpose gives way to user appropriation and evaluation results quickly lose relevance.

Episode: a period of multifocal design work that starts with a set of DAFs and CoFs and ends with a pause for reflection and deliberation. Episodes replace the single arena phases and stages of RILED processes. They can be time boxed like agile iterations, but they are not iterations. They are progressions (as is the project as a whole) where concurrent work in design arenas has no imposed sequences, such as Scrum's closed window rule (Cockton, 2016a).

ERG: Existence, Relatedness, and Growth, the three groups of needs in Alderfer's (1972) theory of motivation, which is shaped by dynamic interactions between these groups.

Evaluation: one of four design arenas. Ephemeral and curated. With the anyficiaries arena, this includes HCD practices in BIG.

Existence: Individual needs in ERG.

Expressive: a resource becomes expressive when it manifests itself in design work. Activation and realisation of expressive functions is automatic for explcit design resources (Cockton, 2013b).

Expressivity Meta-Principle: requires a design team to maintain sufficient expressive resources to support tracking, reflection, deliberation and integration. A potential with eventual diminishing returns. Associated resource functions include expressive and informative.

FCM: Frame Creation Model.

Field: in a non-homogeneous social-spatial "field," people manoeuvre and struggle in pursuit of desirable resources (Bourdieu, 1984). Forming a field is the fifth FCM step. Synonymous with social arena.

Frame: An organising device or structure. Dorst (2015) has two forms of frames, logical and pragmatic (but not named or distinguished as such), which are formed in the sixth FCM step. His pragmatic form is used in DAFs and CoFs.

Frame Creation Model: a procedure for innovating with design frames (Dorst, 2015), beginning with intensive dialogue and research (archaeology), and proceeding through eight further stages: establishing the core paradox, themes, the context, Bordieu's field, frames, futures, transformation, and integration. Each stage can be modelled as a MADS.

Feature Benefit Table: a table (Douglas, 2000) with two columns, one for artefact features, the other for benefits (purpose). An unrestrained concourse structure with connection modes that are implicit at best and sublatent at worst.

Generosity: a meta-principle for design focused on the purpose arena, overlooked in Cockton (2009a). Core to BIG Design as a result of rejecting HCD, engineering requirements specification, or design/strategic vision as the sole basis for design purpose. Donating unexpected benefits (Cockton, 2005) is the main test of generosity. A potential with eventual diminishing returns.

Grafted connection: a connection to/from a connection, rather than to/from a design arena.

Grounded Design: a second wave HCI approach to literate development (Cockton, 1998) that used expressive resources to expose (mis)fit between three design arenas. Superseded by VCD, which added a fourth design purpose arena.

Growth: dynamic needs in ERG. Humans grow and develop, and not only until adulthood. Designing for people means designing for people who grow and change (Marzano, 1998).

HCD: Human-Centred Design.

HCI: Human-Computer Interaction, knowledge from research that can support UX and IxD work, as well as contributing more generally to understanding the use and impact of interactive digital technologies.

Herzberg's two-factor theory: a motivational theory from occupational psychology that actually has three valences: positive (motivators), neutral (lack of motivators and hygiene factors), and negatives (hygiene factors). A useful informative resource that reminds us that a lack of positives is not a presence of negatives and vice-versa. Overlaps with Kano Model.

Hierarchical Value Map: an approach from marketing and advertising that was the origin of W/AMs and Worth Maps (Cockton et al., 2009a).

HTM: Hierarchical Task Modelling, the only non-artefact resource in the 1990s Vista tool (Brown et al., 1998). An artefact-independent higher level model than UAN.

Human-Centred Design: one of three major design paradigms.

HVM: Hierarchical Value Map.

Hybrid Connection Modes: explicit modes of connection requiring judgement, currently argument, articulation, and realisation.

Ideative: (1) a resource function that yields options for design arena items and connections. Ideative functions were identified after Cockton (2013a). (2) a CREAM mode for explicit connections where the connection structure is explict but the connection itself is only tacitly appreciated and understood. Such connections may be better evidenced before or after user evaluation, when the connection is or is not realised as imagined.

IKK: three basic social structures, institutions, kin, and kind, for collective value in the L-ERG-IKK model.

Implicit: a CREAM mode for concourse connections, where the structure is incomplete but some basis for a connection is apparent and could become more explicit after reflection or further progression of a design.

Improvability Meta-Principle: requires a design team to commit to effective evaluation through three subprinciples: evaluability, understandability, and responsiveness. EMS enable evaluability. MECs enable understandability and adroitness enables responsiveness. Although focused on one design arena (evaluation), connections to other arenas are needed by the subprinciples. A potential with eventual diminishing returns (Cockton, 2009a).

Inception: the first episode of design work after initial approval of a project (approval may have required some design work already, which should feed into the inception).

Inclusiveness Meta-Principle: requires a design team to commit to an appropriate balance of beneficiaries over maleficiaries. Although focused on a single design arena (anyficiaries), connections to other arenas are required to deliver on the subprinciples (Cockton, 2009a). A virtue with a golden mean between the vices of discrimination and indiscriminateness.

Informative: a resource becomes informative when it becomes relevant to design work. Activation of informative functions occurs when introducing resources into design conversations (Cockton, 2013b).

Inquisitive: a resource becomes inquisitive when it prompts questions in design work (Cockton, 2013b). Activation of inquisitive functions can be adventitious or co-occur with other functions (e.g., deliberative, reflective, protective).

Institution: the organisational social structure in L-ERG-IKK, where a narrow view is taken of institutions as being formal organisations with hierarchies, rules, rewards and policies. New Institutionalism (Meyer and Rowan, 1977) is acknowledged, as are 'institutionalized aspects' (North, 1991) of the other two "IKK" social structures, kin and kind, which have some formal rules (e.g., marriage law, familial property rights) and informal restraints (sanctions, taboos, customs, traditions, codes of conduct).

Integration: connecting within, across, and between design arenas, core to BIG Design as a result of rejecting the fixed transitions of RILED processes.

Integrative: a resource becomes integrative when it connects within, across, or between design arenas. Activation and realisation of integrative functions can be adventitious (especially in concourses) or due to planned creation of resources such as worth maps (Cockton, 2013b).

Invigorative: a resource becomes invigorative when it impoves a design team's confidence and motivation. Activation and realisation of invigorative functions is typically adventitious and cannot be planned for. It results from unexpected significant advances in the progression of design work (Cockton, 2013b).

Iteration: (1) In VCD, the fourth process. (2) In RILED processes, going around the same line again, perhaps skipping stages. Replaced by end of episode planning in BIG Design.

Iteration Shift Table: a Wo-Fo partial concourse in table format, with explicit links from rows to the research activity in which they are grounded in one column, and artefact capabilities, likely beneficiaries, benefits, and sacrifices (costs, risks) in the other four columns (George, 2016). The start of a design progression via Artefact Connection Tables to Worth Shift Tables.

IxD: Interaction Design.

Kano Model: a quality model (Kano et al., 1984) with five categories of consumer satisfaction, translated in several ways from Japanese: must-be, indifferent, one-dimensional, attractive, and reverse. The must-be category is like Herzberg's hygiene factors (threshold factors in Section 6.1). The attractive category is like Herzberg's motivators (excitement factors in Section 6.1) and can be a target for generous purpose. One-dimensional is both a motivator and hygiene factor: presence satisfies and non-presence dissatisfies (threshold factors in Section 6.1). The indifferent category neither satisfies or dissatisfies (as with absence of factors in Herzberg). The reverse category is consumer-dependent, motivating some and dissatisfying others.

Kin: the second social structure in L-ERG-IKK (Cockton, 2009b), focused on family and associated relationships ("kith and kin").

Kind: the third social structure in L-ERG-IKK (Cockton, 2009b), communities of kind with no spatial boundaries within organisations (e.g., professions, clients, customers), and in groups (e.g., age, faith, gender, sexuality, race, impairment). Communities of kind bring additional value systems into kin and institutions.

L-ERG-IKK: a simple inquisitive resource (Cockton, 2009b) for those allergic to the theory, which asks design teams what they intend to do in specific locales for intersections of individual (ERG) and collective (IKK) value (Cockton, 2006).

L-ERG-IKK+: L-ERG-IKK with a third dimension in addition to ERG and IKK: Mind, Body and Spirit, resulting in finer-grained intersections that allow specific focuses on cognition, embodiment, and affect.

Lacunation: the formation of cavities in biology. Looking for such gaps (lacunae in Latin) is an important critical strategy (Derrida, 1976/1967). However, advocates of RILED processes can be so blatant about gaps (Archer, 1963/4; Parnas and Clements, 1986; Dym et al., 2014) that there is no need for close reading or deconstruction. Such wilful disconnects with the realities of social arenas clearly expose power hierarchies in design practices. MADS have no gaps, only limitations. New design arenas and connection strucures can be added, but closure will never be achieved due to infinite possibilities for connections.

Latent: a CREAM mode for concourse connections where there is only the slightest hint of what a connection may be. Nevertheless, some form of is felt intuitively and is worth noting in the hope that some basis for a connection will follow progression of a design.

Lean: a form of agile development, specialised for innovative IxD by Lean UX (Gothelf and Seiden, 2013).

Literate Development: an early approach to connecting within and between beneficiary and a_tefact arenas using custom software tools (Cockton et al., 1995; Clarke, 1997).

Locale: a physical or virtual space with multiple senses of place for different co-located social groupings (IKK).

Loop of connections: a chain of connections that starts and ends with the same design arena. A complex structure for reflection and deliberation. Still hypothetical.

M-P4D: Meta-Principles for Designing.

MADS: Most Abstract Design Situation.

Maleficiary: someone who suffers from the use of an artefact (Cockton, 2017) as a primary, secondary, or tertiary user.

Means-End Chain: a usage focused articulation connecting artefact features and qualities via user experiences to usage outcomes. The basic structure underlying UXCs, WoDS, and Worth Maps.

MEC: Means-End Chain.

Memoranda: (Latin) things to be borne in mind, the co-product design arenas that must be connected to an a_tefact to form an axiofact (Cockton, 2017).

Memoranti: (Latin) things that have been born in mind through explcit connection resources.

Meta-Principles for Designing: highly abstract virtues and potentials that need to be instantiated to direct design work. Their abstraction allows them to span or involve multiple design arenas.

(Mis)fit: a RILED connection mode where items from one design arena are matched against items in another to assess the degree of (mis)fit.

Mobilisation: deploying resources in a social arena (Renn, 1992).

Most Abstract Design Situation: an ADS that only indicates the presence/absence of design arenas and connections. Only an ADS template is more abstract.

Multifocal: having a focus on more than one design arena.

MVP: a Minimal Viable Product, a Lean concept (Gothelf with Seiden, 2013), is an artefact with the minimal set of capabilities for success in a market.

MVP Experiment: an evaluation designed to test ungrounded assumptions behind a design-led product (Gothelf with Seiden, 2013).

Opportunity Identification: the first VCD process (Cockton, 2005), renamed to Worth Identification by (Vu, 2013).

Organisation: an alternative name for Institution as understood for L-ERG-IKK, but useful as a generalisation of design's beneficiaries with the "growing recognition that the main arena in which design is practiced is not business, but the organization" (Junginger, 2017).

PADS: Proportional Abstract Design Situation.

Palette: a design team's repertoire of resources, approaches, and progression patterns (Friedland, 2019).

Parti: short for *parti pris* (French), a departure point, a concourse beyond the Primary Generator, a conjecture with some analysis (Stolterman, 1999). The term originates in architecture, along with *charette*.

Partial Concourse: a concourse with some explicit connections.

Pattern: a more explicit concourse than codes, a semi-structured mix of design arenas with implicit and explicit connections (Alexander et al., 1977).

Performative: a resource becomes performative when it is used in social settings to inform, account, or persuade. Performative functions are activated by the anticipation of a social setting (Cockton, 2013a).

Persistent design arenas: artefact and anyficiaries, arenas that continue to exist after a project ends. Artefacts persist as long as the programmes that support them. Anyficiaries precede and outlive products and programmes.

PEW: Perceived and Expected Worth (Camara et al., 2013a). See ARROW above, which renamed PEW.

Playbook: a palette with an overlay of something akin to codes (Hillier et al., 1972) that triggers specific plays of resources, approaches, and progression patterns in specific contexts for design work (Gajander, 2019).

Pragmatic Frame: an organising principle, perhaps using metaphor or analogy, or elaborated as a coherent set of statements that characterise a current understanding (Dorst, 2015). A more useful framing of frames than logical frames.

Primary Generator: an antecedent of a proposed solution or conjecture (Darke, 1979); a concourse structure spanning the antefact and other design arenas.

Product: the "goods or services" (Junginger, 2017) developed by or for any organisation, regardless of sector (private, public, voluntary).

Programme: a co-ordinated series of projects to develop and maintain a product or product line (i.e., a family of related products such as an app, website, and kiosk).

Progression: a narrative of design work (Jones, 2020). What actually happens in a design project, as opposed to what should happen according to some imposed normative idealised process.

Proportional Abstract Design Situation: an ADS that shows extents of effort and/or results for each design arena. Connections are usually omitted and design arena indicators laid out in rows (George, 2016).

Protective: a resource becomes protective when it challenges and seeks to redirect a current design progression (Cockton, 2013a). Protective functions can be triggered along with ameliorative ones bearing on the quality and direction of design work. This function can be understood as keeping a project on the rails.

Purpose: one of four design arenas. This ephemeral curated arena does not exist in any major design paradigm, but is absorbed into others by Applied Arts (designer's vision), Engineering Design (requirements specifications), and HCD (users' needs, wants, and pain points).

QOC: Questions, Options, and Criteria, a framework for Design Rationales.

Quaternary connection: a connection of any structure between four design arenas.

Realisation: (1) for a resource, a potential function is realised when it contributes to a design move, with its impact ususaly inscribed in design resources. Realization of all relevant functions completes mobilization of a resources (Renn, 1992); (2) a hybrid connection mode where items in one design arena are re-expressed as items in another. Unlike direct transfer, there are significant differences between the originating and receiving arenas. Unlike translation, where sentences or phrases in one language are used to re-express sentences or phrases about the same topic in another, the topic can change with realisation connections, e.g., from things that matter to anyficiaries (descriptive, fact) to specific goals for design purpose (axiological, value). Extensive interpretation and transformation are needed.

Receptiveness Meta-Principle: a design team's openness to ideas, concepts, information, and challenges. A virtue with a golden mean between parsimony and extravagance. Related resource functions include inquisitve, informative, and ideative.

Reflective: a resource becomes reflective when it proposes options for design arena items and connections. Ideative functions have been identified since (Cockton, 2013a).

Relatedness: social needs in ERG that connect individuals to social groupings (IKK).

Resource: any co-product, knowledge, or element of practice that can support design research. Resources are mobilized by activating and realising potential functions. Activation is rarely automatic. Resources typically require work to set them to work.

Resource Function Analysis: the analysis of resources' potential functions and their activation and realisation in design work, especially conjunction and sequencing of function realisation (Jones, 2020).

RFA: Resource Function Analysis.

RILED: Rational Idealised Linear Engineering Design (Parnas and Clements, 1986), a normative process model with no basis in fact and contrary to 50 years on creative design.

RILED Connection Modes: explicit systematic modes of connection, currently direct transfer, statistical, and (mis)fit.

Rootstock connection: a simple connection onto which another connection is grafted.

Secondary user: a stakeholder who does not use an interactive artefact but has some responsibility (e.g., as a manager supplier or parent) towards primary users who do (and may thus benefit or suffer indirectly).

Simple Connection: a single connection of any arity, with no grafts.

SoMADS: a sequence of MADS, representing process, procedure, and progression using a MADS for each phase, stage, step, and episode of activity.

Statistical: a RILED connection mode where quantities/rankings in one design arena are used to determine quantities/rankings in others, based on descriptive or inferential statistics. For example, user rankings of needs or priorities can determine priorities for purpose or of a_tefact items for agile backlogs or MVP planning.

Subarena: any subdivision of a design arena. Subarenas can nest. Overlapping sets of subarenas are common. For example, the anyficiary subarena sets (beneficiaries, maleficiaries) and (primary users, secondary users, tertiary users) overlap. Suppliers are a subarena of secondary users. Sponsors could be a subarena of secondary or tertiary users depending on how the achieved worth of a system impacts them.

Ternary connection: a connection of any structure between three design arenas.

Tertiary user: a stakeholder who does not use an interactive artefact and has no responsibility for primary users who do (e.g., an associate of someone with accessibility problems, the public sphere for fake news), but who still benefit or suffer indirectly.

UAN: User Action Notation.

UCD: User-Centred Design.

Unary connection: a connection from a design arena to itself, indicating a significant change to it as a result of a current activity or episode. An additional grafted connection indicates when changes originate from another arena.

User-Centred Design: an extremist approach to design that only cares about primary users, ignoring other anyficiaries and related purpose.

User Action Notation: a tabular keystroke level representation of user interaction with digital artefacts (Hartson et al., 1990).

User Experience Case: an articulated connection resource. A use case table extended with columns for mental and sociomaterial memoranti. Originally called a User Experience Frame (UEF or UXF) but renamed to avoid confusion with other BIG uses of "frame."

UXC: User Experience Case.

Valencing: giving positive, neutral, or negative appraisals, along with some indication of strength of feeling.

Value: something beneficial that is appraised positively.

Value-Centred Design: a relaxed RILED framework of four processes for: positive design purpose, evaluation (planned before designing, resumed when test a_tefact beomes available), design, and iteration. Iteration is a process that plans what to do next based on whether value has been donated, delivered, degraded, destroyed, or denied (Cockton, 2005). Vu (2013) renamed the processes to align them with WCD (Cockton, 2006).

Value-Sensitive Design: an approach to design that is sensitive to users' values and seeks to respect them, avoiding adverse consequences of use for primary and other users (Friedman et al., 2006).

Values: abstract reifications that guide human behaviours and appraisals towards positives.

VCD: Value-Centred Design.

W2C: Working to Choose.

WCD: Worth-Centred Design.

WoDS: Worth Delivery Scenario.

Wo-Fo: Worth-Focused, a more balanced concept than worth-centred. Some design activities are worth-focused, others aren't. Design is a complex multifocal activity that cannot have a single centre without causing imbalance and distortion (Cockton, 2013b).

WOP: Worth-Oriented Persona.

Work product: an alternative term for co-product. Carroll's (1990) latter term is preferred. All work products in (Parnas and Clements, 1986) are in the a_tefact arena.

Working to Choose: a framework for understanding design work as a progression through design situations guided by M-P4D and supported by approaches, resources, and functions (Cockton, 2013b).

Worth: a sufficiently positive balance of benefits over sacrifices (costs, risks) that motivates people to buy, learn, use or recommend an interactive digital artefact (Cockton, 2006).

Worth Board: a mood board format where images of worthwhile outcomes replace or complement visual style and brand direction elements (Cockton et al., 2009a).

Worth-Centred Design: a revision of VCD that replaced value with worth and opportunity identification with a broader focus on individual and collective value (Cockton, 2006).

Worth Delivery Scenario: a usage scenario with a happy ending that indicates the worth achieved through an interaction.

Worth Integration Table: a Wo-Fo partial concourse in table format, with explicit links from rows to the research activity in which they are grounded in one column, and artefact capabilities, likely beneficiaries, benefits, and sacrifices (costs, risks) in the other four columns (George, 2016). The start of a design progression via Artefact Connection Tables to Worth Shift Tables.

Worth Map: a worth sketch with MECs threaded through it (Cockton et al., 2009a).

Worth-Oriented Persona: a persona based on a multi-arena template, providing direction on design purpose as well as information on the persona as an anyficiary, including their experience with, and preferences for, interactive digital artefacts. It should also be useful as a profiling resource for recruiting evaluation participants.

Worth Shift Table: a Wo-Fo table with two columns, one for an element of an existing situation, and one for a preferred situation, with the rows as a whole showing how a design can progress to change "existing circumstances into preferred ones" (Simon, 1969). The concourse structure here connects existing anyficiaries' circumstances to design purpose (George, 2016).

Worth Sketch: a vertical layout of worthies (Cockton et al., 2009a), with rows stacked up from the centre for positive MECs ,and down for negative ones, i.e., for the Worthy Types below, materials are in the middle row, worthwhile outcomes at the top, and adverse outcomes at the bottom

Worthy: an element in a MEC (plural worthies).

Worthy Types: the different types of elements in a MEC. For Worth Maps in Vu (2013), these are worthwhile outcomes, positive user experiences, qualities, features, materials, defects, negative user experiences, and adverse outcomes.

References

Abrams, R. 2003. Byker revisited. *Built Environment,* 29(2), 117–13. DOI: 10.2148/benv.29.2.117.54463. 56

Adolph, S., Bramble, P., Cockburn, A., and Pols, A. 2002. *Patterns for Effective Use Cases.* Addison-Wesley. 60

Alderfer, C. 1972. *Existence, Relatedness, and Growth.* Free Press. 19, 36, 117, 172

Alexander., C. 1964. *Notes on the Synthesis of Form.* Harvard University Press. 38, 51

Alexander, C. 1971. State of the Art in Design Methodology: Interview with C. Alexander, *DMG (Design Methods Group) Newsletter* 5(3), 3–7. 3

Alexander, C., Ishikawa, S., and Silverstein, M., with Jacobson, M., Fiksdahl-King, I., and Angel, S. 1977. *A Pattern Language: Towns, Buildings, Construction.* Oxford. 57, 177

Allingham, M. 2002. *Choice Theory.* Oxford Paperbacks. DOI: 10.1093/actrade/9780192803030.001.0001. 30

Anscombe, G. E. M. 1958. Modern moral philosophy. *Philosophy,* 33(124), 1–19. DOI: 10.1017/S0031819100037943. 10

Archer, L. Bruce. 1963/4. Systematic method for designers. *Design.* 176

Ashby, W. R. 1958. Requisite variety and its implications for the control of complex systems, *Cybernetica,* 1(2), 83-99. 15

ATELIER (Project: Thomas Binder, Giorgio De Michelis, Pelle Ehn, Giulio Jacucci, Per Linde, and Ina Wagner). 2011. *Design Things.* MIT Press. 171

Ballantyne, A. 2002. *Architecture: A Very Short Introduction.* Oxford. DOI: 10.1093/actrade/9780192801791.001.0001. 27

Bangor A., Kortum, P. T., and Miller J. T. 2008. An empirical evaluation of the system usability scale. *International Journal of Human-Computer Interaction,* 24(6), 574–594. DOI: 10.1080/10447310802205776. 121, 122

Barnes, J. 2000. *Aristotle: A Very Short Introduction.* Oxford. DOI: 10.1093/actrade/9780192854087.001.0001. 31

Beaney, M. 2017. *Analytic Philosophy: A Very Short Introduction.* Oxford. DOI: 10.1093/actrade/9780198778028.001.0001. 154

Beck, K., Beedle, M., Van Bennekum, A., Cockburn, A., Cunningham, W., Fowler, M., Grenning, J., Highsmith, J., Hunt, A., Jeffries, R., Kern, J., Marick, B., Martin, R. C., Mellor, S., Schwaber, K., Sutherland, J., and Thomas D. 2001. *Manifesto for Agile Software Development*, http://www.agilemanifesto.org. 28, 65, 155, 157, 167

Benedek, J. and Miner, T. 2002. Measuring desirability: New methods for evaluating desirability in a usability lab setting. Presented at the *Usability Professionals' Association Conference*, Orlando, Florida, July 8, 2002. 27

Bentham, J. 1789. *An Introduction to the Principles of Morals and Legislation*. London. Available from https://www.earlymoderntexts.com/assets/pdfs/bentham1780.pdf. DOI: 10.1093/oseo/instance.00077240. 8

Biedenbach, T. and Jacobsson, M. 2016. The open secret of values: The roles of values and axiology in project research. *Project Management Journal*, 47(3), 139–155. DOI: 10.1177/875697281604700312. xv

Blandford, A., Hyde, J. K., Green, T. R. G., Connell, I. Blandford, A., Hyde, J. K., Green, T. R. G., and Connell, I. 2008. Scoping usability evaluation methods: A case study. *Human Computer Interaction Journal*, 23(3), 278–327. DOI 10.1080/07370020802278254. 38, 43

Boehner, K., Vertesi, J., Sengers, P., and Dourish, P. 2007. How HCI interprets the probes. *Proceedings of the SIGCHI Conference on Human Factors in Computing Systems (CHI '07)*, ACM, 1077–1086. DOI: 10.1145/1240624.1240789. 37

Bourdieu, Pierre. 1984. Distinction: a social critique of the judgement of taste. Routledge. 173

Boztepe, S. 2007. Toward a framework of product development for global markets: A user-value-based approach. *Design Studies*, 28(5), 513–533. DOI: 10.1016/j.destud.2007.02.010. 10

Brooke, J. 2013. SUS: A retrospective. *Journal of Usability Studies*, 8(2), 29–40. 120

Brooks, B. M. 1981. Bus design: A study of passenger capabilities and requirements. *Design for Work and Use*, Vol. 2., eds. Maule, H. G. and Weiner, J. S. Taylor and Francis, 15–48. 35

Brown J., Graham T. C. N., and Wright T. 1998. The vista environment for the coevolutionary design of user interfaces. *Proceedings of Human Factors in Computing Systems (CHI'98)*, ACM. 376–383. DOI: 10.1145/274644.274696. 89, 158, 174

Brown, T. 2009. *Change by Design: How Design Thinking Transforms Organizations and Inspires Innovation*. Harper Business. xvi, 30, 102, 143

Browne, M. W. (1983). Disaster on I-95. *Discover*, September, pp. 14–15, 18–20, 22. 38

Buchenau, M. and Suri, J. F. 2000. Experience prototyping. *Proceedings of 3rd Conference on Designing Interactive Systems: Processes, Practices, Methods, and Techniques (DIS '00)*, eds. Boyarski, D. and Kellogg, W. A. ACM, 424–433. DOI: 10.1145/347642.347802. 39

Camara, F., Demumieux, R., Calvary, G., and Mandran, N. 2010. Cocoon, un système de recommandation sensible au contexte: analyse de la valeur par une étude qualitative. *Proceedings Ergonomie et Informatique Avancee Conference (Ergo'IA '10)*, ACM, 211–218. DOI: 10.1145/1868650.1868685. 116, 125

Camara, F. 2012. Retours d'expérience sur la conception centrée valeur de Cocoon: vers des arbres de vie. Ph.D. Thesis Université de Grenoble. https://tel.archives-ouvertes.fr/tel-00848189/document. xviii, 66, 73, 86, 115, 124, 125, 127, 139, 158

Camara, F. and Calvary, G. 2015. Worth-centered design in practice: Lessons from experience and research agenda. *Human-Computer Interaction—INTERACT 2015*, eds. Abascal, J., Barbosa, S., Fetter, M., Gross, T., Palanque, P. and Winckler, M. LNCS 9299. Springer, 123–139. DOI: 10.1007/978-3-319-22723-8_10. 115, 124, 125, 126, 127, 128, 129, 137, 144, 168

Camara, F. and Calvary, G. 2017. Bringing worth maps a step further: A dedicated online-resource. 2017. *Human-Computer Interaction—INTERACT 2017*, eds Bernhaupt R., Dalvi G., Joshi A., K. Balkrishan D., O'Neill, J., and Winckler ,M., LNCS 10515. Springer, 95–113. DOI: 10.1007/978-3-319-67687-6_8. 115, 124, 129, 135, 144, 157, 158, 162, 168

Camara, F., Calvary, G., and Demumieux, R. 2013a. The PEW framework for worth mapping. *Human-Computer Interaction—INTERACT 2013*, eds. Kotzé P., Marsden G., Lindgaard G., Wesson J., and Winckler M., LNCS 8120. Springer, 667–674. DOI: 10.1007/978-3-642-40498-6_59. 115, 124, 125, 126, 127, 130, 134, 140, 178

Camara, F., Parmentier, T., and Kharab, M. 2013b. Colibri: Towards a new generation of advanced planning systems. Demonstration paper. IHM'13. Published as hal-00879554 at https://hal.inria.fr/hal-00879554/document. 127, 128

Cao, X., Lindley, S. E., Helmes, J., and Sellen, A. 2010. Telling the whole story: anticipation, inspiration and reputation in a field deployment of TellTable. *Proceedings of the 2010 ACM Conference on Computer Supported Cooperative Work*, ACM, New York, 251–260. DOI: 10.1145/1718918.1718967. 50, 103, 125, 126, 142, 144

Carroll, J. M. 1990. Infinite detail and emulation in an ontologically minimized HCI. *Proceedings Conference on Human Factors in Computing Systems (CHI '90)*, eds. Chew, J. C. and Whiteside, J. ACM, 321–328. DOI: 10.1145/97243.97303. 35, 60, 105, 181

Carroll, J. M. 2000. *Making Use: Scenario-Based Design of Human-Computer Interactions.* Cambridge, MA: MIT Press. 29, 87, 169

Carroll, J. M. 2002. Scenarios and design cognition. *Proceedings IEEE Joint International Conference on Requirements Engineering (RE'02)*, eds. Dubois, E. and Pohl, K. 3–5. 78

Casner, S. M. 1991. A task-analytic approach to the automated design of graphic presentations. *ACM Transactions on Graphics*, 10 (5), 111–151. DOI: 10.1145/108360.108361. 60

Choi, B., Lee, I., Kim, J., and Jeon, Y. 2005. A qualitative cross-national study of cultural influences on mobile data service design. *Proceedings of the SIGCHI Conference on Human Factors in Computing Systems*, ACM, 661–670. DOI: 10.1145/1054972.1055064. 54

Clarke, S. 1997. Encouraging the effective use of contextual information in design, Ph.D. thesis, Department of Computer Science, University of Glasgow. http://theses.gla.ac.uk/71754/. xxi, 54, 85, 86 , 87, 89, 91, 97, 103, 106, 107, 113, 141, 155, 157, 158, 176

Clarke, S. and Cockton, G. 1998. Linking between multiple points in design documents. *CHI 98 Conference Summary*, eds. Karat, C-M. et al. ACM, 223–224. DOI: 10.1145/286498.286713. 88, 89

Christensen, C. M. and Kaufman, S. P. 2008. Innovation killers: How financial tools destroy your capacity to do new things. *Harvard Business Review*, 86(1), 98–105. 1, 152

CNVC, 2005. Needs Inventory. Center for Nonviolent Communication. Available from https://www.cnvc.org/training/resource/needs-inventory. 15, 17

Cockburn, A. 2000. *Writing Effective Use Cases.* Addison Wesley. 61

Cockton, G. 1998. Let's get it all together: Literate development and the integration of HCI research. *ACM CHI 98 Basic Research Symposium*, eds. Konstan, J. and J. Siegel, J. Version 1.2 (2001) at http://northumbria.academia.edu/GilbertCockton/Papers/1847746/Lets_Get_It_all_Together_Literate_Development_and_the_Integration_of_HCI_Research. 86, 91, 111, 173

Cockton, G. 2004a. From quality in use to value in the world. *CHI 2004 Extended Abstracts*, ACM, 1287–90. DOI: 10.1145/985921.986045. 26, 54, 85, 111, 119, 123

Cockton, G. 2004b. Value-centred HCI. *Proceedings Third Nordic Conference on Human-Computer Interaction*, ed. Hyrskykari, A. 149–160. DOI: 10.1145/1028014.1028038. 9, 26, 116, 119

Cockton, G. 2005. A development framework for value-centred design. *CHI 2005 Extended Abstracts*, ed. Gale, C. ACM, 1292–95. DOI: 10.1145/1056808.1056899. 9, 85, 115, 116, 119, 120, 125, , 145, 146, 147, 148, 173, 181

Cockton, G. 2006. Designing worth is worth designing. *Proceedings NordiCHI 2006*, eds. Mørch, A. I., Morgan, K., Bratteteig, T., Ghosh, G., and Svanæs, D. 165–174. DOI: 10.1145/1182475.1182493. xvi, 11, 35, 85, 116, 119, 123, 126, 144, 146, 176, 181, 182

Cockton, G. 2007. Make evaluation poverty history, alt.chi paper, *CHI 2007*, available from https://www.academia.edu/1906725/Make_Evaluation_Poverty_History. DOI: 10.1145/1240624.2180964. 43, 52, 92, 93, 97, 119, 126

Cockton, G. 2008a. Designing worth: Connecting preferred means with probable ends. *Interactions*, 15(4), ACM, 54–57. DOI: 10.1145/1374489.1374502. 91, 96, 97, 98, 105, 108, 119, 120, 123, 125, 126, 128, 129, 144

Cockton, G. 2008b. Revisiting usability's three key principles. *CHI 2008 Extended Abstracts*, 2473–2484. DOI: 10.1145/1358628.1358704. 80, 119

Cockton, G. 2008c. What worth measuring is. *5th COST294-MAUSE Open Workshop Meaningful Measures: Valid Useful User Experience Measurement*, eds. Law, E. L-C., Bevan, N., Christou, G., Springett, M., and Lárusdóttir, M. 60–66. 26, 52, 72

Cockton, G. 2008d. Sketch worth, catch dreams, be fruity. *CHI 2008 Extended Abstracts*, eds. Czerwinski, M., Lund, A. M., and Tan, D.S. 2579–2582. DOI: 10.1145/1358628.1358716. 119

Cockton, G. 2008e. Putting value into e-valu-ation. *Maturing Usability: Quality in Software, Interaction and Value*, eds. Law, E., Hvannberg, E., and Cockton, G. 287–317, Springer. DOI: 10.1007/978-1-84628-941-5_13. 119

Cockton, G., 2008f. Load while aiming; Hit?", in *Usability Professionals 2008*, eds. Bau, H., Diefenbach, S., Hassenzahl, M., Koller, F., Peissner, M., and Röse, K. 17-22, German Chapter der Usability Professionals Association e.V.. Invited Keynote Address, available at https://tinyurl.com/rkjy2l4. 119

Cockton, G. 2009a. Getting there: Six meta-principles and interaction design. *Proceedings CHI 2009*, eds. Olsen Jr., D. R., Arthur, R. B., Hinckley, K., Morris, M. R., Hudson, S., and Greenberg, S. ACM, 2223–2232. xvii, 21, 24, 30, 31, 32, 35, 60, 62, 65, 85, 86, 108, 119, 120, 141, 147, 149, 155, 167, 173, 174

Cockton, G. 2009b. When and why feelings and impressions matter in interaction design. *Kansei 2009: Interfejs Użytkownika—Kansei w praktyce, CD Rom Proceedings*, Polsko-Japońska Wyższa Szkoła Technik Komputerowych, 7–31. http://repin.pjwstk.edu.pl:8080/xmlui/bitstream/handle/186319/126/kansei2009_Cockton.pdf?sequence=1. 19, 22, 23, 48, 60, 62, 63, 77, 79, 119, 176

Cockton, G. 2010. Design situations and methodological innovation in interaction design. *CHI 2010 Extended Abstracts*, eds. Mynatt, E. D., Schoner, D., Fitzpatrick, G., Hudson, S. E., Edwards, K. and Rodden, T. ACM, 2745–2754. DOI: 10.1145/1753846.1753859. xvii, 47, 67, 77, 82, 111, 119, 133, 167

Cockton, G. 2012. Making designing worth worth designing. *Position Paper, CHI 2012 Workshop on Methods for Accounting for Values in Human-Centered Computing*. Available from http://ii.tudelft.nl/ValuesInDesign/submissions/cockton.pdf. 30

Cockton, G. 2013a. You (have to) design design, co design. Included *Wer gestaltet die Gestaltung? Praxis, Theorie und Geschichte des partizipatorischen Designs.*, eds, Mareis, C., Held, M., and Joost, G., Bielefeld: transcript. 181–205. xvii, 31, 32, 39, 40, 86, 116, 120, 167, 168, 171, 172, 174, 178, 179

Cockton, G. 2013b. Design isn't a shape and it hasn't got a centre: thinking BIG about post-centric interaction design. *Proceedings MIDI '13*, ACM, Article 2. DOI: 10.1145/2500342.2500344. xvii, 30, 83, 86, 102, 116, 120, 140, 169, 171, 172, 175, 181

Cockton, G. 2013c. A load of cobbler's children: beyond the model designing processor. *CHI '13 Extended Abstracts on Human Factors in Computing Systems*, ACM, 2139–2148. DOI: 10.1145/2468356.2468733. 5, 43

Cockton, G. 2014. A critical, creative UX community: CLUF. *Journal of Usability Studies*, 10(1), 1–16. Invited Editorial, available at http://uxpajournal.org/a-critical-creative-ux-community-cluf/. 34

Cockton, G. 2016a. Integrating both user-ccentred design and creative practices into agile development, in *Integrating User-Centered Design in Agile Development*, eds. Cockton, G., Lárusdóttir, M. L., Gregory, P., and Cajander, Å. , Springer, 1–46. DOI: 10.1007/978-3-319-32165-3_1. 28, 81, 155, 172

Cockton, G. 2016b. Five kanbans for better balanced agile development, Position paper for *NordiCHI 2106 Workshop on Stakeholder Involvement in Agile Software*. Available at https://stakeholdersinagile.wordpress.com/papers/. 105

Cockton, G. 2017. New process, new vocabulary: Axiofact = A_tefact + Memoranda, *CHI '17 Extended Abstracts on Human Factors in Computing Systems (CHI EA '17)*, ACM, 747–757. DOI: 10.1145/3027063.3052755. 167, 168, 169, 170, 177

Cockton, G. 2020a. *Worth-Focused Design: Book 1: Balance, Integration, and Generosity*. Morgan & Claypool, San Rafael, CA. DOI: 10.2200/S01000ED1V02Y202003HCI046. x, xv, xxii, 1, 3, 4, 6, 7, 18, 22, 29, 30, 32, 33, 39, 45, 47, 48, 49, 55, 56, 58, 59, 67, 68, 70, 72, 78, 81, 83, 86, 88, 93, 96, 98, 101, 105, 106, 119, 130, 131, 133, 136, 137, 142, 144, 148, 154, 163, 164

Cockton, G. and Clarke, S. 1999. Using contextual information effectively in design, *INTERACT 99 Proceedings*, eds. Sasse, A. and Johnson, C., 578–585. 88, 91

Cockton, G., Clarke, S., and Gray, P. D. 1995. Theories of context influence the system abstractions used to design interactive systems. *People and Computers X*, eds. Kirby, M. A. R., Dix, A. J. and Finlay, J. E. Cambridge University Press, 387–405. 87, 176

Cockton, G., Clarke, S., Gray, P. D., and Johnson, C. 1996. Literate development: Weaving human context into design specifications. *Critical Issues in User Interface Systems Engineering*, eds. Benyon, D. and Palanque, P. Springer Verlag, 227–248. DOI: 10.1007/978-1-4471-1001-9_13. 87

Cockton, G., Gregory, P., Lárusdóttir, M. L., and Cajander, Å. 2016. Introduction. Integrating user-centred design in agile development. *Integrating User-Centered Design in Agile Development*, eds. Cockton, G., Lárusdóttir, M. L., Gregory, P., and Cajander, Å. , Springer, 1–46. DOI: 10.1007/978-3-319-32165-3_1. 152

Cockton, G., Kirk, D., Sellen, A., and Banks, R. 2009a. Evolving and augmenting worth mapping for family archives. *Proceedings HCI 2009*, 329–338, BCS. DOI: 10.14236/ewic/HCI2009.40. 66, 91, 92, 109, 119, 126, 127, 174, 182

Cockton, G., Kujala, S., Nurkka, P., and Hölttä, T. 2009b. Supporting worth mapping with sentence completion. *Proceedings. INTERACT 2009*. II: 566–581. DOI: 10.1007/978-3-642-03658-3_61. 66, 85, 86, 98, 99, 101, 103, 110, 111, 119

Cockton, G., Woolrych, A., and Hindmarch, M. 2004. Reconditioned merchandise: extended structured report formats in usability inspection. *CHI '04 Extended Abstracts on Human Factors in Computing Systems (CHI EA '04)*, ACM, 1433-1436. DOI: 10.1145/985921.986083. 5, 85

Cockton, G., Woolrych, A. Hornbæk, K., and Frøkjær, E. 2012. Inspection-based evaluations. *The Human-Computer Interaction Handbook*, 3rd ed., ed. Jacko, J. 1275–1293. DOI: 10.1201/b11963-ch-56. 34, 51

Cohn, M. 2004. *User Stories Applied*. Addison-Wesley Professional. 58

Convertino, G. and Frishberg, N. 2020. Impact through alliances: two stories. *Interactions*, 27(1),77–79. DOI: 10.1145/3371289. 35, 39

Cooper, A., Reimann, R., and Cronin, D. 2007. *About Face 3.0: The Essentials of Interaction Design*. Wiley. 42, 77

Covey, S. R., Merrill, R. R., and Merrill, A. R. 1994. *First Things First: To Live, to Love, to Learn, to Leave a Legacy*. Simon & Schuster. 14, 36

Crabtree, A., Rodden, T., Tolmie, P., and Button, G. 2009. Ethnography considered harmful. *Proceedings of the SIGCHI Conference on Human Factors in Computing Systems (CHI '09)*, ACM, 879–888. DOI: 10.1145/1518701.1518835. 37

Cross, N. 2001. Designerly ways of knowing: Design discipline versus design science. *Design Issues*, 17(3). 49–55. DOI: 10.1162/074793601750357196. 102

Cross, N. 2011. *Design Thinking: Understanding How Designers Think and Work*. Berg. DOI: 10.5040/9781474293884. 148

Dallmayr, F. 1998. Habermas and rationality. *Political Theory*, 16(4), 553–579. DOI: 10.1177/0090591788016004002. 108

Dam, R. and Siang, T. 2017. Define and frame your design challenge by creating your point of view and ask "How might we." https://tinyurl.com/yb2c8hfz. 50

Darke, J. 1979. The primary generator and the design process. *Design Studies*, 1(1), 36–44. DOI: 10.1016/0142-694X(79)90027-9. 8, 13, 18, 27, 28, 38, 52, 56, 59, 154, 160, 170, 171, 178

Davies, R. and Talbot, R. 1987. Experiencing ideas; identity, insight and the imago. *Design Studies*, 8(1), 17–25. DOI: 10.1016/0142-694X(87)90027-5. 7, 12, 18, 23, 30, 31, 47, 152, 171

Deci, E. L. and Ryan, R. M. 2000. The "What" and 'Why' of goal pursuits: human needs and self-determination of behaviour. *Psychological Inquiry*, 11(4), 227–268. DOI: 10.1207/S15327965PLI1104_01. 118

DeLanda, M. 2006. *A New Philosophy of Society: Assemblage Theory and Social Complexity*. Bloomsbury. 129, 162

Derrida, J. 1976. *Of Grammatology* (G. Spivak's translation of De La Grammatologie 1967). Johns Hopkins University Press. 176

Dewey, J. 1938. *Logic: The Theory of Inquiry*. Henry Holt and Company. 145, 146, 147

Dilnot, C. 2017. Introduction and notes on editing the manuscript. *Design and the Creation of Value*, eds. Dilnot, C. and Boztepe, S. Bloomsbury, 1–20, 39–42. DOI: 10.5040/9781474274289.0007. xvi, xvii, 159

Doblin, J. 1978. *Innovation: A Cook Book Approach*. Doblin. Available from https://doblin.com/our-thinking/innovation-a-cook-book-approach. 9

Doherty, E. P. Cockton, G., Bloor, C., and Benigno, D. 2000. Mixing oil and water: Transcending method boundaries in assistive technology for traumatic brain injury. *Proceedings ACM 1st Conf. on Universal Usability*, eds. Sholtz, J. and Thomas, J. ACM, 110–117. DOI: 10.1145/355460.355544. 85

Dorst, K. 2015. *Frame Innovation: Create New Thinking by Design.* MIT Press. DOI: 10.7551/mitpress/10096.001.0001. 8, 15, 19, 67, 93, 171, 173, 178

Dorst, Kt. 2017. *Notes on Design: How Creative Practice Works.* BIS. 3, 170

Dorst, K .and Dijkhuis J. 1995. Comparing paradigms for describing design activity. *Design Studies,* 16(2), 261-274. 171

Douglas, L. C. 2000. Marketing features vs. benefits. *HomeOfficeMag.com,* December, archived at http://www.entrepreneur.com/article/34942. 58, 173

Dourish, P. 2001. *Where the Action Is: The Foundations of Embodied Interaction.* MIT Press. DOI: 10.7551/mitpress/7221.001.0001. 30

Dourish, P. 2006. Implications for design. *Proceedings of the SIGCHI Conference on Human Factors in Computing Systems (CHI '06),* eds. Grinter, R., Rodden, T., Aoki, P., Cutrell, E., Jeffries, R., and Olson, G. ACM, 541–550. DOI: 10.1145/1124772.1124855. 53, 89

Dym, C. L., Little, P., and Orwin, E. J. 2014. *Engineering Design: A Project Based Introduction,* 4th ed. Wiley. 176

EL-Qirem F. and Cockton G. 2011. Computer usage and user experience in Jordan: Development and application of the diamond model of territorial factors. *Human–Computer Interaction. Towards Mobile and Intelligent Interaction Environments,* ed. Jacko, J. A. LNCS 6763. Springer. DOI: 10.1007/978-3-642-21616-9_55. 54

Erete, S., Israni, A., and Dillahunt, T. 2018. An intersectional approach to designing in the margins. *Interactions,* 25(3), 66–69. DOI: 10.1145/3194349. 14

Erickson, T. 1996. Design as storytelling. *Interactions,* 30–35 (July). DOI: 10.1145/234813.234817. 81

Fallman, D. 2003. Design-oriented human-computer interaction. In *Proceedings of the SIGCHI Conference on Human Factors in Computing Systems (CHI '03),* ACM, 225–232. DOI: 10.1145/642611.642652. 3, 5, 18, 44, 53, 56, 150, 153

Forester, J. 1999. *The Deliberative Practitioner: Encouraging Participatory Planning Processes.* MIT Press. 107

Frayling, C. 1993. *Research in Art and Design.* Royal College of Art. 1(1). xvii, 161

Friedland, L. 2019. Culture eats UX strategy for breakfast. *Interactions,* 26(5), 78–81. DOI: 10.1145/3344947. 6, 158, 178

Friedman, B. and Hendry, D. 2012. The envisioning cards: a toolkit for catalyzing humanistic and technical imaginations. *Proceedings of the SIGCHI Conference on Human Factors in Computing Systems (CHI '12),* ACM, 1145-1148. DOI: 10.1145/2207676.2208562. 23

Friedman, B., Kahn, P. H., Jr., and Borning, A. 2006. Value sensitive design and information systems. *Human-Computer Interaction and Management Information Systems: Foundations*, eds. Zhang, P., Galletta, D., and Sharpe, M. E. 348–372. 9, 14, 19, 23, 112, 181

Gajendar, U. 2019. Toward a playbook for UX leaders. *Interactions*, 26(2), 24-25. DOI: 10.1145/3305354. 6, 158, 178

Garrett, J. J. 2002. *The Elements of User Experience: User-Centered Design for the Web*. New Riders Publishing. 87

Garnik, I., Sikorski, M., and Cockton, G. 2014. Creative sprints: an unplanned broad agile evaluation and redesign process. *Proceedings NordiCHI '14*, ACM, 1125–1130. DOI: 10.1145/2639189.2670290. 34, 44, 53

Garrett, J. J. 2010. *The Elements of User Experience: User-centered Design for the Web*. New Riders. DOI: 10.1111/j.1948-7169.2006.tb00027.x. 38

Gaver, B., Dunne, T., and Pacenti, E. 1999. Design: Cultural probes. *Interactions*, 6(1), 21–29. DOI: 10.1145/291224.291235. 59

Gaver, W. 2011. Making spaces: how design workbooks work. *Proceedings SIGCHI Conference on Human Factors in Computing Systems (CHI '11)*, ACM, 1551–1560. DOI: 10.1145/1978942.1979169. 18, 26, 38, 39, 58, 59, 141, 156, 160, 162, 170

Gaver, W. and Bowers, J. 2012. Annotated portfolios. *Interactions*, 19(4), 40–49. DOI: 10.1145/2212877.2212889. 3, 10, 12, 16, 18, 38, 39, 54, 58, 59, 141, 143, 149, 159, 162, 170

Gedenryd, H. 1998. How designers work: Making sense of authentic cognitive activities. *Lund University Cognitive Studies* 75. Available from https://lup.lub.lu.se/search/publication/d88efa51-c2f9-4551-a259-00bd36fe8d03. 3, 6, 81, 94, 153

George, J. 2016. A case study of balance and integration in worth-focused research through design, Ph.D. thesis, Northumbria University. http://nrl.northumbria.ac.uk/30326/. xviii, xxii, 5, 33, 52, 58, 68, 70, 86, 115, 130, 133, 137, 139, 140, 141, 143, 144, 153, 157, 158, 162, 169, 171, 175, 178, 182

George, J., Cockton, G., and Greenough, T. 2010. A social approach to accessible social networking using the CAT Model. *ICCHP 2010, Part I, LNCS 6179*, eds. Miesenberger, K. et al. Springer. 216–223. DOI: 10.1007/978-3-642-14097-6_35. 132

Gergen, K. J. 2005. Narrative, moral identity, and historical consciousness: A social constructionist account. *Narrative, Identity, And Historical Consciousness*, ed. Straub, J. Berghahn, 99-119. https://works.swarthmore.edu/fac-psychology/589. 77

Gilmore, D. J., Cockton, G., Kujala, S., Churchill, E. F., Henderson, A., and Hammontree, M. L. 2008. Values, value and worth: Their relationship to HCI? *CHI 2008 Extended Abstracts*, eds. M. Czerwinski, A. M. Lund, and D.S. Tan, 3933–3936. DOI: 10.1145/1358628.1358960. 119

Goldschmidt, G. 2014. *Linkography: Unfolding the Design Process*. MIT Press. DOI: 10.7551/mitpress/9455.001.0001. 170

Gothelf, J. with Seiden, J. 2013. *Lean UX: Applying Lean Principles to Improve User Experience*. O'Reilly. 20, 21, 28, 38, 65, 76, 176, 177

Gould, J. D., Boies, S. J., Levy, S., Richards, J. T., and Schoonard, J. 1987. The 1984 Olympic message system: A test of behavioral principles of system design. *Communications ACM* 30(9), 758–769. DOI: 10.1145/30401.30402. 88, 89

Gould, J. and Lewis, C. 1985. Designing for usability: Key principles and what designers think. *CACM*, 28(3). 300–311. DOI: 10.1145/3166.3170. 30, 31

Gram, C. and Cockton, G. 1996. *Design Principles for Interactive Software*. Chapman and Hall. DOI: 10.1007/978-0-387-34912-1. 39

Green, P. E. and Srinivasan, V. 1978. Conjoint analysis in consumer research: Issues and outlook. *Journal of Consumer Research*, 5(2), 103–23. DOI: 10.1086/208721. 8

Guindon, R. 1990. Designing the design process: exploiting opportunistic thoughts. *Human–Computer Interaction*, 5(2), 305–344. DOI: 10.1207/s15327051hci0502&3_6. 8

Hanfling, O. 2003. *Logical Positivism*. Routledge History of Philosophy. Routledge. 150

Harper, R., Rodden, T., Rogers, Y., and Sellen, A. 2008. Being Human: HCI in 2020. Microsoft Research Ltd. www.microsoft.com/en-us/research/project/being-human/. 67, 146

Hartson, H. R., Siochi, A. C., and Hix, D. 1990. The UAN: A user-oriented representation for direct manipulation interface designs. *ACM Transactions on Information Systems*, 8(3), 181–203. DOI: 10.1145/98188.98191. 180

Hassenzahl, M. 2004. The interplay of beauty, goodness, and usability in interactive products. *Human-Computer Interactions* 19(4), 319–349. DOI: 10.1207/s15327051hci1904_2. 26

Hertzum, M. and Jacobsen, N. E. 2003. The evaluator effect: A chilling fact about usability evaluation methods. *International Journal of Human–Computer Interaction*, 15(1), 183–204. DOI: 10.1207/S15327590IJHC1501_14. 43

Herzberg, F. 1966. *Work and the Nature of Man*. Ty Crowell Co; Reissue Edition. 9, 13, 117, 121

Heskett, J. 2005. *Design: A Very Short Introduction*. Oxford. DOI: 10.1093/actrade/9780192854469.001.0001. 30

Heskett, J. 2017. *Design and the Creation of Value*, eds. Dilnot, C. and Boztepe, S. Bloomsbury. DOI: 10.5040/9781474274289. xvii, 11, 12, 13, 156

Hewett, T. T. 1986. The role of iterative evaluation in designing systems for usability. *People and Computers: Designing for Usability*, eds. Harrison, M. D. and Monk, A. F. Cambridge University Press, 196–214. 34

Hey, E. 2006. Conducting large-scale multi-user user tests on the United Kingdom air defence command and control system: case study. *Journal Usability Studies*, 1(3), 121–135. 34

Hiles, D. R. 2008. Axiology. *The Sage Encyclopedia of Qualitative Research Methods*, ed. Given, L. M. Sage Publications. DOI: 10.4135/9781412963909. 8

Hillier, B., Musgrove, J., and O' Sullivan, P. 1972. Knowledge and design. *Environmental Design: Research and Practice*, edra3/ar8 conference, ed. Mitchell, W. UCLA. 57, 59, 76, 116, 117, 169, 178

Holtzblatt, K. and Beyer, H. 2014. Contextual design. *The Encyclopedia of Human-Computer Interaction*, 2nd ed., eds. Soegaard, M. and Dam, R. F. The Interaction Design Foundation. DOI: 10.1145/291224.291229. 34, 88

Homer P. and Kahle L. R. 1988. A structural equation test of the value-attitude-behavior hierarchy. *Journal of Personality and Social Psychology*, 54(4), 638–646. DOI: 10.1037/0022-3514.54.4.638. 15

Hume, D. (1896 ed.). *A Treatise of Human Nature* [1739] (ed.) Lewis Amherst Selby-Bigge. Oxford. 149

Ísleifsdóttir, J. and Lárusdóttir, M. 2008. Measuring the user experience of a task oriented software. *5th COST294-MAUSE Open Workshop Meaningful Measures: Valid Useful User Experience Measurement*, eds. Law, E. L-C., Bevan, N., Christou, G., Springett, M., and Lárusdóttir, M., 97–101. 26

ISO. 2019. Human-centred design for interactive systems. *Ergonomics of Human System Interaction Part 210 (ISO 9241–210)*. International Organization for Standardization. 21, 48, 78, 85, 147

ISO/IEC 25010. 2011. *Systems and Software Engineering—Systems and Software Quality Requirements and Evaluation (SQUARE)—System and Software Quality Models*. International Organization for Standardization. 39, 53

Jeffries R., Turner A. A., Polson P. G. and Atwood, M. E. 1981. The processes involved in designing software. *Cognitive Skills and their Acquisition*, ed. Anderson J. R., Lawrence Erlbaum, 255–283. 160

Johnson, C. 1996. Literate specification: Using design rationale to support formal methods in the development of human computer interfaces. *Human Computer Interaction*, 11(4), 291–320. DOI: 10.1207/s15327051hci1104_1. 87

Jones, J. C., 1970. *Design Methods*. 1st ed. Van Nostrand Reinhold. 149

Jones, J. C. 1988. Softecnica. *Design After Modernism: Beyond the Object*, ed. Thackera, J., Thames and Hudson, 216–266. 160

Jones, M. 2020. Making scenarios more worthwhile: Orienting to design story work, Ph.D. thesis, Northumbria University. http://nrl.northumbria.ac.uk/xxxx/. xxii, 178, 179

Junginger, S. 2017. Design as an economic necessity for governments and organisations. *Design and the Creation of Value*, eds. Dilnot, C. and Boztepe, S.,30–37. Bloomsbury. DOI: 10.5040/9781474274289.0006. 159, 177, 178

Juran, J. M. 1975. The non-Pareto principle; Mea culpa. *Quality Progress,* 8(5), 8–9. 31

Kalbach, J. 2019. Maximize business impact with JTBD. *Interactions,* 26(1), 80-83. DOI: 10.1145/3292021. 13, 28

Kano, N., Seraku, N., Takahashi, F., and Tsuji, S. 1984. Attractive quality and must-be quality. "Hinshitsu" quality. *Japanese Society Quality Control,* 14(2), 147. 117, 121, 175

Keinonen, T. 2009. Design method instrument, competence of agenda? Multiple ways to design research. *Swiss Design Research Network Symposium 09*, ed. Botta, M., pp.280–219. Available in swissdesignnetwork.ch/src/publication/multiple-ways-to-design-research-2009/SDN-Publication-2009-Multiple-ways-to-design_content.pdf. 113

Keller, A. I. 2005. *For Inspiration Only: Designer Interaction with Informal Collections of Visual Material*. Technical University Delft. www.academia.edu/928676/For_inspiration_only. 24

Kheirandish, S. 2018. *HuValue: A Tool to Enrich Design Concepts with Human Values*. Technische Universiteit Eindhoven. Available at https://research.tue.nl/en/publications/huvalue-a-tool-to-enrich-design-concepts-with-human-values. 10, 15, 24

Kheirandish, S., Funk, M., Wensveen, S., Verkerk, M., and Rauterberg, M. 2019. HuValue: A tool to support design students in considering human values in their design, *International Journal of Technology and Design Education*. DOI: 10.1007/s10798-019-09527-31. 23

Kirk, D. S. and Sellen, A. 2010. On human remains: Values and practice in the home archiving of cherished objects. *ACM Transactions Computer-Human Interactions,* 17(3), Article 10. DOI: 10.1145/1806923.1806924. 21, 24, 92

Kirk, D. S., Izadi, A., Sellen, A., Taylor, S., Banks, R., and Hilliges, O. 2010. Opening up the family archive. *Proceedings of the 2010 ACM Conference on Computer Supported Cooperative Work*, ACM, 261–270. DOI: 10.1145/1718918.1718968. 50, 103

Kjeldskov, J., Skov, M. B., and Stage, J. 2004. Instant data analysis: conducting usability evaluations in a day. *Proceedings of the Third Nordic Conference on Human-Computer Interaction (NordiCHI '04)*, ACM, 233–240. DOI: 10.1145/1028014.1028050. 34

Knapp, J., Zeratsky, J., and Kowitz, B. 2016. *Sprint: How to Solve Big Problems and Test New Ideas in Just Five Days*. Simon & Schuster. 33

Knuth, D. 1984. Literate programming. *Computer Journal*, 27(2), 97–111. DOI: 10.1093/comjnl/27.2.97. 87

Koestler, A. 1964. *The Act of Creation*. Hutchinson. DOI: 10.1177/000271626536000141. 20

Kolko, J.   2018. The divisiveness of design thinking. *Interactions*, 25(4), 28–34. DOI: 10.1145/3194313. 102

Kress, G., and Van Leeuwen, T. 2006. *Reading Images The Grammar of Visual Design*. Routledge. DOI: 10.4324/9780203619728. 65

Kujala, S. and Väänänen-Vainio-Mattila, K. 2009. Value of information systems and products: Understanding the users' perspective and values. *Journal of Information Technology Theory and Application (JITTA)*, 9(4), 23-39. 15, 149

Lawson, B. and Dorst, K. 2009. *Design Expertise*. Architectural Press. 4

Le Dantec, C. A., Poole, E. S., and Wyche, S. P. 2009. Values as lived experience: evolving value sensitive design in support of value discovery. *Proceedings of the SIGCHI Conference on Human Factors in Computing Systems (CHI '09)*, ACM, 1141–1150. DOI: 10.1145/1518701.1518875. 19, 23

Lim, Y., Lee, S., and Kim, D. 2011. Interactivity attributes for expression-oriented interaction design. *International Journal of Design*, 5(3), 113–128. 26

Löwgren, J. 1995. Applying design methodology to software development. *Proceedings Designing Interactive Systems (DIS '95)*, eds. Olson, G. M. and Schuon, S., ACM, 87–95. DOI: 10.1145/225434.225444. 38, 68, 80, 81

Löwgren, J. 2013. Annotated portfolios and other forms of intermediate-level knowledge. *Interactions* 20(1), 30–34. DOI: 10.1145/2405716.2405725. 18, 26, 38, 81, 162

Maclean, A., Young, R., Bellotti, V., and Moran, T. 1991. Questions, options and criteria: Elements of design space analysis. *Human Computer Interaction*, 6(3&4), 201–250. DOI: 10.1207/s15327051hci0603&4_2. 51, 88

Marcus, A. and Chen, E. 2002. Designing the PDA of the future. *Interactions*, 9(1), 34–44. DOI: 10.1145/503355.503356. 116, 117

Marzano, S. 1998. *Creating Value by Design*, 2 volumes. V+K Publishing. 160, 173

McDonald, S., Monahan, K., and Cockton, G. 2006. Using contextual design as a field evaluation method. In *Proceedings NordiCHI 2006*, eds. Mørch, A.I., Morgan, K., Bratteteig, T., Ghosh, G., and Svanæs, D., 437–440. DOI: 10.1145/1182475.1182531. 113

McNeill, W. 1999. *The Glance of the Eye: Heidegger, Aristotle, and the Ends of Theory*. SUNY Press. 170

Meyer, J. W. and Rowan, B. 1977. Institutionalized organizations: Formal structure as myth and ceremony. *American Journal of Sociology*, 83(2), 340–363. https://www.jstor.org/stable/2778293. 20, 175

Mok, C. 1996. *Designing Business*. Hayden Books. 28

Monk, A., Wright, P., Haber, J., and Davenport, L. 1993. *Improving Your Human-Computer Interface*. Prentice Hall. 80

Muller, M. J. 2004. HCI as translation work: How translation studies can inform HCI research and practice. *Proceedings of Reflective HCI: Towards a Critical Technical Practice (A Workshop at CHI 2004)*, eds. Dourish, P., Finlay, J., Sengers, P., and Wright, P., http://www.cs.cornell.edu/people/sengers/ReflectiveHCI/ReflectiveHCIProceedings.pdf. 78

Nelson, J. G. and Stolterman, E. 2003. *The Design Way. Intentional change in an unpredictable world. Foundations and Fundamentals of Design Competence* (1st ed.). Englewood Cliffs, Educational Technology Publications. 56

Nielsen, L. 2002. From user to character: an investigation into user-descriptions in scenarios. In *Proceedings of 4th conference on Designing Interactive Systems*, ACM, 99–104. DOI: 10.1145/778712.778729. 78

North, D. C. 1991. Institutions. *Journal of Economic Perspectives*, 5(1), 97–112. DOI: 10.1257/jep.5.1.97. 20, 175

Nov, O. and Su, H. 2018. Eliciting users' demand for interface features. *Proceedings 2018 CHI Conference on Human Factors in Computing Systems (CHI '18)*, ACM, Paper 305, 8 pages. DOI: 10.1145/3173574.3173879. 9, 10

Osterwalder, A. and Pigneur, Y. 2010. *Business Model Generation: A Handbook for Visionaries, Game Changers, and Challengers*. Wiley. 58, 135

Osterwalder, A., Pigneur, Y., Bernarda, G., Smith, A., and Papadakos, T. 2014. *Value Proposition Design: How to Create Products and Services Customers Want*. Wiley. 13, 26, 28, 66, 71, 158

Otero, N. and José, R. 2009. Worth and human values at the centre of designing situated digital public displays. *International Journal of Advanced Pervasive and Ubiquitous Computing (IJAPUC)*, 1(4), 1–13. DOI: 10.4018/japuc.2009100101. 85, 86, 91, 96, 101, 104, 105, 108, 112, 137, 141, 157

Otero, N., Rego, A., and José, R. 2009. Considering the inclusion of worth and values in the design of interactive artifacts. *Proceedings First International Conference on Integration of Design, Engineering and Management for Innovation (IDEMI09)*, FEUP Edições, 329–339. 86, 96, 97, 104, 109, 111, 113

Oulasvirta, A. 2019. It's time to rediscover HCI models. *Interactions*, 26(4), 52-56. DOI: 10.1145/3330340. 34

Øvad, T. and Larsen, L. B. 2016. Templates: A key to success when training developers to perform UX tasks. *Integrating User-Centered Design in Agile Development*, eds. Cockton, G., Lárusdóttir, M. L., Gregory, P., and Cajander, Å., Springer, 77–96. DOI: 10.1007/978-3-319-32165-3_3. 160

Parnas D. L. and Clements P. C. 1986. A rational design process: how and why to fake it. *IEEE Transactions on Software Engineering*, 12(2), 251–257. DOI: 10.1109/TSE.1986.6312940. 3 , 47, 87, 94, 148, 151, 176, 179, 181

Patton, J. with Economy, P. 2014. *User Story Mapping: Discover the Whole Story, Build the Right Product*. O'Reilly. 137, 138

Petroski, H. 1994. *Design Paradigms: Case Histories of Error and Judgement in Engineering*. Cambridge University Press. DOI: 10.1017/CBO9780511805073. 38, 152, 171

Pifarré, M., Sorribas, X., Villegas, E., Fonseca, D., and García, O. 2009. BLA (bipolar laddering) applied to YouTube. Performing postmodern psychology paradigms in user experience field. *World Academy of Science, Engineering and Technology*, 31, 952–958. Available from https://api.intechopen.com/chapter/pdf-preview/8724. 120

Pifarré, M. and Tomico, O. 2007. Bipolar laddering (BLA): a participatory subjective exploration method on user experience. *Proceedings 2007 Conf. on Designing for User eXperiences (DUX '07)*, ACM Article 2, 2–13. DOI: 10.1145/1389908.1389911. 120

Pinker, S. 2018. *Enlightenment Now: The Case for Reason, Science, Humanism, and Progress*. Penguin. 151

Poggenpohl, S. H. 2017. *Afterword Design and the Creation of Value*, eds. Dilnot, C. and Boztepe, S., 181. Bloomsbury. DOI: 10.5040/9781474274289.0021. 146

Popper, K. 1959. *The Logic of Scientific Discovery*. (author's translation of *Logik der Forschung*, 1934). Hutchinson, London. 150

Pruitt, J. and Adlin, T. 2006. *The Persona Lifecycle: Keeping People in Mind Throughout Product Design*. Morgan Kaufmann. DOI: 10.1016/B978-012566251-2/50003-4. 43, 77, 158

Pye, D. 1968. *The Nature and Art of Workmanship*. Barrie and Jenkins. DOI: 10.2307/3101490. 160

Pye, D. 1978. *The Nature and Aesthetics of Design*. Barrie and Jenkins. 160

Qaed, F., Briggs, J., and Cockton, G. 2016. Social media resources for participative design research. *Proceedings of the 14th Participatory Design Conference*, vol. 2, eds. Bossen, C., Smith, R. C., Kanstrup, A. M., McDonnell, J., Teli, M., and Bødker, K., ACM, 49–52. DOI: 10.1145/2948076.2948081. 34, 53, 159

Quine, W. V. O. 1951. Two dogmas of empiricism. *The Philosophical Review*, 60, 20–43. DOI: 10.2307/2181906. 150, 154

Renaud, K. and van Biljon, J. 2010. Worth-centred mobile phone design for older users. *Universal Access in the Information Society*, 9, 387–403. DOI: 10.1007/s10209-009-0177-9. 115, 116, 117, 118, 119, 122, 140, 143, 157

Renn, O. 1992. The social arena concept of risk debates. *Social Theories of Risk*, ed. Krimsky, S. Praeger, 179–196. 5, 177, 179

Rittel, H. W. J. and Webber, M. M. 1973. Dilemmas in a general theory of planning. *Policy Sciences*, 4, 155–169. DOI: 10.1007/BF01405730. 1

Rodgers, P. and Bremner, C. 2013. Design without discipline. *Design Issues*, 29(3), 4-13. DOI: 10.1162/DESI_a_00217. 45

Rogers, Y., Bannon, L., and Button, G. 1994. Rethinking theoretical frameworks for HCI: report on an INTERCHI '93 workshop, Amsterdam, April 24–25, 1993. *SIGCHI Bulletin*, 26(1), ACM, 28-30. DOI: 10.1145/181526.181530. xxi, 61

Rojas, F., English, S., Young, R., and Spencer, N. 2017. A design-relevant mindfulness device. *The Design Journal*, 20 (sup1). S767–S780. DOI: 10.1080/14606925.2017.1353023. 152

Rokeach, M. 1973. *The Nature of Human Value*. Free Press. 11, 15, 26, 92, 112

Romero, M. 2018. *Introducing Intersectionality*. Polity Press. DOI: 10.1093/cdj/bsz015. 35, 36

Rook, P. 1986. Controlling software projects. *Software Engineering Journal*, 1(1), 7–16. DOI: 10.1049/sej.1986.0003. 48

Rosenbaum, S., Cockton, G., Coyne, K., Muller, M., and Rauch, T. 2002. Focus groups in HCI: wealth of information or waste of resources? *CHI '02 Extended Abstracts on Human Factors in Computing Systems*, ACM, 702-703. DOI: 10.1145/506443.506554. 34

Schön, D. A. 1992. Designing as reflective conversation with the materials of a design situation. *Research in Engineering Design*, 3(1) 131–147. DOI: 10.1007/BF01580516. 2

Schwartz, S. H. 1992. Universals in the content and structure of values: theoretical advances and empirical test in 20 countries. *Advances in Experimental Social Psychology 25*, ed. Zanna, M. Academic Press, 1–65. DOI: 10.1016/S0065-2601(08)60281-6. 15

Shneiderman, B. 1983. Direct manipulation: A step beyond programming languages. *IEEE Computer*, 16, 57–69. DOI: 10.1109/MC.1983.1654471. 30

Shneiderman, B. 2003. *Leonardo's Laptop: Human Needs and the New Computing Technologies*. MIT. DOI: 10.7551/mitpress/4201.001.0001. 14, 35, 36, 37

Siegel, D. and Dray, S. 2019. The map is not the territory: empathy in design. *Interactions*, 26(2), 82–85. DOI: 10.1145/3308647. 37

Simon, H. A. 1969. *The Sciences of the Artificial*, 1st ed., MIT Press. (2nd ed. 1981, 3rd ed. 1997). 8, 132, 182

Sio, U. N., Kotovsky, K., and Cagan, J. 2015. Fixation or inspiration? A meta-analytic review of the role of examples on design processes. *Design Studies*, 39, 70–99. DOI: 10.1016/j.destud.2015.04.004. 161

Song, I-Y., Yano, K., Trujillo, J., and Mora, S. L. 2004. A taxonomic class modeling methodology for object-oriented analysis. *Information Modeling Methods and Methodologies*, eds. Krogstie, J., Halpin, T., and Siau, K., Idea Group Publishing, 216–240. DOI: 10.4018/978-1-59140-375-3.ch011. 54

Spool, J. M. 2004. Inherent value testing. Available at articles.uie.com/inherent_value_testing/. 72

Stebbing, L. S. 1930. *A Modern Introduction to Logic*. Methuen. 153

Stevens, J. and Moultrie, J. 2011. Aligning strategy and design perspectives: A framework of design's strategic contributions. *The Design Journal*, 14(4), 475–500. DOI: 10.2752/175630611X13091688930525. 5, 12, 18, 35, 39, 50, 156, 159

Stickel, O., Ogonowski, C., Jakobi, T., Gunnar, S., Pipek, V., Wulf, V., and Stevens, G. 2016. User integration in agile software development processes: Practices and challenges in small and medium dized enterprises. *Integrating User-Centred Design in Agile Development*, eds. Cockton, G., Gregory, P., Lárusdóttir, M., and Cajande, A., p. Springer, 49–76. DOI: 10.1007/978-3-319-32165-3_1. 34, 53

Stolterman, E. 1999. The design of information systems: Parti, formats and sketching. *Information Systems Journal*, 9, 3–20. DOI: 10.1046/j.1365-2575.1999.00044.x. 57, 178

Street, S. 2012. Coming to terms with contingency: Humean constructivism about practical reason. *Constructivism in Practical Philosophy*, eds. Lenman, J. and Shemmer, Y., Oxford University Press. DOI: 10.1093/acprof:oso/9780199609833.003.0003. 10

Sutcliffe, A. G. 2003. Scenario-based requirements engineering. *Proceedings of: RE'03*. IEEE. 08–12. DOI:10.1109/ICRE.2003.1232776. 78

Takeuchi, H. and Nonaka, I. 1986. The new new product development game. *Harvard Business Review*, 64(1), 137–146. 1, 3, 6, 123, 130, 143, 152, 159

Thakara. J. (ed.), 1988. *Design After Modernism: Beyond the Object*. Thames and Hudson. 160

Tuch, A. N. and Hornbæk, K. 2015. Does Herzberg's notion of hygienes and motivators apply to user experience? *ACM Transactions Computer-Human Interactions*, 22(4), Article 16, 24 pages. DOI: 10.1145/2724710. 9

Umemoto, K., Endo, A., and Machado, M. 2004, From sashimi to zen-in: the evolution of concurrent engineering at Fuji Xerox. *Journal of Knowledge Management*, 8(4), 89–99. DOI: 10.1108/13673270410548504. 1

Van Biljon, J. A. 2007. A model for representing the motivational and cultural factors that influence mobile phone usage variety. Ph.D. thesis, School of Computing, University of South Africa, Pretoria. 116, 117, 118

van de Poel, I. 2013. Translating values into design requirements. *Philosophy and Engineering: Reflections on Practice Principles and Process*, eds. Michelfelder, D. P., McCarthy, N., and Goldberg, D. E., Springer, 253–266. DOI: 10.1007/978-94-007-7762-0_20. 11, 19, 49, 52

van Rekom, J. and Wierenga, B. 2007. On the hierarchical nature of means–end relationships in laddering data. *Journal of Business Research*, 60, 401–410. DOI: 10.1016/j.jbusres.2006.10.004. 98, 126, 128, 141

Vistisen, P. 2015. The roles of sketching in design: Mapping the tension between functions in design sketches. *Nordes*, 6. https://archive.nordes.org/index.php/n13/issue/view/11. 4, 39, 56

Voida, A. and Mynatt, E. D. 2005. Conveying user values between families and designers. *CHI '05 Extended Abstracts*, ACM, 2013–2016. DOI: 10.1145/1056808.1057080. 98, 112

Von Hippel, E. 1986. Lead users: A source of novel product concepts. *Management Science*, 32 (7). 791–806. DOI: 10.1287/mnsc.32.7.791. 35, 71

Vu, P. 2013. A worth-centered development approach to information management system design. Master's thesis, Aalto University. www.soberit.hut.fi/T-121/shared/thesis/di-Phuong-Vu.pdf. 86, 115, 116, 119, 124, 128, 134, 139, 141, 142, 143, 144, 157, 158, 162, 177, 181, 182

Walker, S. 2017. *Design for Life: Creating Meaning in a Distracted World*. Routledge. DOI: 10.4324/9781315312538. 10

Waloszek, G. 2012. *Introduction to Design Thinking*. SAP. https://experience.sap.com/skillup/introduction-to-design-thinking/. 149

Warfield, J. N., with Geschka, H. and Hamilton, R. 1975. *Methods of Idea Management*. The Academy for Contemporary Problems. 13

Weber, C. 2017. A note on John Heskett's economics. *Design and the Creation of Value*, eds. Dilnot, C. and Boztepe, S., Bloomsbury, 21–29. 6, 156

Winkler, T. and Spiekermann, S. 2019. Human values as the basis for sustainable information system design. *IEEE Technology and Society Magazine*, 28(3), 34 –43. DOI: 10.1109/MTS.2019.2930268. 5, 11, 12, 15, 49, 117

Wolf, T. V., Rode, J. A., Sussman, J., and Kellogg, W. A. 2006. Dispelling "design" as the black art of CHI. *Proceedings SIGCHI Conference on Human Factors in Computing Systems. (CHI '06)*, eds. Grinter, R., Rodden, T., Aoki, P., Cutrell, E., Jeffries, R., and Olson, G., ACM, 521–530. DOI: 10.1145/1124772.1124853. 56, 59, 81, 162

Woodward, P. A. (ed.), 2001. *The Doctrine of Double Effect: Philosophers Debate a Controversial Moral Principle*. University of Notre Dame Press. DOI: 10.1353/tho.2003.0046. 10

Woolrych, A. Hornbæk, K. Frøkjær, E., and Cockton, G. 2011. Ingredients and meals rather than recipes: A proposal for research that does not treat usability evaluation methods as indivisible wholes. *International Journal of HCI*, 27(10), 940–970. DOI: 10.1080/10447318.2011.555314. 3, 5, 31, 101, 168

Young, R. A. 2008. An integrated model of designing to aid understanding of the complexity paradigm in design practice. *Futures*, 40(6), 562–576, DOI: 10.1016/j.futures.2007.11.005. 46

Zaman, B. and Vanden Abeele, V. 2010. Laddering with young children in user eXperience evaluations: Theoretical groundings and a practical case. *Proceedings 9th Int. Conference on Interaction Design and Children (IDC '10)*. ACM, 156–165. DOI: 10.1145/1810543.1810561. 22

Author Biography

Gilbert Cockton is a part-time Professorial Research Fellow at the University of Sunderland. He retired as Professor of Design Theory at Northumbria University in 2019, remaining affiliated with NORTH Lab as an Emeritus Professor. His career has balanced teaching, research, and working for and within businesses, government, and the third sector. He has worked in academic computing and design departments since 1984. From 2004, his research has focused on bringing critical creative practice fully and appropriately into software design and evaluation, first through value and worth as centres for design practice, and then through a generous Wo-Fo, progressing design work through balance and integration, developing approaches and resources that support realistic design practice.

Gilbert has held leadership roles in HCI groups in the British Computer Society, IFIP, and ACM, as chair of the BCS HCI group, vice-chair of IFIP TC13, programme co-ordinator for INTERACT'90, and general chair for CHI 2003 and British HCI 2000. He chaired ten technical tracks between 1993 and 2012 for INTERACT, British HCI, CHI, and DIS conferences. He was co-editor in chief of AMC *Interactions* magazine from 2016–2019. He was awarded a SIGCHI Lifetime Service Award in 2020.

Printed in the United States
by Baker & Taylor Publisher Services